Eilee

Teaching Religion, Teaching Truth

Religion, Education and Values

SERIES EDITORS:

Dr Stephen Parker
The Rev'd Canon Professor Leslie J. Francis
Dr Rob Freathy
Dr Mandy Robbins

Volume 1

PETER LANG
Oxford • Bern • Berlin • Bruxelles • Frankfurt am Main • New York • Wien

Teaching Religion, Teaching Truth

Theoretical and Empirical Perspectives

Jeff Astley, Leslie J. Francis,
Mandy Robbins and Mualla Selçuk (eds)

PETER LANG
Oxford · Bern · Berlin · Bruxelles · Frankfurt am Main · New York · Wien

Bibliographic information published by Die Deutsche Nationalbibliothek.
Die Deutsche Nationalbibliothek lists this publication in the Deutsche National-
bibliografie; detailed bibliographic data is available on the Internet at
http://dnb.d-nb.de.

A catalogue record for this book is available from the British Library.

Library of Congress Cataloging-in-Publication Data:

Teaching religion, teaching truth : theoretical and empirical perspectives / edited
by Jeff Astley ... [et al.].
    p. cm.
  Includes bibliographical references (p.   ) and index.
  ISBN 978-3-0343-0818-2 (alk. paper)
  1. Christian education. 2. Islamic religious education. 3. Religious education. 4.
Truth--Religious aspects. I. Astley, Jeff.
  BV1464.T435 2012
  207'.5--dc23
                          2012001458

ISSN 2235-4638
ISBN 978-3-0343-0818-2

© Peter Lang AG, International Academic Publishers, Bern 2012
Hochfeldstrasse 32, CH-3012 Bern, Switzerland
info@peterlang.com, www.peterlang.com, www.peterlang.net

All rights reserved.
All parts of this publication are protected by copyright.
Any utilisation outside the strict limits of the copyright law, without
the permission of the publisher, is forbidden and liable to prosecution.
This applies in particular to reproductions, translations, microfilming,
and storage and processing in electronic retrieval systems.

Printed in Germany

Contents

Preface ... ix

List of Tables ... xi

Introduction ... 1

PART I Catholic and Protestant Studies ... 9

GLORIA DURKA
1 Theology of Religions: Through the Looking Glass of US Roman Catholicism ... 11

FRIEDRICH SCHWEITZER
2 Principled Pluralism and Theology's Contribution to Religious Education: A Protestant Perspective ... 31

MARIO O. D'SOUZA
3 Identity, Diversity, and the Common Good ... 47

FERNANDO A. CASCANTE-GÓMEZ
4 Pluralist Latin American Liberation Theology: Theological Themes and Educational Challenges ... 63

KATH ENGEBRETSON
5 Interfaith Education in the Christian School ... 77

PART II   Islamic Studies   91

MUALLA SELÇUK
6   How Can Islamic Pedagogy Promote an Understanding
     of 'Individualized Religion'?   93

RECAI DOĞAN
7   An Ottoman Example of the Perception of Other Religions
     in Islamic Thought   107

Z. ŞEYMA ARSLAN
8   A Holistic Approach in Education from the Perspective of
     the Islamic Understanding of Human Beings   119

PART III   Empirical and Pedagogical Studies   133

ELISABETH ARWECK AND ELEANOR NESBITT
9   The Interaction of the Major Religions at Microcosmic Level:
     Religiously-Mixed Families in the UK   135

HANS-GEORG ZIEBERTZ
10   The Catholic View on Religious Pluralism in Empirical
     Perspective   155

MARIAN DE SOUZA
11   The Dual Role of Unconscious Learning in Engendering
     and Hindering Spiritual Growth: Implications for Religious
     Education in Pluralist Contexts   185

LESLIE J. FRANCIS AND MANDY ROBBINS
12   The Theology of Religions and Psychological Type:
     An Empirical Enquiry among Participants at the Parliament
     of the World's Religions   205

ÜZEYIR OK
13   How Open is Muslim Youth to People of Other Faiths?   223

PART IV   Theological Critique   239

JEFF ASTLEY
14   A Theological Reflection on the Nature of Religious Truth   241

Contributors   263

Index of Names   265

Index of Subjects   271

Preface

World events at the dawn of the twenty-first century have clearly laid to rest some of the overblown claims of the secularization theorists of the 1960s. Belief in God is not dead, and religion has not retreated to the personal domain and given over the public square to the exclusive claim of secular voices. Rather, the importance of religion is again recognized as a matter of public significance and social concern.

In this context the role of religious educators has also grown in public significance. Today religious educators are called upon to enable young people to develop as fully-rounded human beings in a world, and often in a nation or local society, that is thoroughly multicultural and thoroughly multifaith. No longer is it sufficient to teach about the history of religions: religion is not relegated to the past. No longer is it sufficient to teach about the observable outward phenomena of religions: religion is not restricted to practices, artefacts, and buildings observable in the outside world. In this context it is also necessary to take seriously what it is that religions believe about themselves, and what religions believe about other religions. The theology of religions is what ultimately matters in understanding and interpreting the re-emergence of religion in the twenty-first century as a matter of public significance and social concern.

Seen from the inside religions deal in the currency of truth. For the religions themselves truth matters. Truth-claims can lead to harmony and to peace, but they may also engender discord and violence. What ultimately counts is how one set of truth-claims confronts or embraces the truths claimed by other, different voices. Therefore those who teach religion cannot avoid dealing with matters of truth.

In this collection of original essays, religious educators shaped by both Christian and Islamic worldviews discuss the problems and opportunities that now face educators and believers alike, as they are confronted by the challenge of *teaching religion* and *teaching truth*. The arguments presented and the discussion nurtured among the participants attending the sixteenth conference of the International Seminar on Religious Education and Values, hosted by the University of Ankara, Turkey, are here developed further. We now offer these reflections to stimulate a wider debate, in the hope that this may shape good local practice and ultimately build a better global future for us all.

As editors we wish to express our thanks to the University of Ankara for hosting our Seminar and initiating these debates; to the other contributors for developing their papers for publication; and to the North of England Institute for Christian Education, Durham, UK and especially its Secretary, Evelyn Jackson, for preparing the manuscript.

Jeff Astley
Leslie J. Francis
Mandy Robbins
Mualla Selçuk

October 2011

The International Seminar on Religious Education and Values is an association of over 200 religious education scholars and researchers from over thirty-five countries, representing various religious traditions as well as secular standpoints. It meets biennially to discuss topics of mutual interest in the fields of religious and moral education, whether theoretical, empirical, contextual, or practical. For further details, see <http://www.isrev.org>.

List of Tables

Chapter 10

10.1	Concepts and items of the Scale of Religious Pluralism	166
10.2	Monoreligious perspective (Scheffé-Procedure)	171
10.3	Multireligious perspective (Scheffé-Procedure)	172
10.4	Interreligious perspective (Scheffé-Procedure)	173
10.5	Mono, multi and interreligious perspectives in an international comparison	174
10.6	Monoreligious by religion (Scheffé-Procedure)	176
10.7	Multireligious by religion (Scheffé-Procedure)	176
10.8	Interreligious by religion (Scheffé-Procedure)	177
10.9	Monoreligious by Christian denominations (Scheffé-Procedure)	178
10.10	Multireligious by Christian denominations (Scheffé-Procedure)	178
10.11	Interreligious by Christian denominations (Scheffé-Procedure)	179

Chapter 12

12.1	The sixteen complete psychological types	214
12.2	The Francis Index of Theological Exclusivism (FITE): correlation coefficients for each item with the rest of test and item endorsement	215
12.3	Mean FITE scores by dichotomous type preferences	216
12.4	Mean FITE scores by dominant type preferences	216
12.5	Mean FITE scores by dominant and auxiliary type preferences	217

Chapter 13

13.1	Correlational matrix of variables	230
13.2	Items of Interreligious Exclusivism, Interreligious Dialogue and Interreligious Pluralism, along with response percentages	231
13.3	Multiple regression significance test with Interreligious Exclusivism and Interreligious Dialogue as the dependent variables	233
13.4	Religiosity scales	234

Introduction

This volume represents perspectives on the 'theology of religions', and therefore on religious truth, in the context of various forms of religious education. The essays are written from a wide variety of standpoints: theoretical and empirical; Catholic Christian, Protestant Christian, and Muslim; Turkish, Western European, American, and Australian.

Catholic and Protestant studies

The first five essays address issues at the interface between religious education and the theology of religions from Roman Catholic and Protestant perspectives.

In chapter 1, Gloria Durka writes from the standpoint of Roman Catholicism. She considers the demographic shift in the religious scene in the United States, before exploring the impact of this on Catholic identity. The different theologies of religions circulating within the Catholic Church are sympathetically reviewed and their main themes critically explored. Durka then addresses the question, 'What can Roman Catholicism contribute to religious education such that the fashioning of a theology of religions might be enhanced?'

In chapter 2, Friedrich Schweitzer analyses from a Protestant perspective both the notion of 'principled pluralism', a central goal for religious education, and theology's contribution to religious education. Principled pluralism is an attitude that avoids relativism as well as fundamentalism, and is based on personal autonomy and on shared forms of life guided by tolerance, respect, dialogue, and solidarity. Many take it for granted that this kind of pluralism cannot be supported by a type of religious education that takes theology as one of its starting points. On that view, the social sciences or religious studies, together with the philosophy of education, represent the sole foundations for a religious education understood as an impartial subject that should not deal with truth-claims. But Schweitzer contends that there is a price to be paid for this kind of approach. His chapter argues for the possibility of, and the need for, relating religious education to (certain kinds of) theology, as well as to other disciplines.

In chapter 3, Mario O. D'Souza argues that while democratic pluralist societies are marked by religious and cultural pluralism, they also exhibit various forms of diversity. The current international prominence of religion divides such pluralist societies as to the place and role of religion. There is therefore a real need for a democratic square where religious diversity is brought into relationship with a common good that is essentially unifying and humanizing in ways that include – but are wider than – a narrow adherence to one's religious faith. Religious educators have a role to play in the pursuit of this goal by widening their instruction to include the purpose and role of diversity, and how religious autonomy and freedom must be realized in the context of such diversity. Given the prominence of religion, such an education can play a unifying role in enhancing the common good of a society of persons.

In chapter 4, Fernando A. Cascante-Gómez summarizes recent efforts by Latin American theologians who are concerned to develop a pluralist theology of liberation. He highlights some of the most significant issues and themes of an emerging theological reflection among liberation theologians, with particular reference to the intersections between liberation theology and the theology of religious pluralism. Finally, he identifies some of the challenges that a pluralist theology of liberation raises for the Christian religious educator's overall task, in the context of an increasingly interconnected, multireligious world.

In chapter 5, Kath Engebretson accepts that educators in Christian schools (and other religiously affiliated schools?) seek to engage their students in interfaith education in ways that do not compromise or water down their own beliefs, but help them to develop skills to engage with other religions in productive ways. Her chapter argues first that this *can* be done. It then lays out the philosophical basis for interfaith education

Introduction 3

in the religious school, arguing that this must proceed from a basis of inclusivism. Engebretson then spells out the relevant dimensions of this activity – cognitive, affective, and experiential – and argues that the most appropriate contribution of the school may lie in helping young people know about the religions in their community. The experiential dimension, while essential, should not necessarily seek a kind of religious dialogue for which young people may not yet be ready. Rather, she insists, it should bring young people together in non-threatening and more social ways.

Islamic studies

The next three essays are written from a Muslim perspective, with particular reference to insights from the Turkish traditions.

In chapter 6, Mualla Selçuk argues that Islamic pedagogy must face challenges that have been posed by claims over the inflexibility and universality of Islam. In response, she explores the relationships between God and human being, and those between Islam and Islamic law, using the Qur'anic term *hikmah* (wisdom) as a worthy element of individualized religion. Her thesis is that the Meccan Qur'anic verses can provide a theological framework for religious education in Islam as 'a religion of conscience based on individualistic choice and responsibility'.

In chapter 7, Recai Doğan poses the questions, 'What sort of understanding, and what kind of *religious* understanding, of the other is required of education curricula?' Only by answering these questions can religious education concentrate on how we should behave towards the other, as well as towards fellow members of our own religion. This requires a threefold approach to religious understanding: knowing the tradition, evaluating its positive and negative dimensions, and deciding how much we can take from our tradition in the new world in which we now live. In this chapter, the Islam of the madrasas and takkas of the Ottoman period are analysed, with a view to the formation of a religious education curriculum. The understanding of Islam created by the madrasa is more normative, ideological, and *fiqh* (Islamic law)-based; whereas the understanding of Islam created by the takkas between the eleventh and seventeenth centuries was more human-centered, and gave a greater priority to individuals and universal values – seeking to create a culture of coexistence and to develop morality. The essay presents important historical material that contributes to an assessment of what today's Islamic religious education should teach about other religions, and what its attitude towards them should be.

In chapter 8, Z. Şeyma Arslan investigates the Islamic understanding of the wholeness of the human being, and interprets how this holistic view leads to a holistic perspective in education that educates for full personhood, and recognizes the totality of skills and abilities possessed by the student. The Islamic concept of *fitrah* (human nature) is explored under three headings: a human being as a living creature in existential space, the characteristic features of this being, and personal differences between individuals. While the first category relates most significantly to the ultimate aims of education, such as the ultimate meaning of human existence, the second is related to the content of education and how the human being can be improved. The third category indicates a methodological perspective that should be considered in planning and practising education. Arslan argues that this categorization allows us to think systematically about the relationship between human nature and education, thus enabling us to form a broad and balanced system of education.

Empirical and pedagogical studies

The five essays selected for this third part draw on a range of methodologies that have come to characterize educational research and anchor that research in religious education within empirical and pedagogical studies.

In chapter 9, Elisabeth Arweck and Eleanor Nesbitt present findings from a three-year ethnographic study, conducted within the Warwick

Religions and Education Research Unit at the University of Warwick, concerned with the experiences of young people growing up in religiously-mixed families. This research investigated how young people in the UK come to identify themselves in relation to their parents' faiths, and the factors which had a bearing on their own religious beliefs. The authors draw out themes that emerged from the interviews with young people and their parents, and indicate their implications for religious education in the school context. The chapter provides insight into families where different (faith) cultures are present because the mother and father come from different faith backgrounds. Such families may be said to represent microcosms of processes that occur in the wider society, and thus show how individuals can navigate between different cultural and/or religious traditions, so as to facilitate everyday living and ensure respect and space for 'the other'.

In chapter 10, Hans-Georg Ziebertz presents findings from a quantitative study set up in the Würzburg school of empirical theology in order to offer an empirical perspective on the Catholic view of religious pluralism. Drawing on his earlier work undertaken in association with Johannes van der Ven, Ziebertz conceptualizes, discusses, and operationalizes three models or ideal types that express different theologies of religions, which he styles *mono*religious, *multi*religious and *inter*religious. Drawing on a broad international database of nearly 10,000 people, Ziebertz compares the mean values recorded on all three models across Croatia, Finland, Germany, Ireland, Israel, Netherlands, Poland, Sweden, Turkey, and the United Kingdom. He then compares the mean scores by the three main religious traditions (Christianity, Islam, and Judaism) and by Christian denominations (Anglican, Catholic, and Protestant). Reflecting on these findings, Ziebertz urges the Roman Catholic Church to recognize the impact of life in a pluralist society for the ways in which young people shape their religious beliefs and evaluate received religious teachings.

In chapter 11, Marian de Souza examines the role of non-conscious learning as an element that can nurture or hinder spiritual growth in terms of connecting with the other who is different. She discusses the significance of this for a contemporary world that has witnessed wide-ranging movements and displacements of people and which has, inadvertently, led to cultural and religious differences between people being accentuated, sometimes with disturbing consequences. De Souza argues that these factors have impacted on a new emerging generation that now fills classrooms at primary, secondary, and tertiary level, and carry certain implications for curriculum development. Within the Australian context, de Souza considers, with particular reference to programmes of religious education in the classroom, how the positive aspects of non-conscious learning may be used to enhance the students' understanding of people from different religious and cultural backgrounds; and how the negative aspects of non-conscious learning can be acknowledged and addressed, in order to increase the likelihood that this new generation might grow into considerate, perceptive, and empathetic people.

In chapter 12, Leslie J. Francis and Mandy Robbins present findings from a quantitative study set up in the Wales and Warwick school of empirical theology, employing psychologically-formed personality theory. Drawing on data provided by 580 participants at the Parliament of the World's Religions in Barcelona, this chapter tests the thesis that individual differences in positions on the theology of religions reflects a more basic difference in psychological type. Data generated by the Francis Psychological Type Scales and by a new index of theological exclusivism demonstrated that exclusivism scores were significantly higher among sensing types than among intuitive types, among judging types than among perceiving types, and among thinking types than among feeling types. The orientations (introversion and extraversion) were not predictors of exclusivism scores. Overall, the highest levels of exclusivism were to be found among individuals who preferred sensing as either their dominant or their auxiliary function. The lowest levels of exclusivism were among those who preferred dominant intuition with auxiliary feeling, closely followed by those who preferred dominant feeling with auxiliary intuition.

In chapter 13, Üzeyir Ok also employs a quantitative approach to explore the openness of Muslim young people to people of other religious faiths. In this study, Ok investigated the attitude of 422 Muslim adolescents towards people who profess a faith other than Islam. The sample comprised secondary school students between the ages of thirteen and eighteen in two Turkish secondary schools. The data demonstrate that those who were more religious tended to be more exclusivist / particularist and did not appreciate interreligious pluralism. In other words, they were less inclined to see all faiths as equal in terms of their truth-claims. However, they were not closed to interreligious dialogue. In contrast, people with an open religious orientation or who experience religious stress (contradiction, uncertainty, doubt) favour both interreligious dialogue and interreligious openness.

Theological critique

In chapter 14, the final chapter of the book, Jeff Astley offers a particular form of theological reflection on the nature of religious truth. He argues that both the theology of religions and the practice of religious education raise questions about the understanding of truth within religious traditions. He articulates his fear that the theology of religions may promote a misleading view of religion, and therefore an inadequate account of what is needed for a proper religious education, if it focuses on the religious adherent's cognition alone and ignores the importance of his or her affect-driven, salvific religious response. This 'religious embrace' needs to be better understood in non-confessional RE about the religions. It also needs to be evoked in any confessional education *into* a religion.

PART I

Catholic and Protestant Studies

GLORIA DURKA

1 Theology of Religions: Through the Looking Glass of US Roman Catholicism

A looking glass can be both a mirror and a window. Using the image of a triptych mirror, I begin by considering the unique history of the Roman Catholic Church in the United States with a view to recognize what it can suggest to others about the shared common task of repairing the world and promoting human flourishing through an adequate and appropriate theology of religions. First, I invite us to look at the centre panel to take note of the present context. Then to understand how we arrived at where we are, I briefly consider the left-hand panel of the past. Finally, there will be a brief glance at the third panel to help imagine some possibilities for the future of theologies of religion from the perspective of religious education.

The context: a view of the present

US Catholics are struggling between vestiges of the insularity and rigidity of immigrant Catholicism and postmodern religious pluralism. Prior to the Second Vatican Council, such struggle led to a pervasive anti-intellectualism which affected US Catholicism. But things are changing today. Religious educators especially are striving to remain responsive to the specific living culture in which Catholicism resides and the global society of which it is also a part. Both the United States and the US Catholic Church are undergoing a significant demographic shift. Aptly described by church historian Jay P. Dolan (1985) as an 'institutional immigrant', the 'Americanization' of US Catholicism has been a long, gradual, and sometimes painful process. It was frequently portrayed as a foreign transplant from conservative European churches, and thus ill-suited to the US ideals of religious freedom, separation of church and state, and religious pluralism. Nevertheless, through accommodation and struggle Catholics were deemed to be truly 'American' in the second half of the twentieth century. With the election of John F. Kennedy, the first Catholic president of the US, the Americanization of the Catholic Church was said to have been completed. As a result of postwar educational and economic opportunities, millions of second- and third-generation Catholics had entered the middle class and moved to the suburbs (O'Brien, 1996). But there is more to the picture, to the panel, including the story of Eastern-rite Catholics who were marginalized both within and without the Church; the older presence of native Mexican and African American Catholics; the Asian American Catholics, especially the Chinese, the Japanese, and the Filipinos of the nineteenth and early twentieth century. And there are the faces of Native American Catholics with whom missionaries had been involved since 1529 (Phan, 2004b).

There has been a dramatic transformation in the US religious scene in the last forty years. With the abolition in 1965 of the immigration restrictions imposed on Asians, people arrived in great numbers from Asia, Africa, and Latin America bringing with them not only different cultures but also religious traditions other than Christianity and Judaism: Buddhist, Confucian, Taoist, Hindu, Jain, Sikh, Zoroastrian, Islamic, African, and Afro-Caribbean. This was coupled with a shrinking number of European Catholics, which forced the closing or merging of many so-called 'national parishes'.

All of this helps to explain why new ways of doing theology are being born. Diana L. Eck describes the effects of this phenomenon vividly:

> Envisioning the new America in the twenty-first century requires an imaginative leap. It means seeing the religious landscape of America, from sea to shining sea, in all its beautiful complexity. Between the white New England churches and Crystal Cathedral of southern California, we see the sacred mountains and homelands of the Native peoples, the Peace Pagoda amid maples of Massachusetts, the mosque in the cornfields outside Toledo, the Hindu temples pitched atop the hills of Pittsburgh and Chicago, the old and new Buddhist temples of Indianapolis. (2001, 11)

While Judaism and Christianity are still dominant forces in US society, it should be noted that there are more US Muslims than Episcopalians, more Muslims than members of the Presbyterian Church USA, and as many Muslims as Jews. Today it is widely acknowledged that the presence of non-European immigrants should influence how theology is done. Being an immigrant entails a particular way of perceiving oneself and others, in particular the dominant others, fellow groups of immigrants, the cosmos, and ultimately, God.

And there is yet another factor to be considered in the present-day context. For US inhabitants, 9/11 changed everything. With the rise of religious extremism and of home-grown terrorism, social harmony became and remains a pressing issue. These simultaneous encounters shape theology in complex ways. Religious educators are faced with exploring what authentic theology of religions can contribute to social cohesion in a multifaith society. Their impact on theology of religions and religious education will be suggested below.

Who and what is 'Catholic?'

Many present-day Catholics seem to be constructing their own religious identities even though many are unfamiliar with their religious tradition. Clearly there are various meanings of the word *catholic*, all of which make the question of the identity of the Roman Catholic Church in general, and of Roman Catholics in particular, difficult to define. What makes people Catholic and defines their Catholic identity is not so much what differentiates them from Protestants, Orthodox, or Anglicans (for example, acceptance of the Petrine office), but the religion's fundamental structures even though these may be common to others. Besides doctrines, such deep structures could include rituals, art, institutions, and behaviours.

> Thus, a Catholic's identity is shaped not only be doctrines, but as much as (if not more) by sacramental celebrations (though sacraments are common to the Orthodox, Anglicans, and most Protestants), by episcopal structures (common to the Orthodox and the Anglicans), and by artistic monuments such as architecture, the visual arts, and music. (Phan, 2004a, 55)

This notion helps to explain the results of recent studies and surveys which show that, in the big picture, most Catholics remain Catholic (D'Antonio, et al., 2007). Even if they are unhappy with church leadership or church moral teachings, or though they may attend Mass less frequently or contribute less to church appeals, most Catholics stay Catholic. Contemporary Catholics regard some elements as being central to Catholicism and others as peripheral. The central elements that they believe form the unchangeable core of the faith include helping the poor, belief in credal statements such as Jesus' resurrection from the dead, the sacraments, and devotion to Mary as the Mother of God. Other things are less important and open to change.

Catholic theology of religions

In considering Catholic theology of religions, it is helpful to bear in mind that catholicity cannot be limited to geographical extension; rather, it means to embrace the whole (*kat' holos*). Nor can it be reduced to the fullness of present-day Roman Catholicism. As confessed in the ancient creeds, catholicity means not full or perfect, but universal, in contrast to what is local or particular. Rausch is very explicit:

> For Roman Catholics, Catholicism is not the product of a single reformer or historical movement in post-New Testament Christian history. It does not find its identity in a single doctrine, like Lutheranism, with its emphasis on justification by faith alone. Unlike Reformed or Calvinist Christianity, it is not based on a single theological tradition. It is not defined by a single liturgical tradition, as is Anglicanism, which finds its principle of unity in the Book of Common Prayer. Nor is it committed to a

single method of biblical interpretation, like fundamentalist and much of Evangelical Protestantism, bound to a confessional notion of biblical inerrancy. Catholicism includes within itself a variety of theologies, spiritualities, liturgies, and expressions of the Christian life. (2003, 215)

Therefore, if catholicity means inclusiveness, it would seem that to be truly Catholic one must be open to the 'other' and willing to engage in dialogue. This obligation is shared by all Christians. In the Roman Catholic encyclical, 'Dialogue and Mission' (*Redemptoris Missio*), four forms of dialogue open to Christians are highlighted: *dialogue of life*, by a true Christian witness of charity, mercy, pardon, reconciliation, and peace; *dialogue of collaboration or deeds*, by common efforts in the fields of humanitarian, social, economic, and political activity, directed toward the liberation and advancement of humankind; *dialogue of reflection*, by which the Christian, without ignoring the differences that exist among religions, recognizes the treasures of other religious traditions; *dialogue of religious experience*, through prayer and contemplation.

While theologies of the religions have been developing at least since the time of Justin's Logos theology in the mid-second century, because of Christianity's felt need to situate itself vis-à-vis other religions, they gained prominence in the middle of the twentieth century through the pioneering theological work of several Catholic theologians, and they paved the way for a revision of Catholic theology of religions (Duffy, 1999).

Arguably the most influential Catholic theologian of the twentieth century, Karl Rahner, a German Jesuit, explored uncharted religious terrain. He is regarded by many Catholic theologians to be the first to explore the path toward a new Christian theology of religions, and the Second Vatican Council followed it. In a lecture given in 1961 (published in 1966) he laid out a carefully crafted theological case in which he took standard Catholic doctrines and used them to build a truly revolutionary theology of religions. The centerpiece of Rahner's theology of religion is that *God is love* (1 John 4:8). This means that God *wants* to save all people, and that God *gives* saving grace to every human being. As Knitter (2002) points out, in insisting that people can truly experience God and find salvation outside of the boundaries of the Church, Rahner was confirming a trend in Catholic theology since the Council of Trent. This trend holds that Christianity and other religions are complemented, enriched, and corrected by one another. But then he also added another piece of this theology of religions which was both startling and liberating: *the religions can be 'ways of salvation'.* Thus he established not just the possibility but the probability that God is speaking other languages besides Christian.

Rahner's work was foundational for the dramatic revisions in Roman Catholic approaches to the theology of religions. The documents issued at the Second Vatican Council, along with other post-conciliar church statements, give evidence of this shift. Most notable of the Vatican II documents is 'The Declaration on the Relationship of the Church to Non-Christian Religions' (*Nostra Aetate*, 1966). While it does not present a fully developed theology of the religions, it does reflect the shift from exclusivism to a more inclusivistic stance that was occurring in Roman Catholic approaches to the theology of the religions. For the first time in church history, the Declaration on Religions summarizes briefly the basic beliefs and practices of Hinduism, Buddhism, and Islam and makes positive reference to 'other (primal) religions to be found everywhere'. The Declaration recognizes and applauds the 'profound religious sense' animating all these traditions, and affirms that their teachings and practices represent what is 'true and holy' and 'reflect a ray of the Truth that enlightens all people'. Further, it exhorts all Catholics to 'prudently and lovingly' 'dialogue and collaborate' with other believers and so, 'in witness of Christian faith and life, acknowledge, preserve, and promote the spiritual and moral goods found among these people' (*Nostra Aetate*, 2). It is interesting to note that 'The Decree on the Church's Missionary Activity' (*Ad Gentes*) uses a phrase directly from Rahner when it recognizes in the religions 'elements of truth and grace' (AG 9). It also applies the ancient and rich expression of the Church Fathers in affirming that in the religions one can find 'seeds of the Word', the same Word embodied in Jesus (AG 11, 15). And in the 'Pastoral Constitution on the Church in the Modern World' (*Gaudium et Spes*, 92), we read that in the religions there are 'precious things, both religious and human'.

Clearly, the call to dialogue is evident in Vatican II documents. It becomes more central to the 'mission of the Church' in more recent statements – *Redemptoris Missio* and 'Dialogue and Proclamation'. Both insist

Theology of Religions

that proclamation and dialogue are 'component elements and authentic forms' of the one mission of the church (DP 2; RM 55). But dialogue should proceed with the conviction that the Church is the ordinary means of salvation and that she alone possesses 'the fullness of the means of salvation' (RM 55; also DP 19, 22, 58). So as Knitter (2002) points out, Karl Rahner, the Second Vatican Council, and Pope John Paul II made breakthroughs toward a more dialogical relationship of Christians with other believers. While recognizing the reality of the Spirit in these religions, they also believe that God has done something extraordinary and special in Jesus the Christ: 'Christ is thus the fulfilment of yearning of all the world's religions and, as such, he is their sole and definitive completion' (RM 6). This position has been called the 'fulfilment model' and will be addressed again later.

While a number of Catholic theologians have been working to build on the foundational work of Rahner, Küng, and the second Vatican Council, tensions did arise between them and the Congregation for the Doctrine of the Faith (CDF) which issues official Roman declarations. Heated debate followed the publication in 2000 of what became a notorious declaration known as *Dominus Iesus*. Among other things the declaration stressed (Dominus Iesus, 2002):

- Revelation in Christ is complete (no. 5) and is not complemented by other religions (no. 6).
- Christ is unique and has an absolute and universal significance (no. 5).
- Members of other religions, objectively speaking, are in a gravely deficient situation in comparison to those in the Church (no. 22).
- The Church must be committed to announcing the necessity of conversion to Christ (no. 22).

Since then, numerous clarifications to this declaration have been made by various authorities, not always to the satisfaction of theologians and laity, Catholic, Protestant, or Jewish. A voice from the East is especially noteworthy. The Catholic Bishops' Conference of India (1998) gives a nuanced answer to the question of whether other religions can be regarded as 'Ways of salvation'. They replied:

> Christ is the sacrament, the definitive symbol of God's salvation for all humanity. This is what the salvific uniqueness and universality means in the Indian context. That, however, does not mean there cannot be other symbols, valid in their own ways, which the Christian sees as related to the definitive symbol, Jesus Christ. The implication of all this is that for hundreds of millions of our fellow human beings, salvation is seen as being channeled to them not in spite of but through and in their various sociocultural and religious traditions. We cannot, then, deny a priori a salvific role for these non-Christian religions. (Phan, 2000, 22)

The work of fashioning new models of theology of religions continues. Only a few key figures engaged in that task can be mentioned here. In the United States, Roman Catholic theologian Paul Knitter (1985) began to distinguish four models of theology of religions: (1) the conservative evangelical model (one true religion); (2) the most widespread Protestant model today (all salvation comes from Christ); (3) the open Catholic model (various paths, Christ the sole norm); and (4) the theocentric model (various paths with God as centre). Later, in an article entitled 'Catholic theology of religions at the crossroads' (1986), Knitter partly adopts the categories proposed by H. R. Niebuhr for the relationship between Christ and culture: a Christ *against* the religions, *in* the religions, *above* the religions, and *together with* the religions. Peter Phan has critiqued Knitter's models suggesting these theologies of religions and religious pluralism may be divided into four main types. A brief description according to Phan (2004b) follows.

The first, *'the replacement model'*, is summarized in the slogan 'only one true religion'. It holds either that non-Christian religions are unbelief and must be totally replaced by Christianity, or that they contain some truths but cannot offer salvation. They must be partially replaced by Christianity.

The second, called *'the fulfilment model'*, holds that although non-Christian religions possess elements of truth and grace, only Christianity possesses the fullness of truth and grace. Other religions are fulfilled in it; therefore their adherents can be called 'anonymous Christians'.

The third, *'the mutuality model'*, has as its slogan, 'many true religions called to dialogue'. It holds that all religions are called into dialogue with one another since none of them, though true, possesses the whole and complete truth.

The fourth is called *'the acceptance model'*, with the slogan, 'many true religions: so be it'. It holds that each religion has its own aim and particular way of achieving this aim. Thus, no common ground exists among these diverse religions. However, Christians must maintain that salvation is attained only through Christ and should not attempt to solve the question of whether and how non-Christians will be saved.

Phan suggests that from a Roman Catholic perspective, the third model, now embraced by many Roman Catholic theologians, seems, with some significant amendments, to be most adequate for meeting the challenges of religious pluralism while remaining 'in harmony' with Christian faith. He presents an expanded version of the model which contains the following points.

- The fact that Jesus is the unique and universal saviour and that baptism is required for salvation does not exclude the possibility of non-Christians being saved.
- Nor does it exclude the possibility of non-Christian religions functioning as 'ways of salvation' insofar as they contain 'elements of truth and grace'.
- These two possibilities are realized by the activities of both the Logos and the Holy Spirit. The Logos, though identical with Jesus of Nazareth, is not exhaustively embodied in him, who was spatially and temporally limited and therefore could not exhaustively express the divine saving reality in his human words and deeds.
- The Holy Spirit, though intimately united with the Logos, is distinct from him and operates salvifically beyond him and 'blows where he wills' (John 3:8). Thus, God's saving presence through God's Word and Spirit is not limited to the Judeo-Christian history but is extended to all human history and may be seen especially in the

sacred books, rituals, moral teachings, and spiritual practices of all religions.
- Religious pluralism then is not just a matter of fact but also a matter of principle: i.e., non-Christian religions may be seen as part of the plan of divine Providence and endowed with a particular role in the history of salvation.
- This autonomy of non-Christian religions detracts nothing from either the role of Jesus as the unique and universal saviour, or that of the Christian Church as the sacrament of Christ's salvation. On the one hand, Christ's uniqueness is not exclusive or absolute but *constitutive* and *relational*.
- There is then a *reciprocal* relationship between Christianity and the other religions; they are complemented by each other.
- Although the Christian faith proclaims that Jesus Christ is the fullness of revelation and the unique and universal saviour, there is also a reciprocal relationship between him and other 'saviour figures' and non-Christian religions.
- Complementarity between the Christian claims that Jesus is the unique and universal Saviour and that the Church is the sacrament of salvation is *assymetrical* (cf. Dupuis, below). This means that, according to the Christian faith, Jesus mediates God's gift of salvation to humanity in an overt, explicit, and fully visible way, which is now continued in Christianity; whereas other saviour figures and religions, insofar as they mediate God's salvation to their followers, do so through the power of the Logos and the Spirit.
- Lastly, because of the saving presence of the Logos and Holy Spirit in non-Christian religion, their sacred scriptures, prayers, rituals, moral practices, and ascetical and monastic traditions can be a source of inspiration and spiritual enrichment for Christians. Therefore, they may and should be used, at least by Christians who live in a religiously pluralistic context.

Jacques Dupuis, the Belgian Catholic theologian who lived in India for thirty-six years – and whose work (first published in 1997), *Toward a Christian theology of religious pluralism* (1997/2001), was censured by the

Congregation for the Doctrine of the Faith – offers further refinements in his later work, *Christianity and the religions*. Three of the questions he deals with are: Can members of other religions be saved? If so, can these religions be said to contain 'elements of truth and grace' so that if their adherents are saved by and saved in them and somehow through them? If yes, can it be said that these religions have a positive meaning in God's single overall plan of salvation? Dupuis answers in the affirmative and coins the expression 'inclusive pluralism' to describe his position. He notes that in spite of diverse views regarding the way ahead beyond contradictory inclusivist and pluralistic claims, there seems to be general agreement that absolutism and relativism must be avoided on all sides. The place of plurality in God's plan of salvation is to be stressed in principle. Dupuis affirms, 'A theology of religions must in the last analysis be a theology of religious pluralism' (1997/2001, 201).

Dupuis also highlights a pivotal point when he writes that many theologians today are asserting that the categories within the debate on theology of religions reflect a western way of thinking which cannot bring about a satisfactory solution. Western thinking too often implies an *either-or* mode of contradiction which is not congenial to the Eastern mentality of *and-and* ('*et-et*'). He agrees with those theologians who declare that 'The Western problematic must be abandoned if we should hope to build a theology of religions founded not on mutual contradictions and confrontation but on harmony, convergence, and unity' (Dupuis, 1997/2001, 198). As some theologians have acknowledged, so doing can lead to the possibility of dual religious belonging. Phan points out that edifying examples of such dual belonging are not lacking, at least among Roman Catholics. He cites the case of Raimundo Pannikar, a Spanish-Indian Catholic priest and theologian, who confessed: 'I "left" as a Christian, "found myself" a Hindu, and I "return" as a Buddhist, without having ceased to be a Christian' (Pannikar, 1978). For Pannikar there is no need for one single view of Christ because no single notion can comprehend the reality of Christ. Religions may be incommensurable with one another despite some possible common traits, so when religions encounter each other, they can mutually enrich each other and also destroy each other. If Christians are able to extricate from their own religion the 'christic principle', it can be experienced as a dimension at least potentially present in any human being as long as no absolute interpretation is given. He writes,

> Christians may find in this christic principle the point of union, understanding and love with all humankind and with the whole of the cosmos, so that in this concreteness they find the most radical human, cosmic, and divine communion with reality – notwithstanding other possible homeomorphic equivalents. (Pannikar, 2005, 112)

Jewish/Christian Dialogue

Special mention must be made of Jewish/Christian dialogue since it is where most US Catholics first encounter the need for an adequate theology of religions. Ever since the publication of *Nostra Aetate*, there have been many promising initiatives between Jews and Catholics. Pope John XXIII initiated a fundamental change in Catholic-Jewish relations which was continued throughout the term of Pope John Paul II. The Catholic Commission for Religious Relations with the Jews (CRR) was established in 1974 (under Pope Paul VI) and has been a dialogue partner with the Israeli Jewish Council for Interreligious Relations (IJCIR). One example of the fruits of this dialogue is worth mentioning. At their 2004 meeting in Buenos Aires, with the theme '*Tzedaq and Tzedaqah (Justice and Charity)*: Facing the Challenges of the Future; Jewish and Catholic Relations in the 21st Century', a *Joint Declaration* was published which declared that both faith communities have an equal obligation to work for justice with charity. There is a strong commitment to prevent the re-emergence of anti-Semitism and to struggle against terrorism. The document concludes by saying, 'Terror in all its forms, and killing "in the name of God" can never be justified ... We call on men and women of all faiths to support international efforts to eradicate this threat to life, so that all nations can live together in peace and security on the basis of *Tzedeq* and *Tzedaqah*' (in Cassidy, 2005, 243).

Theology of religions and religious education: through the looking glass of Roman Catholicism

Because religiously and culturally monolithic groups are becoming increasingly rare, it is crucial to help students transcend religious ethnocentricity and deepen their appreciation for diverse religious perspectives (Engebretson, et al., 2010). What can Roman Catholicism contribute to religious education such that the fashioning of a theology of religions might be enhanced? A few modest proposals can be suggested from my perspective as a US religious educator.

- As mentioned at the beginning of this chapter, the US is considered now the world's most religiously diverse nation, and the Catholic Church is the largest denomination endowed with rich financial and intellectual resources. As such it could take a lead in interreligious dialogue. I agree with Peter Phan who declares that the Catholic Church 'can serve as a useful laboratory for interreligious dialogue and its achievement in this field will no doubt have an impact on religious pluralism in the Catholic Church as a whole' (2004b, 6).
- People are exposed daily to the otherness of the others. The genius of the Roman Catholic Church over the centuries has been its ability to preserve unity within diversity (Rausch, 2003, 201). Religious educators can teach that social harmony does not require uniformity. Current pastoral and religious educational practice requires new forms which will preserve the different cultures, especially those of its newest members.
- Fashioners of these new forms can learn from the African, Asian, Latin American, and Pacific rim immigrant Catholics who come from lands in which there are Buddhists, Hindus, and Muslims, often in conflict with one another. While there has been a rise of intolerance and hostility toward those who are different, US Catholic immigrants from these places have a unique opportunity

to model how people of different religions can live together in harmony and work together for world peace. Phan claims, 'Scratch the surface of every Asian Catholic and you will find a Confucian, a Taoist, a Buddhist, a Hindu, a Muslim, or more often than not, an indistinguishable mixture of all these religions' (2004b, 5–6).

- The socialization of Asian and Pacific Catholics in US society, where they rub shoulders daily with non-Christians, is instructive. Many Asian, African, Latin American, and Pacific rim Catholics do not find it strange to inhabit different religious universes because they are regularly exposed to practices, values, spiritualities, proverbs, folk sayings, rituals, and cultural festivals of other religions (Phan and Hayes, 2005, 111). This social experience provides a hospitable context for interreligious dialogue which can be practised by people of faith regardless of educational level, social standing, or religious status. Such dialogue constitutes the very process of peacemaking and reconciliation itself. For religious educators especially, these dialogues are powerful means to correct biases, erase deep-seated hatreds, and heal ancient wounds (Phan, 2007). In formal classrooms and informal educational settings, proposing information about other religions, practising communication skills, nurturing critical thinking, and above all – as many contemporary theologians suggest – sharing experiences of the divine, all help to pave new ways for theologies of religion.
- If religious education were regarded as a deepening and intensification of deep structures that are pervasive in the Roman Catholic Church's faith and practice, and that are possessed in common with other Christians and even with non-Christian believers, then ecumenical and interreligious dialogues would not constitute a threat to the preservation of Roman Catholic identity – nor that of any other believers (Phan, 2004a). Deep structures function as both the religious context and the epistemological warrant for beliefs and practices (Phan, 2006).
- All religious educators, not only in Judaism and Christianity, Islam, and Buddhism, but even in tribal religions, could benefit from a feminist hermeneutics of suspicion. Feminist theologians

have shown that throughout the history of all religions there are expressions of male-dominated cultures that have marginalized women to some extent, although women have been more radically and totally marginalized in some religious systems than in others (Ruether, 2005). As well, liberation theologians have pointed out that the First World development model for promoting the economic welfare of the Third World subtly but effectively leads to further economic dependence and subordination, rather than to true liberation. Tissa Balasuriya puts it bluntly when he writes that it causes one to be suspicious: 'Can the self-understanding of churches that legitimize sexist, racist, classist, and religious oppression be theologically true?' (1985, 202). Knitter (2002) suggests that hermeneutical suspicion about traditional Christian theology of religions, particularly its Christological basis, has impelled many Christian theologians to begin their search for a pluralist theology of religions. Christian feminist theologians in general and Catholic feminists in particular are contributing to this search by continuing to allow the divine to be experienced in ways defined by women (Ruether, 2005).

- There is much to be gained in the refinement of theologies of religion by not absolutizing one's religion while teaching or dialoguing. This suggests scrutinizing our language to avoid uncritical use of terms such as *unique* or *absolute*. For Christians this is a particular challenge in describing the role of Jesus as Saviour (see Moran, 1992). Even so, an attitude of openness to some degree of divine reality is plausible for Christians committed to the 'uniqueness' of Jesus Christ and the Christian religion. Adequate and appropriate language is needed to communicate religious beliefs among people who are other.

- US Catholic religious educators can take courage from the bold action of the Catholic bishops of England and Wales who unanimously approved a new interfaith document, 'Meeting God in Friend and Stranger' (2010), in which they encourage Catholics to pray with people of other faiths. The bishops bravely describe critics of interreligious dialogue as having a 'defective' understanding

of Catholicism. They emphasize that interreligious dialogue is a crucial part of the Catholic Church's mission.
- Religious educators should not resist the unprecedented diversity of faiths that permeate contemporary existence, but should face the challenge head on, recognizing and showing that each faith provides a powerful matrix for ultimate meaning and shaping meaningful lives for global community (King, 2009).
- Religious education processes could give more emphasis to complexity and ambiguity in dealing with matters of religion and life. This implies a willingness to have and to bear tension, both by teachers and learners. Perhaps teachers still need to expand their palette of methods to include more ways of releasing the religious imagination through art, music, drama, architecture, and the like – not simply studying *about* them but *doing* them, *interpreting* them, *playing* with them; and *struggling/wrestling* with them. Such imaginative exploration combined with critical inquiry can greatly enhance the ability to see the world and others 'with eyes wide open'. We have to see differently if we are to live more harmoniously. For many theologians, religion's closest cousin is art not logic. The arts are vehicles for imaginative exploration; when nurtured they enrich the deep structures of religious belonging and religious openness. They help us to be curious rather than certain; they help us to live with mystery.
- The twin voyages into one's own tradition and into other religious traditions can enhance conversation. Although the journey to the new and different can have chaos, it is worth the effort. Teaching students well about their own faith tradition and that of others, that is, in an intellectually honest way, will help them to stay the course. There is no easy way through it. I agree with David Tracy, who wrote,

It cannot be overemphasized that if genuine dialogue is to occur, we must be willing to put everything at risk. Otherwise, we do not allow attention to the logic of questioning elicited by this particular subject matter (however different or other – even at times, terrifying as other ...). (1991, 95)

Towards a conclusion: a glance at the panel of the future

As mentioned earlier, a looking glass can also be a window. It not only reflects light but lets it in. The third panel as mirror is yet to be written, but its traces are already visible in the present. It is already abundantly clear that it takes courage to engage in authentic conversation. The continuities and discontinuities present in the contemporary religious education enterprise should be allowed to emerge and be addressed so that we all might better see the light. The words of David Tracy say it well:

> We understand one another, if at all, only through analogy. Who you are I know only by knowing what event, what focal meaning, you actually live by. And that I know only if I too have sensed some analogous guide in my own life. If we converse, it is likely we will both be changed as we focus upon the subject matter itself – the fundamental questions and the classical responses in our traditions. That analogical imagination seems and is a very small thing. And yet it does suffice.
>
> For the analogical imagination, once religiously engaged, can become a clearing wherein we may finally hear each other once again, where we yet become willing to face the actuality of the not-yet concealed in our present inhumanity in all its darkness – a deepening, encroaching darkness, that, even now, even here, discloses the encompassing light always-already with us. (1981, 454–455)

This is the true light of the looking glass.

References

Balasuriya, T. (1985). A third world perspective. In V. Fabella and S. Torres (eds), *Doing theology in a divided world* (pp. 197–205). Maryknoll, New York: Orbis Books.

Cassidy, E. I., Cardinal (2005). *Ecumenism and interreligious dialogue: Unitatis Redintegratio, Nostra Aetate.* New York: Paulist Press.

Catholic Bishops' Conference of England and Wales (2010). *Meeting God in friend and stranger.* (Cited in *The Tablet*, 24 April 2010, 35.)

D'Antonio, W. V., Davidson, J. D., Hoge, D. R., and Gautier, M. L. (2007). *American Catholics today: New realities of their faith and their church*. New York: Rowman and Littlefield.

Dolan, J. P. (1985). *The American Catholic experience: A history from colonial times to the present*. Garden City, New York: Doubleday.

Dominus Iesus (2002). On the unicity and salvific universality of Jesus Christ and the Church. 6 August 2000. Congregation for the Doctrine of Faith. In S. J. Pope and C. Hefling (eds), *Sic et Non: Encountering* Dominus Iesus (pp. 3–26). Maryknoll, New York: Orbis Books.

Duffy, S. J. (1999). A theology of the religions and/or a comparative theology? *Horizons, 26* (1), 105–115.

Dupuis, J. (2001). *Toward a Christian theology of religious pluralism*. Maryknoll, New York: Orbis Books. (Originally published 1997.)

Eck, D. L. (2001). *A new religious America: How a 'Christian country' has become the world's most religiously diverse nation*. San Francisco: Harper.

Engebretson, K., de Souza, M., Durka, G., and Gearon, L. (eds). (2010). *Handbook of Inter-Religious Education*. Dordrecht: Springer Press.

Hick, J., and Knitter, P. F. (eds). (2005). *The myth of Christian uniqueness: Toward a pluralistic theology of religions*. Eugene, Oregon: Wipf and Stock.

John Paul II. (6 November 1999). *Ecclesia in Asia*. Promulgated following the Special Assembly for Asia of the Synod of Bishops (19 April–14 May 1998).

John Paul II. (1990). Dialogue and Mission *(Redemptoris Missio)*. Rome: Congregation for the Doctrine of Faith.

King, U. (2009). *The search for spirituality: Our global quest for meaning and fulfilment*. Norwich: Canterbury Press.

Knitter, P. F. (1985). *No other name? A critical survey of Christian attitudes to world religions*. Maryknoll, New York: Orbis Books.

Knitter, P. F. (1986). Catholic theology at the crossroads. In *Christianity among world religions. Concilium, 183* (1), 99–107.

Knitter, P. F. (2002). *Introducing theologies of religions*. Maryknoll, New York: Orbis Books.

Moran, G. (1992). *Uniqueness: Problem or paradox in Jewish and Christian traditions*. Maryknoll, New York: Orbis Books.

Nostra Aetate (Declaration on the Relationship of the Church to Non-Christian Religions) (1966). In W. M. Abbott (ed.), *The documents of Vatican II*, Piscataway, New Jersey: America Press.

O'Brien, D. J. (1996). *Public Catholicism*. Maryknoll, New York: Orbis Books.

Pannikar, R. (1978). *The intrareligious dialogue*. New York: Paulist Press.

Pannikar, R. (2005). The Jordan, the Tiber, and the Ganges. In Hick and Knitter (pp. 89–116).

Phan, P. C. (2004a). *Being religious interreligiously: Asian perspectives on interfaith dialogue*. Maryknoll, New York: Orbis Books.

Phan, P. C. (2004b). Cultures, religions, and power: Proclaiming Christ in the United States today. *Theological Studies, 65* (4), 714–740.

Phan, P. C. (2006). Religious identity and belonging amidst diversity and pluralism: Challenges and opportunities for church and theology. In J. Heft (ed.), *Passing on the faith: Transforming traditions for the next generation of Jews, Christians, and Muslims* (pp. 162–184). New York: Fordham University Press.

Phan, P. C. (2007). Speaking in many tongues: Why the Church must be more catholic. *Commonweal, 134* (1), 16–19.

Phan, P. C. (ed.). (2000). *The Asian Synod: Texts and commentaries*. Maryknoll, New York: Orbis Books.

Phan, P. C., and Hayes, D. (2005). *Many faces, one church: Cultural diversity and the American Catholic experience*. New York: Rowman and Littlefield.

Rahner, K. (1966). Christianity and the non-Christian religions. In *Theological investigations, vol. 5* (pp. 115–134). Baltimore, Maryland: Helicon Press.

Rausch, T. R. (2003). *Towards a truly Catholic church: An ecclesiology for the third millennium*. Collegeville, Minnesota: Liturgical Press.

Ruether, R. R. (2005). Particularism and universalism in the search for religious truth. In Hick and Knitter (pp. 137–148).

Tracy, D. (1981). *The analogical imagination: Christian theology and the culture of pluralism*. New York: Crossroad.

Tracy, D. (1991). *Dialogue with the other: The inter-religious dialogue*. Grand Rapids, Michigan: Eerdmans.

FRIEDRICH SCHWEITZER

2   Principled Pluralism and Theology's Contribution to Religious Education: A Protestant Perspective

The relationship between religious education and theology is considered problematic. Ever since Jean-Jacques Rousseau's *Emile* was first published in 1762, many educators have argued against theology as a basis or as a source for religious education. Since the 1960s, there has been a growing debate about whether theology *or* religious studies is the appropriate academic subject or field to which religious education should be related. Consequently, my interest in theology's contribution to religious education will be suspect to many readers from the beginning, especially to those from countries where religious education is based on a multifaith approach, such as England and Wales, or on a so-called scientific approach to the study of religion, as in Sweden. This is why I want to start out with a number of clarifications about what theology should and should not be in religious education.

However, this question will only be treated in a preliminary way here. My main argument is not about the relationship between religious education and theology in general. Instead, my focus is on the situation of religious pluralism, including the corresponding challenges of relativism and fundamentalism. In my understanding, religious education will not be able to face up to this situation unless it is prepared to deal with competing contradictory religious truth-claims. In this respect, it is certainly the case that teaching religion and questions of truth must be closely interconnected, as suggested by the title of the present book. Yet how should religious education actually deal with competing truth-claims? And what, if anything, might theology have to contribute to this task?

In other words, I am interested in the relationship between the selfunderstanding of religion and religious education. Consequently, I must also be clear about my own theological self-understanding. My background is Protestant Christianity and religious education (cf. Schweitzer, 2006a). Since I clearly cannot speak for other religions or even for other Christian denominations (as a Protestant I do not expect, for example, the Pope to agree with me, and neither do I feel obliged to agree with him), I want to be open about my Protestant point of view from the beginning. This point of view is not meant to be exclusive, but naturally it implies a number of presuppositions that others might not share.

In relationship to religious education, I want to be specific as well. It is easy to see that there are many different educational situations and challenges perceived by today's educators around the world. For the present purposes, I will refer to a western context that is characterized by plurality or pluralism, in the sense of the co-presence of different cultures and different religions or worldviews (cf. Osmer and Schweitzer, 2003). It is against this background of multicultural and multireligious societies that I will be considering the role of theology in relationship to religious education.

What theology should and should not be in religious education

It would be an interesting enterprise to study the different references to theology in twentieth-century religious education, a task that, unfortunately, cannot be fulfilled here (interesting starting points for such a study would be the different publications in the *British Journal of Religious Education* over the years, for example, Ballard, 1966; Netto, 1989; Cush, 1999; Hull, 2004, articles that I have consulted in preparing this chapter). Yet a few remarks that indicate my own understanding are in place. Since space does not allow for fully referencing the discussion on theology in relationship to religious education here, I want at least to refer readers to some publications that can be consulted for additional references (cf. Nipkow, 1985; Herms,

1995; Schwöbel, 2003; Rothgangel and Thaidigsmann, 2005; Schweitzer, 2006c; Schweitzer and Schwöbel, 2007). A broader analysis of the present topic would also have to include the different theological traditions that are, at least in some cases, also related to different countries, regions, or denominations (cf. Miller, 1995), but can also be specific to a certain religion, for example, to Islam (Aslan, 2009).

The contemporary situation includes a number of apprehensions and suspicions that should be addressed openly.

Quite often, educators seem to equate theology with some kind of Christian imperialism. Traditionally, as in the case of Rousseau, the suspicion of imperialism referred to the dominance of theology over education. Today, it is directed to the dominance of Christianity over other religions and worldviews. In my own understanding, however, theology is a generic term used for the reflexive understanding of a certain faith and religious tradition, necessarily including – although not limited to – an inside perspective that tries to do justice to the truth-claims of the particular faith. This distinctive characteristic refers to the difference between theology and a religious studies approach that often defines itself exactly by referring to an outside perspective irrespective of the possible truth of a faith (for the corresponding discussion within British religious education, see Copley, 1997, 83, referring to the influence of Ninian Smart: 'The study of religion is strategic to some of the human sciences. It has a broad base and does not make the truth assumptions made by theology'). It should be noted that this self-definition of religious studies is not necessarily shared by theology, at least not in respect to its implications for theology. According to its self-definition, theology often includes outside perspectives as well. Moreover, especially in the present context, theology should not be identified with Christianity. It can be Christian but can also be Muslim or Jewish, etc., provided it includes the inside perspective of the respective faith. Given today's situation, at least in western countries, it should also be obvious that, especially in the context of the state school, theology and the philosophy of education must be partners in dialogue, without any attempt at unilateral domination.

It is also important to be clear that theology cannot be identified with dogmatics and even less with dogmatism. Dogmatics can be one of the theological sub-disciplines but it is not altogether the same as theology. Modern theology is open to different methodologies and epistemologies – historical methods as well as social scientific methods, etc. Like law, it is a normative discipline that works from certain normative or credal presuppositions – the inside perspective mentioned above – but this does not mean that these presuppositions must prevent interdisciplinary partnerships, cooperation, or open dialogue.

While there is no full agreement on the nature of theology even within Christian theology, it is at least widely accepted that theology must be clearly distinguished from religion. Religion is a form of life whereas theology is an academic enterprise, at least in one of its meanings that is most pertinent for the present context. As such, it is related to lived religion in a complex manner, bound to a certain faith yet also to general academic standards. This is why theology is always one or several steps removed from lived religion. Without this distance to lived religion, no academic freedom would be possible.

In a different sense, theology can also mean the ways of making sense of one's faith or religion that are not limited to any academic setting. Sometimes such attempts are called lay theology or ordinary theology (Astley, 2002), as opposed to academic theology. According to this understanding, this kind of theology is present in any human context, in education as well as in the everyday life of the people who are thinking about themselves and about their lives.

The interest in children's theology that has emerged in recent years (Bucher, et al., 2002; Schweitzer, 2006b; Iversen, Mitchell, and Pollard, 2009) can be considered a variety of lay theology or of ordinary theology. The term refers to children's ways of making sense of their faith, of religious images, and of religious ideas that they produce themselves or that they encounter. The reference to children's theology parallels the recent advocacy of children's spirituality (Erricker and Erricker, 2000). In both cases, educators advocate the position that children should not be offered some adult theology boiled down to miniature size, but their own ways of making sense of things by themselves should be respected.

While these considerations could open up a whole discussion on many different ways for relating theology to religious education, the present chapter is focused on theology as a reflexive, most often academic enterprise, and on the context of religious pluralism. Readers should not forget, however, that this enterprise has its roots in everyday life, with ordinary people and not only with academics who consider themselves theologians or with the churches and their representatives.

It is against this background that I now turn to some considerations concerning principled pluralism as an aim of religious education.

Principled pluralism as an aim of religious education

A good opportunity for understanding the tasks of contemporary religious education is relating religious education to the religious situation in western societies. For a long time, secularization was considered the basic challenge for contemporary religious education. Religion seemed to be on the wane, due to the forces of rationalization and modernization. This assumption has turned out to be not very realistic. Social scientists have come to doubt even the concept of secularization itself and most of all its scientific value (for example, Berger, 1979; Luckmann, 1991; Luhmann, 2000). The progressive loss of religion this concept implies has certainly not taken place, at least not in the general sense that many analysts had expected (Casanova, 1994; Berger, 1999). Influential philosophers like Jürgen Habermas now diagnose a 'post-secular' situation or society (Habermas, 2002). Others like Hans Joas, a leading sociologist of religion, maintain that even the reference to 'post' – after – secularization is not appropriate because religion has never disappeared, except perhaps in the minds of secularist philosophers (Joas, 2004). In any case, if religion has ever been absent, it now appears to have come back. And no doubt religion is here to stay, with many different facets. There is also wide agreement that religion is far from being beneficial in all cases, and that religious pluralism holds many challenges.

The social scientific successors of secularization theory are the concepts of plurality, pluralization, and pluralism. In my own understanding, *plurality* refers to the fact that contemporary societies entail different cultures, religions, and worldviews, and that none of them can claim a synthesizing function or demand an overarching influence, at least not successfully. *Pluralization* refers to the process that brings about plurality. *Pluralism*, finally, means a certain order which implies that the different cultures, religions, worldviews, etc. have reached some kind of coexistence that goes beyond fighting or discriminating against one another. This is certainly true for the understanding of political pluralism as a democratic way of dealing with differences, but I assume that it also makes sense to speak of religious pluralism in this fashion.

It is easy to see that religious pluralism entails special demands on the people who live in a situation of religious plurality. They must be able to come to terms with this plurality without either just taking resort to relativism that does not take the different truth-claims seriously, or by entrenching themselves in fundamentalist positions that do not allow for peaceful relationships with others who do not share the respective convictions. Both relativism and fundamentalism exclude religious pluralism as a dialogical order that makes space for the other without devaluing the differences between religious orientations and convictions.

In my understanding, religious pluralism must be based on clear principles such as dialogue, tolerance, and mutual respect. This is why I refer to *principled pluralism* as the aim of religious education. It is such principles that distinguish this pluralism from relativism because the principles must be defensible. They must be based on grounds that can also be convincing to others, at least potentially. At the same time, these principles must guarantee openness towards others who, explicitly and permanently, do not share one's own convictions.

It is quite obvious, at least to most observers, that such principles supporting the kind of pluralism I have described will not develop automatically, neither with children and adolescents nor with adults. This is why education and religious education are important in this context. In particular, religious education must support the acquisition or development of principles that make religious pluralism possible. Yet how can such principles be identified and what role should theology play in this process?

Pluralism with or without theology?

One of the contested questions about pluralism concerns the possible role of theology in religious education. In many places – for example, in the UK but also in a number of other countries – the transition from a traditional understanding of religious education to a more pluralist understanding has been based on giving up all confessional ties. Accordingly, confessional religious education is now considered monoreligious and monolithic or – to put it differently – confessional religious education is considered anti-pluralist and intolerant, or just like indoctrination (cf. the description by Copley, 1997, 101).

More or less automatically, the transition to the non-confessional and pluralist understanding of religious education seemed to imply as well that there should be no special relationship anymore between religious education and theology. After all, theology most often understands itself as a denominational enterprise that is premised on a certain creed or confession. From this point of view, it was the religious studies approach with its claim to religious neutrality that seemed to offer itself most naturally as a new basis for religious education. As Michael Grimmitt recently put it, there is no need for theology in religious education, at least not in the UK (Grimmitt, 2008, 274; Grimmitt also mentions others in the United Kingdom who would not agree with him on this issue).

As the title of this chapter indicates, I want to challenge this apparently natural fit between religious education and religious studies. My critical argument proceeds in two steps. First, I want to point out a number of weaknesses of the combination of religious education and religious studies from an educational point of view, and second, I want to present some perspectives from a Protestant theological point of view. I start with the educational perspective in order to make clear that what is at stake is not some kind of confessional or church-related interest but a general educational problem.

(1) From an educational point of view, the detachment of religious education from theology comes at a high price. It entails the following disadvantages.

(a) *No exposure to the internal or inside perspective of religions and, consequently, no opportunity to learn how to balance internal and external perspectives.* As pointed out above, theology is based on the internal perspective of faith which it develops and systematizes academically, in terms of doctrine and reflexive models. Yet from early on, Christian theology has also included external perspectives, for example, by making use of the Greco-Roman philosophical concept of *logos* in the first Christian centuries or, in later times, by pursuing the dialogue with different kinds of philosophy, anthropology, and with the social sciences as well as with natural science. Today, at least for Protestant theology, the constant interplay between internal and external perspectives is a basic requirement, especially in the areas of systematic and practical theology (a branch of theology that has only been developed to a very limited degree, for example, in the UK). Contrary to this, religious studies most often limits its approaches to the perspective of the outsider. At least according to many representatives of this discipline, the self-understanding of the religious traditions should not play a role for their scientific understanding that must be exclusively explanatory.

Educationally, however, it is the interplay between inside and outside perspectives that is of special importance. The process of education can actually be described as the acquisition of the ability to see oneself from other perspectives, not only those of other individuals but also those of different academic disciplines. Moreover, this process must also entail a balance between the different perspectives. Otherwise education would mean the transformation of human beings into the alloplastic objects of outside perceptions. Both one's own perspective and those of others remain crucial, and both must be brought into a considered balance.

(b) *No connection to the religious bodies, institutions, and communities that make up religious life outside the classroom, and consequently no chance to influence this life.* From its very premises, a religious studies approach will not be interested in having credibility or even authority with any tradition or community of faith. Such credibility would jeopardize the neutrality and scientific objectivity to which this approach aspires. It is easy to see that religious education would have to pay a high price for making this approach its sole basis. It certainly cannot hope to exert any influence on society beyond the classroom – a disadvantage or concern that is often now addressed in the context of fundamentalism.

(c) *No development of dialogical skills that are based on the encounter between different perspectives in the mode of speaking between you and me as I and Thou.* Dialogue needs difference. It depends on the encounter of persons who hold different perspectives or understandings. Even if some dialogues aim at mutual understanding and the overcoming of differences, true dialogue always presupposes that it must be possible for differences to continue to exist. Dialogue is not the end of difference, and differences should not be the end of dialogue. This is especially true for religious differences that, in many cases, can only be expected to dissolve at the expense of deep convictions. Disputes between different faiths have never been settled by scientific arguments. Any approach that does not make space for lasting differences falls short of the task of dialogical education.

(d) *No access to the values embodied in religious traditions that are intrinsically connected to the respective convictions and, consequently, no opportunities really to learn 'from' such traditions.* There is wide agreement in the religious education discussion over the last thirty years that it has been an important achievement to overcome a sterile 'learning about' approach. This approach turned religious education into a prolonged visit to a museum of dead objects on display, or into a rote learning enterprise like the geography classes of the past that tended to cover one country after another applying a set scheme of information. Yet the progression to 'learning from' religion has not really achieved a clear stance towards the need to include the internal perspective of faith and theology. But how can anyone learn from religion if the inner convictions and the values connected to them are methodically excluded? If theology is the reflexive understanding of a certain faith and religious tradition, it holds much potential for learning 'from' a religion or tradition. In fact, any approach to a religion that systematically neglects its reflexive expressions is necessarily incomplete, and must therefore be considered one-sided and questionable. Education is not allowed to present a distorted image of reality to students which intentionally leaves out certain parts or aspects of this reality because these aspects are considered, for example, old-fashioned and dated.

(e) *No access to whatever critical reflexivity religious traditions may have developed internally, consequently a limitation to external critical reflexivity.* There are many examples of the failure of well meant attempts to introduce enlightenment, democracy, or human rights by forcing them on people from the outside. Typically the result of such attempts has been, for example, less tolerance rather than more, because the people subjected to the imperialism of western democracy and values felt threatened in their cultural and religious identities. This is why it is so important to find access to whatever critical reflexivity religious traditions may have developed internally through their different religious traditions – in order to build upon this reflexivity without alienating people. The attempt to identify the religious roots of tolerance carried out in conversation between different religions is a good example of this (Schwöbel and von Tippelskirch, 2002).

(2) To these educational disadvantages, I want to add the following theological shortcomings of an approach to religious education detached from theology.

(a) *Interreligious relationships cannot be comprehended from a God perspective that is superior to the other religious faiths.* This is a crucial point especially for Protestant theology that holds a general scepticism vis-à-vis so-called pluralist theologies of religion. Since faith is about ultimate matters and beliefs, there can be no superior point of view above the different faiths. At least from a religious point of view, such a super perspective is not convincing. This is why pluralist models implying some kind of relativizing judgement of religious differences are not very attractive theologically. They seem to be premised either on a super ethics (as in the case of Hans Küng's global ethics – Küng, 1990) or on some kind of super epistemology (as in the case of John Hick's philosophical scepticism – Hick, 1996) that allow for defining the place of religious ideas. It is quite possible to consider religion from a moral point of view, but it remains equally possible to consider ethics from a religious point of view. The same applies to the relationship between theology and the philosophy of religion. Again, there should be dialogue in place of the claim to superiority.

(b) *Interreligious relationships should not be limited to ethics or to political demands but should include the attempt of understanding the other's faith.* Modern democracies are premised on religious freedom. This premise includes the limitation of state power in the realm of religion. Consequently, the state or the state school cannot have the right to demand or to enforce anything concerning matters of faith. Instead, the relationship between different denominations and religions should be based on religious beliefs rather than on state imposed ethical or political demands. This is also why it should include the attempt to understand the other's faith, as a presupposition for mutuality. Again, in terms of religious education, this implies that any limitation to an outside perspective must be challenged. The exclusion of religious truth-claims and their theological explanation or defence cannot lead to true dialogue.

(c) *The Protestant understanding of certainty in faith entails the view that this certainty is not the result of human decision-making, but is based on the experience of being granted certainty as a gift. The same is assumed for other faiths, so that religious pluralism is a necessity and cannot be overcome through the appeal to any objective prior-to-faith perspective.* The understanding that faith must be granted and that the certainty of faith is not a human achievement is a core conviction of Protestant theology that can already be found with the sixteenth-century reformers. It also excludes, from the beginning, any kind of 'teaching into' religion approach. Contrary to Roman Catholicism, faith can never be an aim of education in the Protestant understanding. This is why the identification of a Protestant confessional approach with indoctrination does not make much sense. From a Protestant perspective, indoctrination can never be accepted. Faith and indoctrination cannot go together, at least not theologically. If it can be shown that certain Protestant religious educators teach into the Christian faith, they must be criticized theologically – as well as educationally – for this attempt. It has taken Protestants a long time, however, to realize that the Protestant understanding of faith must also lead to a positive attitude towards pluralism. Only recently has the Protestant rejection of pluralism, as an external imposition that should be criticized or rejected, been overcome by the new perspective of a plea for pluralism based on the internal demands of faith itself (Herms, 1995; Schwöbel, 2003).

In this section, I have limited myself to theological views of religious education which means identifying theological demands on religious education. Yet it is clear that we must also consider the reverse perspective. What are the educational demands on theology?

Educational demands on theology

The considerations of why theology may have to play an important role for religious education in plural situations entail far-reaching implications for theology itself. In other words, not all kinds of theology will be suitable for the tasks and purposes described above. In a similar vein, for example, the German philosopher of education, Dietrich Benner, one of the leading representatives of this field in Germany, is in favour of relating religious education to theology. At the same time, he speaks of the need for non-fundamentalist approaches to religion as a presupposition for their integration in education (Benner, 2008).

In my own work, I refer to the following tasks that theology must fulfil in the context of religious education (for a general background, cf. Schweitzer, 2006a). Theology must be able to afford believers with a language and with concepts that can enable them to participate in dialogue across different cultures and different religions. In the first place, religious language is directed at insiders. It develops in the context of religious practice, ritual, and narrative. This implies that the ability to be in conversation about religious matters with outsiders requires additional skills at the interface between internal and external communication. If theology should be used for developing such skills, it must itself hold the potential of communicating with others that are not part of one's own community of faith, which is not automatically the case. A theology that only aims for discourse within one's own community falls short of the demands of education.

Moreover, religious traditions are not automatically supportive of tolerance and they do not develop dialogical attitudes and skills by themselves. This is why we need a theology that operates as the reflexive attempt of making sense of religious beliefs in the context of today's world. This kind of theology can only be developed in dialogue with different worldviews, with philosophy and with ethics, with natural science and with the social sciences. And we should add explicitly that this theology must also be in constant conversation with other religions. In this sense, it must become a theology of religions that tries to make sense of the coexistence of different religious traditions. This does not imply, however, that theology should give up its roots in a particular tradition.

If in fact theology is to be better equipped for this task than other disciplines – such as, for example, the philosophy or the sociology of religion; or a religious studies approach – it must focus on the roots of tolerance or of peace and justice within the religious traditions themselves. Such a theology can have a degree of credibility and authority among believers that religious studies approaches can never have.

Saying this, it should again be clear that I do not want to limit theology to the perspective of the insider. Theological statements should not be confused with a confession of faith. Confessional principles may be axiomatic for theology, but the work of theology itself must be strictly academic. Academic theology, however, has always – or, to make the claim more modest, most often – been premised on interdisciplinary and conversational structures. The inclusion of the perspective of the other may not have been equally visible in theology at all times, but it certainly should be made visible today and it should be recognized as the prerequisite for a theology that can serve as the basis for education for tolerance, peace, and justice.

Conclusion

It is my conviction that the pluralist situations of multiculturalism and multireligiosity do not imply that we need less theology in religious education. The rejection of theology as a partner that can inform religious education is based on the identification of theology with confessionalism and with dogmatism, or even with Christian imperialism. The kind of theology I have tried to describe in the present chapter is neither confessionalist nor dogmatic in the traditional sense. This theology will not only be of help in understanding religion, it is also indispensable for any kind of true 'learning from religion' as well as for interreligious dialogue that goes beyond relativism and fundamentalism.

References

Aslan, E. (ed.) (2009). *Islamische Erziehung in Europa/Islamic Education in Europe.* Wien et al.: Böhlau.
Astley, J. (2002). *Ordinary theology: Looking, listening and learning in theology.* Aldershot: Ashgate.
Ballard, P. H. (1966). Theology and religious education. *Learning for Living, 5,* 16–17.
Benner, D. (2008). Religiöse Bildung. Überlegungen zur Unterscheidung zwischen 'fundamentalen' und 'fundamentalistischen' Konzepten. In F. Schweitzer, V. Elsenbast, and C. T. Scheilke (eds), *Religionspädagogik und Zeitgeschichte im Spiegel der Rezeption von Karl Ernst Nipkow* (pp. 151–164). Gütersloh: Gütersloher Verlagshaus.
Berger, P. L. (1979). *The heretical imperative: Contemporary possibilities of religious affirmation.* Garden City, New York: Anchor Press.
Berger, P. L. (ed.). (1999). *The desecularization of the world: Resurgent religion and world politics.* Grand Rapids, Michigan: Eerdmans.
Bucher, A., et al. (2002). *Jahrbuch für Kindertheologie.* Stuttgart: Calwer.

Casanova, J. (1994). *Public religions in the modern world*. Chicago and London: University of Chicago Press.

Copley, T. (1997). *Teaching religion: Fifty years of religious education in England and Wales*. Exeter: University of Exeter Press.

Cush, D. (1999). The relationships between religious studies, religious education and theology: Big brother, little sister and the clerical uncle? *British Journal of Religious Education, 21,* 137–146.

Erricker, C., and Erricker, J. (2000). *Reconstructing religious, spiritual, and moral education*. London and New York: Routledge.

Grimmitt, M. (2008). England. In F. Schweitzer, V. Elsenbast, and C. T. Scheilke (eds), *Religionspädagogik und Zeitgeschichte im Spiegel der Rezeption von Karl Ernst Nipkow* (pp. 265–277). Gütersloh: Gütersloher Verlagshaus.

Habermas, J. (2002). *Glauben und Wissen: Friedenspreis des Deutschen Buchhandels 2001*. Frankfurt am Main: Suhrkamp.

Herms, E. (1995). Pluralismus aus Prinzip. In E. Herms, *Kirche für die Welt: Lage und Aufgabe der evangelischen Kirchen im vereinigten Deutschland* (pp. 467–485). Tübingen: Siebeck.

Hick, J. (1996). *Religion: Die menschlichen Antworten auf die Frage nach Leben und Tod*. München: Diederichs.

Hull, J. (2004). Practical theology and religious education in a pluralist Europe. *British Journal of Religious Education, 26,* 7–19.

Iversen, G. Y., Mitchell, G., and Pollard, G. (eds). (2009). *Hovering over the face of the deep: Philosophy, theology and children*. Münster et al.: Waxmann.

Joas, H. (2004). *Braucht der Mensch Religion? Über Erfahrungen der Selbsttranszendenz*. Freiburg: Herder.

Küng, H. (1990): *Projekt Weltethos*. München and Zürich: Piper.

Luckmann, T. (1991). *Die unsichtbare Religion*. Frankfurt/M.: Surkamp.

Luhmann, N. (2000). *Die Religion der Gesellschaft*. Frankfurt/M.: Suhrkamp.

Miller, R. C. (ed.). (1995). *Theologies of Religious Education*. Birmingham, Alabama: Religious Education Press.

Netto, B. (1989). On removing theology from religious education. *British Journal of Religious Education, 11,* 163–168.

Nipkow, K. E. (1985). Can theology have an educational role? In M. C. Felderhof (ed.), *Religious Education in a Pluralistic Society: Papers from a Consultation on Theology and Education held at Westhill College, Selly Oak* (pp. 23–38). London: Hodder and Stoughton.

Osmer, R. R., and Schweitzer, F. (2003). *Religious education between modernization and globalization: New perspectives on the United States and Germany*. Grand Rapids, Michigan: Eerdmans.

Rothgangel, M., and Thaidigsmann, E. (eds). (2005). *Religionspädagogik als Mitte der Theologie? Theologische Disziplinen im Diskurs*. Stuttgart: Kohlhammer.

Schweitzer, F. (2006a). *Religionspädagogik*. Gütersloh: Gütersloher Verlagshaus.

Schweitzer, F. (2006b). Children as theologians: God-talk with children, developmental psychology, and interreligious education. In D. Bates, G. Durka, and F. Schweitzer (eds), *Education, religion and society: Essays in honour of John M. Hull* (pp. 179–190). London and New York: Routledge.

Schweitzer, F. (2006c). Let the captives speak for themselves! More dialogue between religious education in England and Germany. *British Journal of Religious Education, 28*, 141–151.

Schweitzer, F., and Schwöbel, C. (eds). (2007). *Aufgaben, Gestalt und Zukunft Theologischer Fakultäten (Veröffentlichungen der WGTh Vol. 31)*. Gütersloh: Gütersloher Verlagshaus.

Schwöbel, C. (2003). *Christlicher Glaube im Pluralismus: Studien zu einer Theologie der Kultur*. Tübingen: Siebeck.

Schwöbel, C., and von Tippelskirch, D. (eds). (2002). *Die religiösen Wurzeln der Toleranz*. Freiburg et al.: Herder.

MARIO O. D'SOUZA

3   Identity, Diversity, and the Common Good

Introduction

I offer my thoughts from my Canadian perspective, a country that has traditionally been divided by the accolades of 'English' and 'French', and has also been referred to as the two solitudes (see Taylor, 1993). Immigration has not so much changed the reality of English and French Canada as it has drawn attention to the limitation of these categories. Contemporary Canada is a multicultural society, as well as religiously and educationally pluralist. And while the country has two official languages, English and French, it has no official culture. Canada's aboriginal peoples, or First Nations, are also part of this landscape, each with their own culture, language, and *Weltanschauung* and all that it entails. The Canadian political landscape has also been challenged by French nationalism, and even though this is confined to the province of Quebec, it shows its strains across the political landscape. Some have maintained that while Canada is socially a multicultural society, it is not so politically (see OECD, 1985, 8). Finally, Canada's educational plurality allows for the establishment of private educational institutions, and while all the provinces have fully-funded primary and secondary education, some provinces offer publicly-funded forms of Catholic education. This rough politico-sociocartography of Canada acts as my backdrop.

Pierre Trudeau, one of Canada's most visionary and charismatic leaders, saw federalism as a superior form of government, because in being more pluralist than monolithic it respected diversity among peoples (see Axworthy and Trudeau, 1990, 360). What Trudeau did not develop, however, was the foundation upon which diversity is grounded.

Today, the absence of such a foundation impoverishes not just Canada but the liberal democratic state in general in understanding the nature and purpose of its various diversities. The circular and generally unhelpful slogan, *diversity for diversity's sake*, is not particularly enlightening. Diversity seems to be deprived of a social and political *telos*, an end point: a place of communal arriving, striving, and living. However, one must in fairness recognize that a political and social system that enables peoples of different cultural identities to live out their aspirations in the same society is both 'recent' and 'genuinely new' (Lovin, 1992, 4). Today, however, the prominence of religion as a source of primary identity is calling into question the liberal agenda of the celebration of diversity for its own sake. The political and cultural tussle appears to be between those who see religion as private and apart from the public square, and those who see it as public and part of the public square – and informing and shaping the very nature of the state. Either way, religion now occupies a place of prominence, and it has led to disagreements, debate, and discussion in ways that would have been unimaginable to citizens of liberal democratic societies just twenty-five years ago. Internationally, religion dominates the global agenda: identities, nationhood, and moral positions are often read through the univocal lens of religion. Amartya Sen, in his work *Identity and violence: The illusion of destiny* (Sen, 2006), rightly wonders whether confining human identity to religion and culture does not in fact lead to the 'miniaturization' of human beings. The illusion of destiny, especially when it is suffocatingly bound up with religion, has resulted both in violence and in persecution. Sen admits that religion and cultures are enormously formative in shaping human identity, but they need not be the only sources of identity leading to the rejection and even persecution of those who are not part of the same religious fold: 'the recognition of multiple identities and of the world beyond religious affiliations, even for very religious people, can possibly make some difference in a troubled world in which we live' (Sen, 2006, xvi, 79).

The modern liberal democratic state has two immediately identifiable features: first, its social and economic structures and programmes, and second, the support of individual and group rights and tolerance in the midst of religious and cultural plurality. The nature of a liberal welfare state and the components of individual rights are usually contained in public documents and are usually not difficult to identify. On the other hand, while violations of tolerance are relatively easy to recognize, what actually constitutes the existence and practice of tolerance is more difficult to corroborate. The very word tolerance itself has a reductionist tone, and suggests a level of interaction that is minimal, suspicious, and latently xenophobic. Jacques Derrida suggests substituting 'hospitality' for 'tolerance' (Borradori, 2003, 16), while Jacques Maritain prefers 'fellowship' (Maritain, 1972, 116). Furthermore, defining and situating the common good, given the prominence of religion and its increasingly uneasy relationship with the ever expansive stage of liberalism, pluralism, and multiculturalism, all under the ever widening umbrella of democracy, becomes increasingly bulky and tricky. In spite of this, however, we need to agree on some basic features of the common good. We need to agree, for example, that the common good is more than a collection of private goods; that the common good is the collective good of human persons living virtuously, justly, and fairly in a pluralist society, and that in ultimate terms – *ultimate* in earthly terms not *absolute ultimate* in religious terms – the common good leads to human development and perfection. There is no doubt that in a pluralist context, terms like *common good*, *human person*, *human development*, and *human perfection* will not find universal agreement; but they have enormous implications for society, and they must not become the intellectual possession of political philosophers and politicians alone. All citizens must engage with these concepts, thus enriching the democratic and political dialogue: a dialogue that must be perennial if it is to be healthy. Discussions of the common good must also recognize its terrestrial and sociopolitical nature; this good does not have to be justified in exclusive and narrow religious terms. In this light, one can still affirm the intellectual, material, and moral components of the common good (see Maritain, 1953, 142). I plan to pursue this discussion through two sections: the first dealing with the relationship between religious identity, diversity, and the common good; the second reflecting on the education of persons and religious education, a relationship that is vital for the health of democratic society and the collective striving for the common good.

Religious identity, diversity, and the common good

What is the relationship of religious identity and diversity to the common good? Aristotelian influences on our understanding of the common good include the distinct nature of the individual parts that comprise this good. The individual citizen is a part contributing to the social whole where the common good is to be located: 'thus the common good is the good of individuals as parts and members of society, and is sought by them precisely as *members of society and as being not all alike*.' Further, since the common good extends to what 'is most determinate and actual in individuals, it is not for that reason to be identified with the singular, private good of these individuals; rather it is common by reason of its *communicability* to these many different individuals, and not because it includes the singular good of all of them' (McCoy, 1963, 52). It is also worth noting that understanding the common good as essentially related the social and communal nature of human persons secures it on an anthropological foundation. Human beings, human persons, require membership in society by virtue of their 'dignity and needs', but also in response to the person's 'inner urge to the communications of knowledge and love which require relationship with other persons' (Maritain, 1966, 47). Karl Hosteler identifies three characteristics of the common good: first, the common good as 'general welfare in contrast to what is merely personal and parochial'; second, the common good as 'a resource that is rightly public property ... and ... should not be privatized'; and third, the common good 'in the sense of a value that is held to be of benefit to all or nearly all human beings; something that would be part of a worthwhile human life regardless of what particular persons or communities believe' (Hosteler, 2003, 350).

Today, liberal democratic societies have, at best, a vague idea of the common good, and it is usually politico-economic in nature. However, what is troubling is that it seems to understand this good as a collection of individual goods monitored by various legal, political, and narrow social policies that guarantee the distribution of services to all citizens. What appears to be missing is a sense of 'deliberating with your fellow citizens about the common good and helping to shape the destiny of the political community ... [A deliberation that requires] a knowledge of public affairs and also a sense of belonging, a concern for the whole, a moral bond of the community' (Gairdner, 2001, 427). The difficulty with confining the common good to politico-economic categories, and situating it in exclusively material, individual, and terrestrial terms, is that the mystery of human personhood is relegated to the world of religion, and often culture, and deemed to be private. Citizens are expected to relate to one another within the politico-economic sphere but divorced from these other dimensions of human identity. So while there is an acknowledgment of religious and cultural diversity, as well as a tendency of most citizens to categorize each other according to these identities, the state proceeds towards this politico-economic good separated from the formative identities of religion and culture. In remaining true to its principle of not favouring a particular religion or culture, the liberal state sees diversity for diversity's sake, but is unable to respond to the complexity and mystery of human personhood and the various diversities of identity and human flourishing that now exist side by side. Thus religion runs the risk of going from one extreme of being deemed private to the other extreme of becoming the sole verification of human identity. Today, human flourishing, with the exception of economic and material welfare, is relegated to the private worlds, particularly to religion. Thus the constricted liberal understanding of the common good as life bound in economic and political union results in the further miniaturization of human beings. This leads, on the one hand, to a tension between the secular understanding of the common good reduced to the individual's good and welfare as realized through the framework of a liberal democratic state, a good understood in individual and politico-economic terms; and, on the other hand, a narrow religious, and often fundamentalist, understanding of the common good – and with increasing antagonism as to which of these two should be the exclusive measure of the good of the citizens. Either model reduces the common good to narrow categories because of a limited understanding of human flourishing. Neither the secular nor narrowly religious models include the intellectual, moral, material, and social dimensions of the common good, particularly in the context of the pluralist state; nor do they have an adequate understanding of the temporal good of human society with ends and goals universal enough to merit common recognition, but that need not be reduced either by materialism or by religious and cultural fundamentalism.

In responding to the demands of religious diversity and cultural plurality, as well as recognizing the seeming oppression of a univocal conception of the common good, some have called for the recognition of 'secure common goods in the sense of basic rights, material resources, education, and other goods that individuals can use to pursue whatever good life they deem proper for themselves' (Hosteler, 2003, 348). Pragmatic though the suggestion may be, it only leads to the further fragmentation of liberal democratic societies already burgeoning with diversity and divided between an ever-expanding secular understanding of what the good life constitutes, and a narrow understanding based on religion. Once again, both models lead to the miniaturization of the citizen as a person. The state exists to ensure the development and the flourishing of its citizens, and the key lies in interpreting those two nouns. Immigration has widened the religious and cultural plurality of Europe and North America, and immigrants usually cite three fundamental reasons for their translation: economic welfare, political freedom, and religious liberty. Soon after their arrival, however, they realize that religious liberty is relegated to the private sphere and political freedom is constitutionally guaranteed. Of these three reasons economic welfare is, by and large, left to their own ingenuity. Material and economic welfare becomes the measure of success, and the lens of viewing the common good, the good life, and human flourishing.

But who is the citizen? The concrete existing human being is a citizen, but never just a citizen. And why live in society? Are not the state's guarantees an encouragement for citizens to live private lives? If so, then any idea of the increasing perfection of one's nature as a citizen would have to be laid to rest, for such perfection depends upon the communal nature, aspirations, and objectives of political society. Society enables the citizen, who is more than just a citizen, to develop perfections as a whole person through communal values, shared knowledge, and truly human communications. Society also enables the citizen to make up for the deficiencies of the human condition, both physical and material, and in so doing it enables the individual citizen to attain a truly human life. Thus one develops and grows as a citizen and as a person (see Maritain, 1966, 47–48). The Aristotelian claim that 'man is by nature a political animal; it is his nature to live in a state' (Aristotle, 1967, 28) is the starting point for understanding the political being of the citizen and how it develops. Civil society is not bestowed by nature; it is a human creation, and human beings are inclined toward it for the perfection of their rational natures (see Fortin, 1987, 253). It is the perfection of this inclination that holds the clue to understanding the Aristotelian claim. In a pluralist state, the perfection of the citizen's political nature is not dependent on metaphysical and religious principles, but on practical civic ones; it is dependent on a 'fundamental agreement between minds and wills on the basis of life in common'; it is a life based upon a '*civic or secular* faith, not a religious one' (Maritain, 1951, 109, 110).

One must conclude, then, that the pursuit of the common good is a real means of uniting the religiously diverse democratic state. But it is a unity that cannot ignore the nature of the citizen as a person whose aspirations rise above the confines of politico-economic society. In spite of this, the challenge is in agreeing upon an understanding of the citizen's nature and of human flourishing that is not measured by the exclusivity of material welfare, on the one hand, or religious beliefs on the other.

The education of persons and religious education

What is the connection between the education of persons and religious education, a relationship that is vital for the health of democratic society and the collective striving for the common good? Religious education depends upon an implicit theological anthropology. What increasingly seems to be in question is whether there are implications for life in common stemming from this anthropology. While religions understand societal responsibilities and relationships in different ways, all religious leaders have experienced the strains of educating their adherents for life in pluralist societies, particularly in light of the labyrinth of postmodernity, and the cultural implications of globalization often presented in 'terms of material well being [alone]' (Blair, Daly, and Priestley, 2002, 240). In the face of a sea of religious, cultural, social, and moral plurality and materialism, one can understand, therefore, the temptation of religious educators to reject this seeming confusion in favour of concentrating on and retreating into the seeming security of an inward-centered and conservative religious practice.

Education and democracy have a natural relationship, but what has shown increasing strains is relating them to the common good in the context of religious pluralism. To paraphrase Lady Macbeth, the *sticking place* for the perfection of the political collectivity now seems to depend upon educators and political leaders coming to see the relationship between education, democracy, and the common good secured upon human nature, irrespective of religious differences. Philosophers have explored what a common human nature means (see, for example, Reid, 1964). Others have critiqued such a universalist understanding, but see the importance of affirming a 'disposition common to all people', a 'natural solidarity', and 'a measure of mutual forbearance, helpfulness, and trust' (Lazari-Pawlowska, 1970, 583, 584). In the face of religious diversity, then, religious educators must educate with an eye towards this human nature or to this human commonality and its influence on life in common. Political leaders must broaden their economic and materialist conceptions of political society, not simply in acknowledging the phenomenon of religious differences but also in recognizing the contribution of religious belief to the common life of civic society. All this widens our conception of human nature in relation to the common good. Religious educators and political leaders have public responsibilities to the common good. Indeed, the wider questions: 'What is life for?' and 'What are schools for?' provide foundations for the relationship between the common good and religious education (see Vryhof, 2005, 125), because both questions engage students, future active citizens, in ways that are broadly communal and not narrowly religious or materialistic. Both questions, therefore, widen how we understand the relationship between the broader task of the education of persons and the more focused task of religious education.

One of the finest works on the topic of religious education and liberal democracy is Walter Feinberg's work, *For goodness sake: Religious schools and education for democratic citizenry*. It is worth quoting him at some length:

> Religious education is a matter of faith in more than the familiar sense of the term. To fail to broaden the debate about the appropriate aims of religious education in liberal, democratic societies beyond the confines of a single faith community is to assume that the attitudes, skills, and dispositions required to reproduce liberal, democratic society can be placed on automatic and grow themselves. This assumption is false. The skills required for liberal democracy are multifaceted, the dispositions deep, and the attitudes complex ... They are satisfied not just when people vote. They are expressed in the way citizens treat one another at home, at work, and on the street. (Feinberg, 2006, xiii–xiv)

Feinberg says that democratic pluralism should favour schools where contact between different groups is encouraged, and where religious distinctiveness does not monopolize the person's identity (see Feinberg, 2006, 43). While the democratic principle of such contact is to be applauded, there is no denying that though pluralism by definition emphasizes religious diversity – 'plurality' being a recognition of 'multiplicity', while 'pluralism' being an evaluation of the multiplicity in a 'positive' light (see Skeie, 2002, 48) – the secular, liberal state is unable to engage human distinctiveness beyond economic and political relationships. However, while religions strive to develop a deep sense of enduring identity in the believer, citizens also have the freedom to proceed by the conviction that their 'lives are not predetermined by birth and social origin, and that each and every one has the right and also the responsibility to shape his or her own life according to their wishes and life plans. It seems that this well-known characteristic of modern and postmodern societies has far reaching religious implications' (Schweitzer, 2007, 90). Such freedom is advocated by philosophers of education who, while recognizing the right of parents to educate their children in their faith and distinct religious practices, go on to remind us of the children's right, on reaching the age of reason, to embrace, fall away from, or reject those beliefs and practices (see McLaughlin, 1984; Callan, 1985). Such freedom is an undeniable characteristic of the modern democratic pluralist state and influences one's conception of the common good, particularly if this good has been conceived of and taught in exclusively religious terms.

While reason and rationality are essential to the education of persons, what is their relationship to religious education? The relationship between faith and reason, or doctrine and reason, or the revealed word and reason is different in each religion. In addition, there is the challenge that while students today have vast amounts of information and ready access to it, they appear to be lacking in methods, systems, and values that prioritize and evaluate this information, and from the perspective of religious education they appear to have very different ways of evaluating this information. Dividing knowing and information into secular and religious categories only complicates matters as it is the one knowing, learning, and acting human person who receives and responds to this information. Added to this mix is the fact that 'modern plurality' is not only characterized by 'fragmentation' but also that different groups have 'competing and often contradictory rationalities' (Jackson, 2004, 8). Pluralist societies lack 'traditional metaphysical comforts' (Blacker, 2007, 12).

Alan Bloom's *The closing of the American mind* (Bloom, 1987) marks the beginning of a sustained discussion on the role of the liberal arts and the humanities in a pluralist and multicultural society. These categories of knowledge and learning did, by and large, introduce students to wider questions such as: 'How should I spend my life?', 'What do I most care about and why?', 'For the sake of what or who am I living?', 'What is my life for?' (see Kronman, 2007, 9). Only the one asking these questions can answer them for they are fundamentally personal, but the fact that others have a propensity to ask the same questions would suggest a common human yearning: a shared condition which situates the origin and the exploration of such and similar questions. All this is to say that in the midst of pluralism, reason and faith can provide the platform to seek not doctrinal or theological commonality but human and civic commonality, and a yearning for a truly human common good that is of a higher order than material categories alone. In light of the fact that western education has become increasingly less liberal (in the classical sense of the term *liberal education*), religious educators have an ideal opportunity to play a more conscious and deliberate role to educate persons for life in community nourished by more than just religious ideals. The inclusion of the virtues of reason, intelligence, personal responsibility, public and civic responsibility and accountability, etc., must also be included. However, the seeming timelessness of the classics has been challenged; Plato and Aristotle's portrayal of human nature and equality, for example, are insufficient. Liberal education must be humanistic for our time, and chief among its qualities must be the realization that, in the midst of pluralism, the citizen's identity – as one striving for the common good – depends upon 'dialogical relations with others' (Taylor, 1992, 34).

A great deal has been written on citizenship education and its implications for religious education. Religious education, whether taught communally or exclusively, must educate the student to see their civic and political participation in ways that are wider than the economic and the material alone. While the kind of actions, choices, and decisions of interest to religious educators and political leaders may well be different, each group has a responsibility to prepare believers and citizens for a life in political society: the evolution of pluralist societies and the evolution of an integral history depend upon it. Religious educators must form students to look upon religious plurality as a distinctive feature and the inevitable result of human freedom, and not just as a characteristic of the historic evolution of political society, or worse as a historic accident culminating in the pluralist state. What is needed is for citizens to engage one another in a comprehensive human manner, because the citizen is more than just a political animal bound by economic and political relationships. The citizen also transcends the confines of political society, but with a transcendence that is not to be narrowed by religious identity alone. 'Citizenship education', therefore, 'is about knowledge *and* action' (Watson, 2004, 261). However, in the face of a pervasive plurality of beliefs, engaging in this comprehensive manner may be better served through dialogue, conversation, and interaction rather than by succumbing to the temptation to draw up a complete list of absolute values and agreements (see Smith, 2000, 412–413). And though some values and agreements are already put in place by the state, a more relational starting point is required: some foundation from which mutual engagement and dialogue can proceed. Is not the commonality of human nature such a starting point? Are not the autonomy, freedom, and the equality of the knowing and acting human person, irrespective of religious, cultural, ethnic, and social identities, the foundation for this comprehensive interaction?

Conclusion

I have maintained that striving for the common good, one that is not narrowly conceived through religious or cultural categories nor by economic and material ones, gives religious educators an opportunity to strive for the unity of a religiously pluralist society. Of course, this position presumes a few things, including the acceptance by religious leaders to see a value and a need to live in harmony beyond political and economic relations alone. They also need to see the perfection of the citizen's nature as a citizen, and not exclusively as a religious believer, to be a good – and one that can only occur in the midst of diversity and through diverse levels of human interaction. There is also the fundamental presupposition of the freedom of religious belief, as well as the freedom to reject such a belief. Neither acceptance nor rejection of religious belief can become the measuring rod of the common good of a pluralist society.

However, in an attempt to engage a religiously diverse citizenry to work together for the common good, educators make, in my estimation, one of two mistakes. Either they attempt some form of interreligious dialogue to show common religious and moral principles, or they argue for the elimination of religiously-based education and religious education, replacing them with a secular education for citizenship. In either case they move towards extremes: either they attempt to minimize religious differences or they banish those differences to the isolated worlds of ethnicity and race, and risk ghettoization. The credal and doctrinal differences of religions are too fundamental, and the foundational reality of religious identity too rudimentary, to endure such banishment. Becoming aware of the commonality of our religious principles is undoubtedly important, as indeed is the understanding of our religious distinctiveness.

However, just as a previous classical philosophy stressed the primacy of being over becoming, perhaps the time is now ripe to stress the societal responsibilities of becoming without negating the primacy of religious being. Religious educators spend much time and analysis on the role of becoming as a result of one's religious identity and affiliation. Religious becoming has inward and outward dimensions. While historically, the inward dimension has been given sustained attention, today there is a pressing need to attend to the outward or public dimension of religious becoming and its implications for life in society. Herein is to be found an important feature of the relationship between the education of the person and religious education. Pluralist societies present religious educators with the formidable challenge of bringing believers not only to agree on the common good, but also to see their striving and working for the common good as an activity rooted in their religious beliefs and identity. Reason and intelligence are fundamental human traits, and they ennoble the citizen as a person. In narrowing the political arena, the pluralist state has also narrowed the function of intelligence. The pursuit of the common good by a diverse religious citizenry may well be one means of liberating political and societal intelligence. Perhaps the summons of religious education and the responsibility of religious educators will be to draw out the implications of religious becoming as a means for sociopolitical unity.

References

Aristotle (1967). *The politics.* (T. A. Sinclair, trans.). Harmondsworth: Penguin Books.
Axworthy, T., and Trudeau, P. (1990). *Toward a just society: The Trudeau years.* (P. Claxton, trans.). Markham, Ontario: Viking.
Blacker, D. (2007). *Democratic education stretched thin: How complexity challenges a liberal ideal.* Albany: State University of New York Press.

Blair, C., Daly, E., and Priestley, J. (2002). Three reflections for ministry and education. *Religious Education*, 97 (3), 238-253.
Bloom, A. (1987). *The closing of the American mind*. New York: Simon & Schuster.
Borradori, G. (2003). *Philosophy in a time of terror: Dialogues with Jürgen Habermas and Jacques Derrida*. Chicago: University of Chicago Press.
Callan, E. (1985). McLaughlin on parental rights. *Journal of Philosophy of Education*, 19, 111-118.
Feinberg, E. W. (2006). *For goodness sake: Religious schools and education for democratic citizenry*. New York and London: Routledge.
Fortin, E. (1987). St Thomas Aquinas. In L. Strauss, and J. Cropsey (eds), *History of political philosophy* (pp. 248-275). Chicago: University of Chicago Press.
Gairdner, W. (2001). *The trouble with democracy: A citizen speaks out*. Toronto: Stoddart.
Hosteler, K. (2003). The common good and public education. *Educational Theory*, 53 (3), 347-361.
Jackson, R. (2004). *Rethinking religious education and plurality: Issues in diversity and pedagogy*. London and New York: RoutledgeFalmer.
Kornman, A. (2007). *Education's end: Why our colleges and universities have given up on the meaning of life*. New Haven and London: Yale University Press.
Lazari-Pawlowska, I. (1970). On cultural relativism. *The Journal of Philosophy*, 67 (17), 577-584.
Lovin, R. (1992). Must we disown our past to become multicultural? *Liberal Education*, 78, 2-9.
Maritain, J. (1951). *Man and the state*. Chicago: University of Chicago Press.
Maritain, J. (1953). *The range of reason*. New York: Charles Scribner's Sons.
Maritain, J. (1966). *The person and the common good*. (J. J. Fitzgerald, trans.). Notre Dame, Indiana: University of Notre Dame Press.
Maritain, J. (1972). *Ransoming the time*. (H. L. Binsse, trans.). New York: Gordian Press.
McCoy, C. (1963). *The structure of political thought: A study in the history of political ideas*. New York: McGraw Hill.
McLaughlin, T. (1984). Parental rights and the religious upbringing of children. *Journal of Philosophy of Education*, 18 (1), 75-83.
OECD – Organization for Economic Cooperation and Development (1985). *Education: Cultural and linguistic pluralism in Canada*. Ottawa: Multiculturalism Directorate, Department of the Secretary of State of Canada.
Reid, J. P. (1964). Marx on the unity of man. *The Thomist*, 28 (3), 259-301.
Schweitzer, F. (2007). Religions and individualization: New challenges to educate for tolerance. *British Journal of Religious Education*, 29 (1), 89-100.

Sen, A. (2006). *Identity and violence. The illusion of destiny*. London: Allen Lane.
Skeie, G. (2002). The concept of plurality and its meaning for religious education. *British Journal of Religious Education*, 25 (1), 47–59.
Smith, S. (2000). Morality, civics, and citizenship. *Educational Theory*, 50 (3), 405–418.
Taylor, C. (1993). *Reconciling the solitudes: Essays on Canadian federalism and nationalism*. Montreal and Kingston: McGill-Queen's University Press.
Taylor, C. (1992). *Multiculturalism and the politics of recognition*. A. Gutman (ed.). Princeton, New Jersey: Princeton University Press.
Vryhof, S. (2005). A system where everyone wins: The legitimacy of faith-based schools in a system of choice. *Educational Horizons*, 83 (2), 125–142.
Watson, J. (2004). Educating for citizenship – the emerging relationship between religious education and citizenship education. *British Journal of Religious Education*, 26 (2), 260–271.

FERNANDO A. CASCANTE-GÓMEZ

4 Pluralist Latin American Liberation Theology: Theological Themes and Educational Challenges

Introduction[1]

For decades the theology of religious pluralism and the theology of liberation developed separately, 'in their own circles', without much contact or conversation. But in recent years, Latin American theologians have been at work developing a 'pluralist theology of liberation'. In the present context of globalization, they are examining the crucial role religions can play in the restoration of justice and peace. Thus, at the turn of the new millennium, with the title 'Along the many paths of God', a series of five books was planned to develop a liberation theology of religions.[2] Under the auspices

1 This article is an enlarged and updated version of my article 'Latin American Theology and Religious Pluralism: A Latin American Voice' in *Religious Education, 104* (5), 2009, 556–563.
2 These are the Spanish titles of the series:
   1. *Por los Muchos Caminos de Dios I: Desafíos del Pluralismo Religioso a la Teología de la Liberación*. Colección Tiempo Axial. ASETT/Verbo Divino, Quito, 2003.
   2. *Por los Muchos Caminos de Dios II: Hacia una Teología Cristiana y Latinoamericana del Pluralismo Religioso*. Colección Tiempo Axial. ASETT/Abya-Yala, Quito, 2004.
   3. *Por los Muchos Caminos de Dios III: Teología Latinoamericana Pluralista de la Liberación*. Colección Tiempo Axial. ASETT/Abya Yala, Quito, 2006.
   4. *Por los Muchos Caminos de Dios IV: Teología Liberadora Intercontinental del Pluralismo Religioso*. Colección Tiempo Axial. ASETT/Abya Yala, Quito, 2007.
   (These four books were edited by José María Vigil, Luiza Tomita y Marcelo Barros.)
   5. *Por los muchos caminos de Dios V: Hacia una Teología Planetaria*. Colección Tiempo Axial. ASETT/Abya Yala, Quito, 2010. (Edited by José María Vigil.)

of the Ecumenical Association of Third World Theologians (EATWOT, or ASETT in Spanish), and coordinated by its Theological Commission for Latin America, a group of Latin American liberation theologians began to reflect and write in response to their new, enhanced awareness of the 'many paths of God in the world'. The first three books of the series were intentionally written from and for the particular Latin American historical and theological context. Book four incorporates the reflections of Christian theologians from five continents, in search of a Christian 'inter-continental' pluralist theology of liberation. The final book, published in 2010, gathers the results of a consultation among theologians from around the world and from different world religions concerned with a 'planetary theology': that is, a 'multireligious', pluralist theology of liberation.

To summarize or analyse what the different authors say in these books, or what they are saying as whole, is beyond the scope of this chapter. My purpose here is much more modest. On the one hand, I simply want to depict the development of an ongoing dialogue between the theology of liberation and the theology of religious pluralism. On the other hand, as a Christian religious educator, I want to highlight some of the fundamental themes and educational challenges of a theology of religious pluralism conceived from the particular perspective of the Latin American theology of liberation. First, I present a short description of what the authors tried to do in each of the books of the series. Second, I draw attention to what I consider are the most critical theological insights presented in the third book of the series, wherein the goal was specifically to outline what a Latin American pluralist theology of liberation would be. Finally, I draw attention to some of the central challenges a pluralist theology of liberation raises for the task of Christian religious education.

The developing path of a pluralist theology of liberation

According to Latin American theologians, their recent interest in and efforts for a pluralist theology of liberation should be understood not as a delayed response to academic discussions about the need and importance of interfaith dialogue and of a theology of religions, but mainly as a response to a new movement of the Spirit. For decades, 'without books and theology', people have intuited a 'spirituality of religious pluralism' in academic settings, as well as in informal conversations in homes and in public places. José María Vigil, one of the organizers of the five-volume series and coordinator of the Theological Latin American Commission, explains it this way:

> We are facing a new great *wave* of the Spirit upon history. The previous one was undoubtedly a spirituality of liberation, which awoke Christianity around the world to a commitment to love-justice, making it aware of the socio-political dimension [of the gospel] to which it was partially blind ... At the dawn of the 21st century we are witnessing the full expansion of a new and still growing wave, that of becoming aware of religious pluralism, which is going to profoundly transform Christianity and all religions, as a milestone clearly indicating a before and an after.[3]

The planning and the writing of the series, *Along the Many Paths of God*, therefore constitutes a 'second act' that, on the one hand, assumes an existing Christian praxis with regards to the intersection of theology of liberation and religious pluralism and which, on the other hand, invites more praxis towards a theology of religious pluralism by all religions. The following is an overview of the growth of this 'second act'.

In the first book of the series (*Along the Many Paths of God I: Challenges of Religious Pluralism to Theology of Liberation*, 2003) the authors look at the main issues that religious pluralism presents to liberation theology. They look at the past and present reality of religious pluralism in the world, and more particularly in Latin America where Christianity, in its Protestant and Catholic expressions, has been in contact mostly with Afro-Caribbean and Indian-native religions. From the perspective of Indian, Afro-Caribbean, and feminist Latin American theologies, authors in this book analyse the religious intolerance that has characterized and still characterizes the male-dominant versions of Christianity imposed by the European Catholic conquerors and colonizers, and later continued by the Protestant missions from the North. Liberation of the

---

3   Freely translated from the epilogue by José María Vigil in book IV of the series, *op. cit.*, accessed at <http://tiempoaxial.org/textos/TA8Epilogo.htm>.

poor and the call for justice continue to be the hermeneutical criteria for their reflections. The book makes a strong call to develop an awareness of the new spirituality emerging from religious pluralism and the need to develop a new sense of the missionary activity which is intrinsic to the Christian religion.

In book two (*Along the Many Paths of God II: Toward a Christian and Latin American Theology of Religious Pluralism*, 2004) another group of authors discuss the possibilities and limitations of 'classical' liberation theology to respond congruently and constructively to the challenges presented by religious pluralism. It represents a 'first step' to outlining a Latin American liberation theology of religious pluralism. They realized that, although liberation theology has explicitly inclusivist roots (e.g. the Second Vatican Council acknowledges the spiritual value of other religions as means of salvation), this was not enough to engage in genuine religious dialogue with people of other faiths. Thus, attention is given in this book to the religious experience of indigenous and Afro-Caribbean populations and the increasing role of women in church and society. In addition, more explicit connections are proposed between a theology of liberation and a theology of religious pluralism.

A new paradigm is explicitly assumed in book three (*Along the Many Paths of God III: Latin American Pluralist Theology of Liberation*, 2006): the 'pluralist paradigm' for a theology of liberation that values the 'many paths of God' in the world. In a world where the majority of people are not Christian, only a pluralist theology of liberation can enable a global interreligious dialogue that could move all of humanity towards a world of justice and peace. This pluralist paradigm assumes respect and value of the 'religious other'. It requires a revisiting of central theological loci, in order to move towards a deeper and broader understanding for developing a pluralist theology of liberation. In the following section, in light of the purpose of this chapter, I will briefly refer to some of these central theological themes as they are currently being revisited by some Latin American theologians.

In book four (*Along the Many Paths of God IV: Christian and Intercontinental Theology of Liberation of Religious Pluralism*, 2007) eighteen theologians from Latin America, Asia, Africa, North America, and Europe reflect on the reality of religious pluralism in their own contexts, as well as on some of the particular challenges that religious pluralism raises for Christian theology in those parts of the world. On balance, it is accepted that the development of a theology of religious pluralism is in its initial steps in each of the continents. However, it is also acknowledged that a theology of religions is present in much lesser degree and not in all continents. Similarly, it is accepted that the proportion of theologians who are concerned with, and who are responding to the reality of religious pluralism from, a 'pluralist paradigm' is very small. Nevertheless, there is an incipient awareness that a new way of doing theology is in the making: one that uses the pluralist paradigm for the creation of the only theology that may have a future in the world – that is, a theology of religious pluralism.

It is precisely the concern for the development of a theology of religious pluralism that is at the base of the final book of the series (*Along the Many Paths of God V: Toward a Planetary Theology*, 2010). This is the only title that has been published in English,[4] in addition to the customary Spanish, Portuguese, and Italian editions of the previous four books. In this last book, twenty theologians, representing some of the major world religions (Christianity, Baha'i, Islam, Hinduism, and Buddhism) and African indigenous religions, reflect on the challenges and possibilities of a planetary theology. Some of them prefer to use the term 'interfaith theology', others call it 'transreligious theology', and still others name it 'post-religious or post-confessional theology'. In the form of a consultation, the questions posed to them were the following:

---

4   A free digital version of this book can be accessed at <http://tiempoaxial.org/AlongTheManyPaths/>.

- Is an 'interreligious, multireligious, planetary, world theology' possible?
- What are the concrete elements, themes and suggestions for developing an interfaith theology?
- What is the relationship between an interfaith theology and the universal 'golden rule' and the option for the poor?
- Is an interfaith spirituality possible? Beyond being pluralist, will it be secular? Post-religional?[5]

As expected, different, contrasting, and even opposing views are expressed in response to these questions. Nevertheless, its value is seen in the gathering of voices from around the world regarding the reality of religious pluralism, and the possibility of a pluralist theology beyond confessions. For this final book 'assumes the concrete exercise of dialogue as a spiritual and human path that ... might one day be the daily practice of the religions of all humanity'.[6]

Key themes of a Latin American theology of religious pluralism

The central themes of a Latin American theology of religious pluralism are present throughout the first three books of the series. The first two books constitute an effort to look for a 'pluralist paradigm' in light of those key themes. But the third book actually represents the efforts of looking at those themes in light of an explicit 'pluralist paradigm'. Therefore, *Along the Many Paths of God III: Latin American Pluralist Theology of Liberation* is possibly the first book ever written with the clear intention to overcome

---

5   José María Vigil (ed.), *Along the Many Paths of God V: Toward a Planetary Theology*, digital version, 15.
6   Ibid., 13.

the inclusivist perspective of 'classical' liberation theology, and to assume an unambiguous pluralist perspective. The book is a collection of essays that show the praxis and reflection of lay and professional theologians.[7] Moved by the 'pluralist paradigm' they revisit classical theological loci such as revelation, Christology, ecclesiology, soteriology, Christian spirituality, ethics, and missiology. They are increasingly concerned about the pluralist manifestation of humanity's religious experience and its connection with the struggle for justice and peace in the world.

The authors of the third volume offer as a 'first draft' their reflections and search for new emphasis and new readings of biblical texts (e.g. primeval story in the book of Genesis), doctrines (e.g. of the Spirit), and of New Testament teachings (e.g. Logos, reign of God). In assuming the 'pluralist paradigm', Latin American liberation theologians[8] continue to value the role of the Scriptures as a crucial source of theological categories for looking at religious pluralism from a liberating, life-giving perspective. The identity of the Church is affirmed as something in process, open to an interdependent and hospitable dialogue with other religious communities. In Jesus, God calls all human beings and all religions to convert to the vision of and mission for another kind of world, one characterized by justice and peace. A pluralist Christian spirituality involves a return to the centrality of God and God's reign in the life and teachings of Jesus. But it is also a spirituality that invites people to pray and worship from a cosmic dimension, reassuming the sacramental value of the body and all the natural elements from the environment. The main emphasis for the Church's mission is on collaboration with what God is already creating in history. This requires a

---

7 For a list of authors and chapter titles in this book, see <http://latinoamericana.org/tiempoaxial/textos/TA6Indice.htm>.

8 As is the case for the other books in the series, some of authors in book three were born in Latin America, while some of them have made Latin America their home and the place for their Christian praxis and reflection. Some of them are world-renowned theologians (e.g. Leonardo Boff, José Comblin, Jose María Vigil), while others probably are unknown outside Latin America, or even unknown in their own countries beyond their work contexts. But all of them are convinced that in today's globalized world we have no option but to be plural.

spirit of dialogue in order to discern what God is doing through others. It also demands a willingness to be inserted in the midst of society, with all its conflicts, in order to witness to it and serve in it.

While keeping in mind the overall perspective of the poor and oppressed, and its ethical demand to all religions, some authors emphasize the particular plight of women and of the Afro- and indigenous populations whose voices and religious experiences have not been equally heard, or heard at all, within some forms of inclusivist Christianity. In one case, the plurality of the religious experience is affirmed from the gender perspective, which questions the hegemony or primacy given to male biblical and theological interpretations. In another case, a plurality of divine revelations is validated in the encounter of God with the history of black people and the particular appropriation of Jesus by indigenous Andean communities.

Other authors incorporate secular voices from the natural and human sciences and philosophy to propose a view of God's grace and of Jesus and his message that seriously questions exclusivist and inclusivist theological affirmations which, in the end, do not contribute to interreligious dialogue or peaceful living for all people in the world. For pluralist theology of liberation, 'ecological and anthropological' hermeneutics becomes as relevant for reading both Scripture and historical reality as the 'socioeconomic' hermeneutics was for classical theology of liberation. For example, it is affirmed that in the same way all natural species witness to the mystery of life, so all religions reveal something of the mystery of God. The multiple manifestations of what it is to be human (e.g. cultures), as well as the multiple expressions of human religious experience (that is, religious pluralism), have an incommensurable value that deserves to be preserved in the same way that the immense biodiversity in nature deserves to be preserved. At the same time, a new value is given to scientific progress and human knowledge that allows a humanist perspective to understand God's revelation in the secular realm of life of groups and societies. Since the Spirit of God is in everything, and since everything that makes human life more human comes from God, it is possible to say that 'there is salvation outside religions.'

For pluralist liberation theologians religions (including Christianity) reveal the many ways we should walk in fidelity and love for God, neighbour, and all of creation. Religions serve their goal as long as they lead people to love and serve the poor, and work for peace and justice in the world. Jesus' life and teachings provide definite criteria for Christians to judge any doctrine and practice of institutionalized Christian religion, and to discern what is best in other religions. This is so because his life and teachings were centered in the love and service for our neighbours as signs of our love for God. Jesus never intended to create a new religion. There are no signs in the Gospels that he presented himself as God. Therefore exclusivist theologies are a distortion of the core message of Jesus and an obstacle to becoming his true disciples. Likewise, inclusivist theologies, although a step forward, fall short of God's ultimate desire for personal, social, and cosmic liberation. Finally, the pluralist liberation theologians' critique of exclusivist and inclusivist theologies requires feminist, Afro-, and Indian perspectives to overcome representations of divine authority in Christian religion which are usually dominated by white-male perspectives. Religious ethnocentrism, in the end, is what has made it difficult for Christian theology to encounter the different-others (e.g. as female or as black), and discover that God is revealed in and through them.

Challenges for Christian religious educators

Arguably, the main challenge of a pluralist theology of liberation is the fact that theologies of liberation still have a rather marginal status within current dominant forms of Christianity. It is true that, after decades of struggle, persecution, criticism, and even martyrdom of many of its proponents, liberation theology, in its classical and new expressions (e.g. socioeconomic, feminist, Afro-Caribbean, indigenous, Black, Asian, ecological), has gained a place of respect among mainstream Protestant and Catholic theologies. Nevertheless, these theologies of liberation that speak on behalf of and from the perspective of those on the margins of society continue to be themselves at the margin of the discourses and practices of most Christian institutions and denominations. They continue to be either rejected or ignored by conservative sectors and movements in the Protestant Church (not to mention fundamentalist groups). Similarly, they continue to be either questioned or persecuted by an increasing number of conservative high-ranking officials in the Catholic Church. In addition, as mentioned earlier, the number of liberation theologians involved in the development and promotion of a pluralist theology of liberation is still very small. Christian religious educators who want to advocate a pluralist theology of liberation must therefore be aware that they are joining a group of Christians who are 'a minority among a minority', doing theology with a pluralist paradigm that is just in its initial stage, and which has not much of a place within the dominant theological and ecclesiastical institutions. This means that much is still to be discovered in terms of content and methodologies for doing and teaching a pluralist theology of liberation.[9] And, paradoxically, much of the spiritual support and intellectual resources available to this new breed of Christian religious educators seems to be found outside their institutional church and theological institutions, rather than inside them.

However, a pluralist theology of liberation, as briefly sketched here, offers important insights and opportunities for Christian religious educators concerned about and committed to religious pluralism. Particularly helpful for Christian religious educators is the emerging understanding of 'Christian mission' within the new pluralist paradigm of liberation theology. This new understanding does not focus on proselytism, or on the transmission of presumed universal dogmas, or on the planting of new churches. It focuses on three activities that could help advance our educational efforts towards a pluralist Christian religious education. They are testimony, dialogue, and service. Here I offer a brief commentary of how I understand the ways that these clues could support our educational reflection and practices in Christian religious education.

---

[9] At the moment, the books in this series are probably one of the best resources available to Christian religious educators and faith community leaders concerned with the meaning of Christianity in a multireligious context. *Theology of Religious Pluralism* (2008) by José M. Vigil is also an excellent educational resource.

Testimony

Although it is not a word equally emphasized or understood among different Christian traditions, *testimony* is, without a doubt, an important word in Christian religious vocabulary. On the one hand, *testimony* has to do with what one says in public (e.g. teaching and preaching). On the other hand, it has to do with how a person and a community live out their religious beliefs in the midst of people who have different religious beliefs, opposing beliefs, or none at all (e.g. acts of love and justice in the world). In sum, *testimony* has to do with the deeds and words of a religious community.

This means that, in light of a pluralist theology of liberation, the challenge for Christian people is to review afresh what we are saying about our faith in connection with other people's faiths. We need to go back and re-examine the testimony of God's multifaceted revelation in Scriptures, the texts and traditions that reveal God's universal love for all peoples of the world, the reign-oriented life and teachings of Jesus, and the life-giving manifestations of God in the natural and human world. At the same time we need to find ways to nurture a style of life that shows, at the personal and communal level, evidence of God's love for all peoples of the world. This kind of testimony draws from our religious sources and needs to be nurtured within the contexts of practice of our religious lives (e.g., home, congregation, and community). This kind of *testimony* invites the inclusion of a 'theology of religions'[10] as an essential part of the training of leaders and pastors in seminaries and Bible institutes; it invites open conversations within congregations about their Christian faith in light of other people's faiths; and it invites open conversation between parents and children at home when they come with questions such as 'Is God a girl or a boy?'[11] The

---

10 See, for example, Paul Knitter's book, *Introducing Theologies of Religions* (New York: Orbis Books, 2003).
11 This question generated a lively conversation among four- and five-year-old children in a private pre-kindergarten hosted at a theological institution. This conversation showed the crucial role of parents (mothers in this case) in shaping children's religious beliefs. Here are some of the verbatim expressions of some of the children documented

reality of religious diversity permeates people's lives from pre-kindergarten to higher education, from rural areas to small and large cities, from parks and malls to the workplace. It is increasingly coming to us through visual images and messages on TV and the Internet. Therefore, this is the kind of testimony we ought to undertake, and these are invitations we have no option but to accept, sooner or later.

Dialogue

Knowing the content and practices of the *testimony* of one's faith tradition is a necessary step to move into intelligent, respectful, honest, and open-minded *dialogue* with people of other faiths. For this *interreligious dialogue*, Christian religious educators need to learn or develop (or both) educational principles and practices that enable persons and congregations to discern God's activity in the different-others, as well as in themselves. This pedagogy should promote and expand a capacity for 'decentring' our religious beliefs and practices. This means that, in our dialogue with people from other faiths, we should not use those beliefs and practices as the core around which everything else in life should spin, in order to understand and value what other people believe, and how and why they live out their beliefs in the way that they do.

Efforts and experiences of interreligious dialogue have a long history. But it is a history that has involved only a few and that, until recently, has involved mostly people from academic and theological spheres, or those high in denominational church structures. Fortunately, we are now seeing hopeful signs of new interests and efforts among people of different reli-

---

during their conversation: 'My Mom says God is a girl'; 'In my religion God is a boy'; 'In my country God is a boy'; 'My Mom says that God is a girl, and my Mom makes good pancakes'; 'I think God is a girl and a boy.' Arguably, conversations that relate to religious pluralism are happening more frequently in pre-school and elementary school settings than in churches and seminaries.

gions that see the urgency and the importance of this dialogue.[12] If the *interreligious dialogue* was once initiated and promoted from the 'top', today it is being initiated and fostered at and from the 'bottom'. It is, therefore, a theological imperative that pastors in churches and professors at seminaries pay attention to what they are doing and saying, if they want the congregations they serve to become part of this *interreligious dialogue*.

Service

Finally, as religious educators we need to incorporate service as both the means and goal of our educational efforts. We need to translate the preaching that happens in places of worship into a 'faith that expresses itself through love' in the world. We need to transform the teaching that happens in Sunday School buildings so that concrete forms of Christian testimony to and dialogue with those who live around us can take place. This is the kind of service that Christians, at the personal and communal levels, ought to give to the world for the sake of God's reign in the world. Of course, it is not just any kind of service. From the perspective of a pluralist theology of liberation, it is service oriented to personal and social transformation and the promotion of life for the whole planet. More particularly, it is service done in solidarity with the poor and oppressed, and against the realities that oppress them. It is service done in collaboration with the poor and all others who care for the full wellbeing of persons, groups, and the whole of creation. For it is in service for the sake of justice and peace of the world that the Christian religion, in collaboration with other religions, bears testimony to the central message of love for God and neighbour for which Jesus gave his life.

---

12   See *Interfaith Dialogue at the Grass Roots*, edited by Rebecca Kratz Mays and published by Ecumenical Press, Philadelphia, 2008. This book is a collection of essays written by people representing the three Abrahamic faith traditions (Judaism, Islam, and Christianity) and who have been very involved in developing principles, practices, and programmes for interfaith dialogue.

Conclusion

To see plurality of life as a 'good thing' (as God sees it in the account of creation according to the book of Genesis)[13] is the beginning of a pluralist spirituality and, therefore, of a pluralist theology of religion. But, as has been demonstrated by the contributors to the series *Along the Many Paths of God*, this theology has to be developed and nurtured from the inside out, from an 'intrareligious' dialogue among Christians who are open to an 'interreligious' dialogue with people of other faiths. From the perspective of Latin American liberation theologians, such theology has to be at the service of seeking justice for all, of seeking peace among all peoples of the earth, and of defending and promoting all forms of life in this planet and the whole cosmos. It should be a theology of life with justice, and of justice with life. To assume the challenges that pluralist liberation theologians present is not only difficult but risky in an ecclesial, political, economic, and cultural context that still imposes itself as exclusive and hegemonic. But if we, as religious educators, see the 'many paths of God' in the world as the way God acts in it, and are therefore willing to rethink our Christian faith in light of a pluralist paradigm, then we have to prepare ourselves for censorship, rejection, and even persecution by those in Church and academy who still do not see religious pluralism as an expression of the 'polyphony of life' for the good of all creation.

---

13 See Genesis 1:4, 10, 12, 18, 21, 25, 31.

KATH ENGEBRETSON

5 Interfaith Education in the Christian School

What is interfaith education?

Interfaith education is that process by which we learn new ways of thinking about and behaving towards those whose religious worldviews, systems of meanings and belief, religious narratives, and symbols are different from our own. Ultimately it seeks personal, attitudinal, and behavioural transformation. Often the terms interfaith education, multifaith education, and interreligious education are used interchangeably. I choose to use the term interfaith education based on Patel's definition of interfaith (cited in Puett, 2005, 272). 'Interfaith' is when our experience of the diversity of modern life and our connections to our religious traditions cohere such that we develop faith identities which encourage us to interact with others in intentional and appreciative ways. It is the goal of being rooted in our own traditions and in relationship with others. Interfaith educators not only seek that their students develop an understanding of different religious worlds, but they also see as their ultimate task the development and sustaining of social cohesion and peace, and the continuing of a dialogue of mutual understanding, respect, and solidarity which can address the most significant issues of our times.

Interfaith education has two movements which are inextricably linked with each other. Objective, cognitively-based interfaith education about religions is the starting point, but it is when the affective and experiential dimensions come into the dialogue that education in its fullest sense occurs. In this chapter, I critically discuss what part interfaith education can play in the Christian school and how these two aspects of the process may be played out.

Considering the philosophical position for interfaith education in the Christian school[1]

Exclusivism

All interfaith educators need first to consider the various philosophical stances that may inhibit or enhance good interfaith education. They need to consider which of these stances is most meaningful for themselves as learners, and to discuss and critique these with students. This is especially important when it can be assumed that most of the students will have had some socialization into Christianity and some may be committed Christians. One issue that interfaith educators must face is that of exclusivism in religious belief and its relationship to tolerance of other religions. When the followers of another religion are considered to be heretics or infidels, tolerance, dialogue, and good education are impossible. The exclusivism that argues that only one religion, or one interpretation of it, leads to salvation is a significant barrier to interfaith education (Franzmann and Tidswell, 2006).

Exclusivism is often manifested in a fundamentalist approach to one's own religion, a position which can bring the believer into tension even with his or her own tradition. Fundamentalist students in any religion have often had a dramatic and emotional conversion experience, especially at a time when they sought a new sense of identity or deliverance from a disordered and unhappy lifestyle. The euphoria of conversion at first means that the fundamentalist strongly resists any challenge to their conviction that their path is the exclusive path to salvation. The convert's initial euphoria is buoyed up by community and institutional networks of fellow believers, which provide social and emotional frameworks that exclude other points of view except as objects of criticism (Brown, 1992; Strieb, 2007).

Fundamentalism is of its nature exclusive. It is certain that there is only one way to salvation, and adopts a crusading mentality which assumes that

---

[1] This section follows the analysis in Engebretson, 2009.

the fundamentalist view, to whatever religion it belongs, is correct and all other views are incorrect. Along with this comes a commitment to convert others to this way of thinking (Brown, 1992). For the fundamentalist to hold on to his or her claim to exclusive truth, other claims must be untrue or even evil (Franzmann and Tidswell, 2006). Fundamentalism is therefore incompatible with the openness, good will, listening, and evaluation that are the qualities of interfaith education. It follows that a first and ongoing task for the interfaith educator is to observe the presence of fundamentalism in various forms among the students, and to ensure that they have the language to name and critique these. For some students of a fundamentalist frame of mind, interfaith education may not be possible, and a perceptive teacher may well recognize this, while not desisting in the work of challenging and critiquing the exclusivist mindset.

Relativism, agnosticism, atheism, and indifference

Another stance which some students bring to interfaith education is relativism. This is often described as an outcome of a 'postmodern' view of the world, which claims that there is no objective truth that can be known, but that there are endless ways of seeing truth, each valid for the person who holds that view. Relativism is very often applied to cultures, religions, morals, and values, and is very prevalent among the Generation Y students in our schools and universities. In this argument, any religion is historically and culturally conditioned, and can only be understood in that context. There is no one overarching truth or archetypal story, but many theories about truth and many stories which purport to explain the world. Each of these is valid for those who hold them. Typical of a relativist view of truth are the statements: 'Whatever works for you'; 'If that's true for you that's fine, but it's not true for me. We can agree to differ'; 'You can't judge others by your own standards.'

Similarly, a relativist view of the world refuses to make absolute judgements about right and wrong. It argues that we cannot judge right and wrong because we cannot know all of the cultural, social, and personal circumstances that led to a particular decision and action. The natural outcome of relativism is agnosticism, which is the view that the existence of God or the gods, the afterlife, and other belief propositions are unknown and cannot be known. There is a reluctance to commit oneself to an opinion about whether God exists or not, and it is argued that the question cannot be approached objectively. From the agnostic position, anyone who holds such beliefs holds them as their own truth: but they are not universal truth, only truth for that person.

One problem with relativism for the classroom and university is that it can engender intellectual laziness. It does away with the need to deconstruct, critique, and evaluate religious claims and practices; and it glosses over religions in a superficial acceptance. One does not have to argue that God exists or even think about it very deeply, because if one believes that God exists then that is true for the individual who holds that belief, but not necessarily for anyone else. Relativism does not promote good interfaith education (Küng, 1988), for its ultimate end is indifference to all religions. Arising from the postmodern fear of making judgements about any belief-system because all are culturally and historically bound (Wright, 2000), it trivializes questions of truth (Küng, 1988). It leads to bland, uncritical interfaith education which is limited to an accumulation of facts, eschewing critical judgements. Ultimately, Küng (1988) argues, it is demeaning of all religions.

Relativism is also related to atheism, a view which argues that all religious claims are untrue. This position challenges all religions, claiming that they are all built on illusion, and that beyond human life there is nothingness. In this view, interfaith education is a study of idiosyncratic ways of seeing the world, which are no more than cultural and historical curiosities and which have no relation to the life of the student. In refuting the atheistic position, Küng (1988) argued that we must honestly take account of the fact that the earliest accounts of human life, right through to the present, portray a need and desire to open up to the transcendent. Atheism is grounded in the western world, Küng argues, and is therefore a minority position. In short, relativism, indifference, agnosticism, and atheism all need to be identified, deconstructed, and evaluated, as first steps in interfaith education.

Pluralism

A stance that many take in their approach to interfaith education is pluralism, whose key proponent is the philosopher, John Hick (1989). Hick's view is that people are inherently religious, and that each of the religions of the world is a different human response, arising from this inherent religiousness, to one divine Reality which does exist. Each religion has arisen in its own time and culture as a response to this Reality, and while each religion gives the Reality a different name, the Reality that is the focus of their worship is one and the same, and is the fundamental ground of human experience. In other words, all religious paths have the same purpose and lead to the same destination. More than this, religions promote the good, for almost every religious tradition positively changes the lives of its followers. 'The great post-axial faiths constitute different ways of experiencing, conceiving and living in relation to an ultimate divine Reality which transcends all our varied visions of it' (Hick, 1989, 235).

The question arises, if all religions point to the same fundamental Reality, why are there so many differences between religions? Hick explains that these differences exist because human beings do not have direct access to the Real. Their access is mediated through religious traditions which, while they are authentic, are human constructs, each putting its own interpretation and array of concepts on the Real. The religion itself, acting on the imagination of the community and the individual, shapes perceptions of the Real. Therefore perceptions differ among religions and often conflict. These differences need not be a barrier to the study of religions, but are accepted as inevitable when the limited human mind attempts to comprehend and explain the ineffable.

In summary, Hick argues: first, that there is one divine Reality which he calls the Real; second, that among the multiplicity of religions in the world none has direct access to and therefore an unbiased perception of the Real; third, each religion is an authentic way in which the Real is conceived, mediated, and experienced; fourth, the Real is beyond any of the descriptions, positive or negative, which human institutions and individuals may give it. Study of religions is then a study of the various ways in which peoples approach the fundamental reality, the Real.

There is much to attract interfaith educators in Hick's pluralistic view of religions. It accepts religions as authentic ways to the Real, but acknowledges these as lenses through which the Real is apprehended only dimly. Therefore the various ways in which religions express their beliefs, the ways in which they celebrate and the stories they tell can be studied in an ongoing quest to come closer to understanding the Real. It is clear, however, that a pluralist approach to the study of religions will not be the right approach for every student or group of students, for often the situation is more complex than acknowledging that all religions are equally valid paths to truth. In Christian schools and universities there are students who are committed to their own religions, who although ready to engage with and learn about other religions and to enter into dialogue with them, hold to the superior – if not to the unique – revelation of their own religion. This will also be the case to a lesser extent in non-religiously-affiliated schools. For example, the committed Muslim respects what has gone before in Judaism and Christianity, but sees Islam as the true fulfilment of these religions, and as the fullness of God's revelation. The Christian student wants to assert the unique place of Jesus Christ in salvation. And the Jewish student, while respecting the later developments of Christianity and Islam, sees them as departures from the original covenant. The question arises, then, whether for students to study religions authentically, they need to forsake their convictions about the uniqueness or fullness of truth of their own religion. Ultimately this is what is required in a pluralistic approach to the study of religion.

For students and educators who want to hold to individual religious convictions, and yet openly to engage in education about other religions, the philosophical position with which they are most comfortable is inclusivism.

Inclusivism

Küng (1988, 235) has argued that the position he describes as a 'generous, tolerant inclusivism' is the solution in interfaith education for the committed believer. Those who take this position believe that while the fullness of truth resides in their religion, all religions share in the truth of this one religion. The contemporary Catholic position, for example, recognizes the truth and the action of the Holy Spirit in other religions, and this makes true dialogue possible. In this scenario, committed religious belief in one tradition is not only compatible with interfaith education, it would seem that committed religious belief which is open to truth and goodness in other religions is more desirable in interfaith education than either relativism or indifference. For the open committed believer, interfaith education will bring a heightened sense of the contexts of one's religious beliefs and feelings, a questioning of their assumptions, and a realization of alternate perspectives. The committed believer is challenged to probe assumptions and to search more deeply into the history and theology of their own religion (Boys, Lee, and Bass, 1995). Ultimately, interfaith education has the potential to affirm, educate, and transform committed religious belief, a process which Swidler (1986) has argued is one of the three goals of interfaith education, alongside knowing the other ever more authentically, gaining a friendly understanding of others as they are, and establishing a more solid foundation for community life and action among people from different religious traditions.

Interfaith education in the Christian school as one stage in a transformative religious education

I have claimed that interfaith education is transformative. I will now describe what I mean by transformative education, using Boyd and Myers (1988) theory of transformative education, and linking this with the religious education development theory of Moran (1983). Boyd and Myers adopt a psychological approach to transformative education, seeing it as working towards the integration by the individual of their inner and outer worlds. On the part of the learner this entails the achievement of individualization, as a prelude to the expansion of consciousness which attends the adult journey. The journey is first inward to achieve identity, corresponding with the tasks of identity formation of the school years, and then outward to integrate identity with many other meanings, a journey typical of adulthood (Boyd and Myers, 1988). So the process of transformative education is developmental and lifelong, and it has a particular stage that belongs to the school years. In these years, individuals accommodate the demands encountered in their worlds, and assimilate what they need to obtain their goals. The main task is differentiation: that is, determining personal and work identities, and developing the knowledge, abilities, and skills that are required to establish themselves within their society. The more transformative aspects of education play a secondary role to this instrumental education, through which the individual is enabled to take their place in the community. In the second half of life, Boyd and Myers (1988) claim, the process moves increasingly away from differentiation to integration and wholeness. Questions such as, 'Where am I going from here?', 'What really counts in life?', and other questions related to the more inward journey, begin to gain prominence. The movements in transformative education in the adult years are receptivity and listening to other ways of seeing the world, the recognition that these other ways may have something to say to me, sometimes 'grieving' for the older ways of seeing the world, leading ideally to a hope-filled sense of restabilization and reintegration (Boyd and Myers, 1988).

I find this theory of transformative education helpful for thinking about interfaith education, especially in its treatment of the tasks of the school years. Boyd and Myers' naming of the fact that school education is largely instrumental, meant to give students the knowledge and skills they need to achieve individualization, resonates with what I instinctively know as an educator. Moreover, I find that this theory of transformative education complements Moran's (1983) theory of religious education development, which has given many religious educators a theoretical framework, and which I will now briefly outline.

Moran's developmental theory of religious education begins with the years of infancy. In this *Simply Religious* stage, whatever contributes to the child's education also provides the foundation for a more complex religious education later. His second stage is *Intermediary* and relates to school education. Examination of his theory reveals that in the school years he also advocates instrumental religious education. He argues that this is the time to give young people 'the solid substance of a particular religious tradition' (189). They should learn about the 'nature and influence of religion in our lives' (189), and also about their own religious tradition. In addition, they should be immersed in the rituals and practices of their tradition. 'Even if they wish to reject religious practice later', he argues, 'they ought to have an elementary knowledge of what they are rejecting' (189). The third stage is *Religiously Christian (Jewish, Muslim)*. The point of the third level is for the person's religious identity to develop in a deeper and richer context. 'The Christian way, to become more fully intelligible to an adult, needs to be put into relation with at least Judaism and Islam' (190). If such dialogue is preceded by 'solid grounding in one's own tradition' (190), the result is usually an enrichment (transformation) for everyone concerned. Jews become more Jewish, Christians become more Christian. 'An added benefit', Moran remarks, 'is that differences within each group also get illuminated by conversation beyond the group' (190).

What do these theories of transformative education offer to interfaith education in the Christian school?

Boyd and Myers (1988) and Moran (1983), each from their respective disciplines, advocate an instrumental approach to education in the school years, and I believe that their developmental theories can help us to respond to the question of what the Christian school can achieve in interfaith education. My argument is that the school has a particular role in interfaith education, a role that is fundamental and absolutely necessary, but limited. The role is instrumental education, defined by Boyd and Myers (1988) as 'differentiation' (276): that is, determining personal and work identities, and developing the knowledge, abilities, and skills that are required for young people to establish themselves within their society. The individual defines and develops their individuality. Through instrumental education the individual is enabled to take their place in the community. Moran also sees the task of religious education in the school years as instrumental, assisting the students to gain 'the solid substance of a particular religious tradition' (189).

There are therefore two tasks in the school years that will assist a later involvement in transformative interfaith education and dialogue. The first task is the immersion of the Christian student in knowledge about, and experience of, their own tradition – so that they may develop an informed understanding of it, suitable to their age group, but developed to some level of sophistication by the end of the secondary school. This informed (even committed) position is the best stance from which transformative interfaith education may continue into the adult years. The second task is also instrumental: that is, assisting the student in the Christian school to acquire a correct and rich education about the range of religions in the local community, and deeper education in the major ones. Although a cognitive study, this will have experiential aspects, and it may be provided in many different ways. This acquiring of basic knowledge about other religions will again allow the more sophisticated interfaith education and dialogue of the later years to be informed and sensitive. As Ratzinger – now Pope Benedict XVI – has pointed out, this dialogue cannot even begin unless there is first some basic education in the phenomenon of religion, and its expressions in the religions of the world. This is the task of the school.

> We first have to try and understand them as they are, in their historical dynamic, in their essential structures and types, as also in their possible relations with each other or as possible threats to each other, before we try to arrive at any judgments (Ratzinger, 2004, 10).

Attention to this cognitive goal will allow for an enriched understanding and appreciation of one's own religion, and the establishment of a foundation for common life and action for justice in the school (Swidler, 1986).

The aims, principles, and skills of good instrumental interfaith education in the Christian school

The aims of instrumental interfaith education in the Christian school include: (1) the development of greater understanding and appreciation of the people and groups in the community, leading to enhanced tolerance, appreciation of religious diversity, and social cohesion; (2) the rejection of prejudice and intolerance based on misinformation; (3) the acquisition of basic knowledge about religious traditions such as their historical roots and foundational stories, and the doctrinal basis for religious practices; (4) the development of critical and informed awareness of the religions in local and national communities; (5) the enabling of a deeper understanding of the religious perspectives of others in the community as a basis for shared action for peace and justice; and (6) provision of the opportunity for an enhanced knowledge and appreciation of the student's own religion, and an expansion of religious consciousness through learning about others.

Good instrumental interfaith education has these characteristics. It clearly communicates its purposes for the students themselves, for the community, and for the wider world. It respects religions as they are holistically in their cultural settings. It does not seek to syncretize religions, to condense them, or to relativize them; but treats each religion as it is. At first it adopts a *macro* approach introducing students to the big picture of a religion, its beliefs, rituals, values and ethics, foundational stories, sacred text, social organization, key symbols, and ways of praying. The fundamental element of these which flows into all other elements is belief, and this interdependence between the elements of religions is made clear. While respecting the *macro* view of the religion, it recognizes religions as dynamic systems which continually adapt to new contexts. It seeks the common ground between religions such as a mutual language about or images of God, respect for certain sacred texts, mutual approaches to social and ethical issues, mutual appreciation of certain virtues, and even shared history. Nevertheless, it does not gloss over the differences between religions, but treats these as sources of education and interest. As much as possible it seeks information and explanations from people who practise the religion being studied, always with a realization that there is diversity of religious expression and practice within a religion, and that these need to be historically and culturally located within the wider tradition. Finally, it presents religious commitment as life-enhancing for believers and does not confuse religious passion and conviction with proselytism.

Good interfaith education seeks to develop these skills in the students: the ability to put aside their own religious assumptions in order to enter empathetically in the world of the other; attentive listening, questioning, and discussion in ways that respect the faith of others; skills to critique the presentation of religions in Internet material, news items, and political views; the ability to weigh up a diversity of views and to distinguish between extremist and more moderate views; and the development of skills in communicating about their own religion.

What of the experiential aspect of interfaith education in the Christian school?

An open-minded, committed religious believer holds to the foundational truth of their own religion, but acknowledges truth in other religions; indeed, seeks to understand this truth and to incorporate it into an ever developing religious understanding. He or she seeks interfaith dialogue. I argue that the very best starting point for genuine experiential interfaith education is a strong yet inclusive commitment to one's own religion, against which interfaith education becomes interfaith dialogue. This becomes complicated, however, when we think of interfaith education in the school. Rummery (1975) and others (Fowler, 1981) have convincingly argued than the natural position of adolescents is a certain confusion and questioning in relation to their inherited faith, a position Rummery has referred to as 'suspended belief' (185). Given this state of suspended belief, Rummery argued for an approach to religious education that would put fewer demands on the uncertain faith of the young person. Can there, therefore, be an experiential element to interfaith education in the Christian school? Yes, but it is limited. Rather than expecting the dialogue in faith of which open, committed believers are capable, the Christian school can provide the opportunity to establish connections between young people of different religions: bringing them together socially and helping then to develop friendships over shared food and games, discussion about mutually interesting issues, visits to each others' schools, and working on projects together. This non-demanding experiential accompaniment to instrumental interfaith education can help to break down the cultural barriers that keep young people isolated in their own cultural groups, and indirectly can help to attain many of the goals of interfaith education in schools. It may also be a platform towards deeper interfaith dialogue in adult life.

References

Boyd, R., and Myers, G. (1988). Transformative education. *International Journal of Lifelong Education*, 7 (4), 261–284.

Boys, M., Lee, S., and Bass, D. (1995). Protestant, Catholic, Jew: The transformative possibilities of educating across religious boundaries. *Religious Education*, 90 (2), 255–276.

Brown, C. (1992). Witness or dialogue? Christian fundamentalists at bay. *Australian Religious Studies REVIEW*, 5 (1), 1–4.

Engebretson, K. (2009). *In your shoes: Interfaith education for Australian schools and universities*. Ballan, Victoria: Connorcourt.

Fowler, J. W. (1981). *Stages of faith: The psychology of human development and the quest for meaning*. Blackburn, Victoria: Dove Communications.

Franzmann, M., and Tidswell, T. (2006). Education for tolerance of world religions. *Journal of Religious Education*, 54 (3), 39–42.

Hick, J. (1989). *An interpretation of religion*. New Haven, Connecticut: Yale University Press.

Küng, H. (1988). *Theology for the third millennium*. New York: Doubleday.

Moran, G. (1983). *Religious education development*. Minneapolis, Minnesota: Winston Press.

Puett, T. (2005). On transforming our world: Critical pedagogy for interfaith education. *Cross Currents*, 55 (2), 264–273.

Ratzinger, J. (2004). *Truth and tolerance: Christian belief and world religions*. (H. Taylor, trans.). San Francisco: Ignatius Press.

Rummery, G. (1975). *Catechesis and religious education in a pluralist society*. Sydney: E. J. Dwyer.

Streib, H. (2007). Faith development and a way beyond fundamentalism. In C. Timmermann, D. Hutsebaut, S. Mels, W. Nonneman, and W. van Herck (eds), *Faith-based radicalism: Christianity, Islam and Judaism between constructive activism and destructive fanaticism* (pp. 151–167). Brussels: Peter Lang.

Swidler, L. (ed.). (1986). *Towards a universal theology of religion*. Maryknoll, New York: Orbis Books.

Wright, A. (2000). *Spirituality and education*. London: Taylor and Francis.

PART II
Islamic Studies

MUALLA SELÇUK

6 How Can Islamic Pedagogy Promote an Understanding of 'Individualized Religion'?

Introduction

Religions, including Islam, understandably endorse unalterable basic theological principles and beliefs. However, the believers of any religion also carry a religious culture, which includes social and historical contexts. Religion and culture are therefore inevitably interrelated. In particular, the view that arises from the fundamental sources of Islam and the common understanding formed within history calls for a religion that is present in all spheres of social life. In our day, however, what belongs to the religious domain and what may be left to the individual are matters of controversy. Islamic pedagogy faces the tension between preserving religious identity, on the one hand, and responding to the demands of modernity, on the other. Claims over the inflexibility and universality of Islam with regard to its contextual, indigenous, and ephemeral dimensions confront educators as challenges that must be dealt with in Islamic pedagogy. Will these challenges continue to suppress religious education, or will the field be able to open up new thinking within contemporary pedagogy?

In the process of answering this central question I will explore the relationship between *Rabb-abd* (God-human being), as well as the *Islam-sharia* (Islam-Islamic law) relationship. I shall introduce the Qur'anic term *hikmah* (Wisdom) as a working element of individualized religion. I also offer the messages of the Qur'anic Meccan verses for shaping the content of religious education.

I hope this chapter will contribute to an understanding of Islam not only as a matter of communal affiliation but also as an aspect of individual choice.

The contribution of RE to the life journey with regard to individualized religion

What I mean by individualized religion is the unique relationship between the individual and Allah (*Abd* and *Rabb*). I also mean that individuals have the freedom and responsibility to contemplate and to argue over religious matters, and to choose any religious interpretation from their religious tradition. Here, individuals do not see themselves as passive recipients of the past; rather, they put themselves in charge of questioning and improving the intellectual legacy of the past. An individualistic perception of religion requires a form of education that leads towards a reason-based faith for which individuals are responsible for their choices.

Towards the end of the 1990s, I was preparing an article dealing with the question whether religious education can be a libertarian process. I formulated my expectations of religious education as follows:

> Religious education should be allowed to be an intellectual education, it must teach the individual how to use his/her mind in order to live a humane life. Religious education is not indoctrination; it must not be seen only as catechetical knowledge. It must also be interested in the personal development of the individual. Critical thinking, discovering the meaning of life, making decisions, solving problems, and self-expression must be among the aims and content of religious education. Religious education must put a person into such contact with our holy sources (the Qur'an and Sunnah) that the person must be able to understand both what God and the Prophet said in history, and what these words mean in the present.

A young person whom I interviewed objected. He found my expectations extremely theoretical, even impossible. 'If you can't organize your own life, if you don't have power over your fate, what freedom are you talking about?' He added:

> Let me, first, tell you something. I have never felt any sympathy for religion and religious matters. I yearned in my heart for a life that is entirely contrary to the religious one: that is, a free life in which no power will have control over me. But fate always kept me in this environment.

Islamic Pedagogy and Understanding 'Individualized Religion' 95

> I never knew my father. He died when I was only one year old. My mother suffered serious difficulties and was mistreated by her relatives. She saw religion as a way to get rid of her problems, and promised God and herself that she would educate me in line with the rules of religious life. I am exactly 23 years old. That is why I am attached to God who from that day forth has had control over all my behaviour.
>
> But now I resent living in accordance with religion. As I think of all that has happened to me, I began to suspect the wisdom of God and his justice. (Selçuk, 1998, 81)

As a teacher, my first impression from these statements was that it was of great importance to bring theology and educational theory into dialogue.

Such statements reflect a widespread understanding among young people. Despite the risk of generalization, I would like to make the following claim. The young hold two understandings of belief, almost side by side: one of them they articulate but cannot put into practice, the other is what they put into practice but of which they have no knowledge (practice without theory).

Empirical study is helpful in clarifying the nature of these understandings. In a study examining the role of belief about 'freedom of choice' on the behaviour of high school students, it has been found that most of the students held a fatalistic understanding with a Jabri/fatalistic inclination, which may be described as classical. (Jabriyya refers to a school of thought according to which acts of human beings in fact belong to God. As they are determined by God, human beings have no choice other than to engage in these acts.) Others, however, held to a Mutazilite view, which brings free will to the fore, and rejects ideas of the 'appointment' and 'determination' of one's behaviour. (According to the Mutazila, the individual is the creator of his/her own acts and is completely free in doing them. Unless the individual is free, he/she could not be held responsible for his/her acts. Yet God is just and merciful towards his servants.) However, when the dimensions of their belief in and understanding of fate are considered, there appears to be no harmony, cohesion, and consistency between the participants' understanding of fate and their attitudes towards fate and related behaviour (Özarslan, 1994, 100). For example, most of the participants who held that people's acts and behaviours are determined by God also said that the calamities and troubles that happened to people stemmed from their own mistakes. These same participants also believed that people should be free in choosing their partners; whereas those participants who held a contrary understanding reported that in times of trouble they recalled fate and blamed it for what was happening to them.

In a questionnaire study conducted in 2004, similar problems were found. The researcher stated that education could not find a solution between the Jabri/fatalistic understanding received from the cultural environment and the Mutazilite one which appears in the academic milieu. In this context, the researcher draws attention to the following questions raised by the participants.

> Why am I not rich? Why am I not a single child? What do the concepts of divine decree (*qadâ*) and fate (*qadar*) mean? What does it mean to believe in divine decree and fate? If God knows everything, why are we being tested? Is it God who causes earthquakes, if so, why? Does fate restrict our freedom? Can fate be changed? Is there any relation between events in nature and religion, and between increasing immorality and earthquakes? Does fate depend on man, or does God determine it? Who really determines our fate? What is the crime of a child born disabled? Why did God create evils, disasters and diseases? Why does not God present everybody with equal conditions? Why do people suffer? If God helps the good, why are the good always oppressed? Why was I born from this particular mother and father without my will? If had been born in America, I would be a Christian; what crime did they commit that they are damned? (Altaş, 2004, 174)

So features of a strong belief in fate have not been consistently observed among young people. Rather, uncertainty, confusion, and distortion are all present, together with a lack of clarity.

We cannot say that the beliefs of adolescents and young adults have any strong base. Hence we cannot talk about their belief-action consistency; their knowledge has developed from childhood onwards largely through imitations of and suggestions by the parents. Young people's beliefs are mostly characterized by uncertainty and error. And yet, are there not many books about religion? Are students not being taught during their religious education courses? Are the publications of theologians, who choose religion as their profession, and the attempts of the university faculties of divinity being ignored? Sermons are regularly delivered in our mosques; the number of journals is increasing day by day; many organized religious panels and lectures exist. Are these all ignored? Do not the TV and radio broadcasts on religion and morals, and newspaper columns assigned to religious matters and their supplements in Ramadan, provide adequate information in this area?

These various channels meet certain needs, of course. But we are talking about the lack of provision that impacts on the learner's life, explains, and interprets it; and which thus connects us with the past and allows us to reach out towards the future. The question facing us is the future of religious education itself, and with it the future of the individual.

The complexity of content knowledge in religious education: the religion-sharia relation[1]

While one of the two main sources of Islam is the Holy Qur'an, the other is the Sunnah that comprises the sayings and acts of Prophet Muhammad. In Muslim societies many areas of life are shaped in the light of these two sources. As we learn from the Qur'an and Sunnah, Islam consists of believing in God, worshipping God, and moral principles. Faith, worship, and morals, as the three fundamental elements, constitute the principal values of Islam – the unchangeables that are beyond the ages. Islam also provides judgements organizing interpersonal relations. These judgements are related to our human environment and consist of social, political, cultural, economic, and historic factors, and include law.

The principles of Islam concerning faith, worship, and morals have not been much discussed, since they contain universal values. However, in the case of sharia, which is also called Islamic jurisprudence and *muamalât*, different considerations have been proposed. Treating these judgements as unchangeable despite the changing nature of life leads to theoretical and

---

1 I first discussed this complexity in Selçuk (2007). Some paragraphs here are from this paper.

practical difficulties. Questions concerning the unchangeable, universal dimensions of Islam, and its judgements in relation to history, place, and time confront us as important challenges to religious education. Will these challenges continue to constrain religious education, or will the field be open to new ideas?

In general, there are three understandings regarding the universal and historical message of Islam:

- a literal understanding;
- an interpretative understanding;
- a progressive understanding.

On a literal understanding, the legal arrangements of Islam about social life are regarded as unchangeable and beyond history; hence life must be adapted to them. All judgements found within sharia regarding marriage, divorce, bequests, trading, shopping, military matters, politics, etc., are included in the nature of religion. This understanding defends the claim that judgements of sharia must be carried out in every time and every place. Yet they are absolute and universal, not time bound. This understanding brings form rather than principle and goals to the fore. It does not give way to common approval and public participation. Thus it has an oppressive, dogmatic, and authoritarian nature.

The interpretative understanding also holds that the judgements of sharia constitute the unchangeable and constant values of religion. However, as it is an order of religion that no authority has a right to impose any judgement to disturb the considerations of public interest (*maslahah*), this approach holds that the sharia can be interpreted. From time to time it qualifies the sharia, saying that practice should depend on the development and progress of society. Thus the Qur'an 'abolished' slavery when the source of slavery dried up. Comments such as 'Islam comes to an agreement with democracy', 'Islam is in harmony with secularism', and 'Monogamy is essential in Islam' all stem from attempts to adapt Islam to the age.

According to the progressive understanding, such arrangements are not included in the essence and nature of religion, but are the model solutions offered in line with the main principles and aims of religion in a certain time and society. They change and develop with the growing and changing circumstances of the age: that is, they take shape or are cancelled. Islam's statements on political, military, and legal matters are related to Muslims' concrete historical needs. In different cultural milieus, it is possible to rearrange these statements in accordance with the scientific and intellectual experience of human society. This viewpoint emphasizes that from the very beginning such terms as reason (*akl*) and science (*ilm*) became the dominant terms in the religion-life relationship in Islam.

A Turkish professor of theology comments on locally-bounded legislation in the Qur'an as follows:

> Apart from the examples I gave so far, there are many examples in the Qur'an concerning the legal situation of society; acceptance of these seems almost impossible in developed countries. For example, you cannot expect the modern woman with higher education to be regarded as an eye witness who only carries half the weight of her uneducated brother just because it has been stated to be so in the Qur'an. For example, you cannot persuade a Muslim woman who became a doctor, engineer, or manager of a firm to accept the verse in the Qur'an that gives daughters a half share compared with that of their brothers. If asked whether there is any revolt on behalf of justice against the Qur'an, we have to say No! While keeping the Qur'an's local values as expressed fourteen centuries ago as historical facts, we must be able to validate its universal principles. (Hatiboğlu, 2004, 12, my translation)

The same scholar addresses the researchers of Islam as follows: 'Without some objective consideration of the sources of Islamic culture over the centuries, and without distinguishing the changeable from the unchangeable, to speak definitely on behalf of Islam is unscholarly behavior' (Hatiboğlu, 1986, 24).

Although it seems difficult for Islamic scholars to adopt the view stated above, there are many attempts in Turkey to realize this goal. Scholars in the faculty where I work approach historical experience through a critical method, trying to distinguish the historical from the universal, and bringing into the light the libertarian approach that for many reasons has remained obscured in history. The main motivation for these studies is as follows. Faith, worship, and moral principles are unchangeable and binding as *al-Islam*. But the sharia as a solution to the problems caused by social change is historical. The sharia is renewable, changeable, and abolishable. We must distinguish 'the fact of religion' from 'thinking about the fact of religion'. Thus, it is the thought that must be explained and reinterpreted in the face of new circumstances, not the main principles of religion. As each generation has its own problems, each generation must solve these problems in accordance with the concepts of their own time, their own forms of thinking, and the practical problems they meet. It is only possible by way of such an attempt to show that Islam will be able to live across the ages.

However, the information produced in academic circles is not yet sufficient to constitute the theological bases of religious education, nor to develop reflection on religious education in the context of individual and social facts of a democratic society. It is an open question how much progress in terms of individualized religion these new theological ideas has really produced.

From tension to opportunity: a vision

I suggest here some opportunities in religious education, inspired by the hadith of the Prophet Muhammad: 'Wisdom (*hikmah*) is the lost property of the believer; he is the most rightful person to take it wherever he finds it.'[2]

The concept of *hikmah* has a very important place in Islamic tradition. The search for *hikmah* is strongly commended by the Prophet through any decent means possible. Words derivative of the root *h-k-m* are mentioned 210 times in the Qur'an, in both predicative and substantive forms. The primary meaning of the root *h-k-m* is 'to restrain' in English. The restraint in question could be from injustice (*zulm*), ignorance (*jahl*), or foolishness (*safah*). Accordingly, *hikmah* can be defined as justice (*adl*), knowledge

---

[2] In this context 'he' is interpreted as including 'she'.

(*ilm*), or forbearance (*hilm*), respectively. In this context, everything that prevents a person from acting in a corrupt manner, or from committing a blameworthy deed, can be described by the verbs derived from the root *h-k-m*. *Hikmah*, therefore, has epistemological as well as practical components (Yaman, 2008, 3–4). In other words, it is a combination of knowledge and action.

The Qur'an employs the term *hikmah* in passages where it expounds the place of the individual in the cosmos, the aim of creation, and the core of the prophets' message; and gives various warnings about the past and future of humankind, and the positive and negative results of individual preferences. According to the Qur'an, God is the ultimate possessor of *hikmah*. He is called *al-Hakim*, one of the Most Beautiful Names of God (*al-asma' al-husnâ*). The Qur'an states that God has given *hikmah* to the prophets in general:

> God took a pledge from the prophets, saying, 'If, after I have bestowed Scripture and wisdom upon you, a messenger comes confirming what you have been given, you must believe in him and support him. Do you affirm this and accept My pledge as binding on you?' They said, 'We do.' He said, 'Then bear witness and I too will bear witness.' (Al-Imran 3:81)

The Qur'an mentions the name of prophets such as David, Jesus, and Muhammad as those who are given *hikmah*:

> ABRAHAM: 'Do they envy (other) people for the bounty God has granted them? We gave the descendants of Abraham the scripture and wisdom ...' (Nisa 4:54).
> DAVID: '... and God gave him (David) sovereignty and wisdom and taught him what He pleased.' (Bakara 2:251). 'We strengthened his kingdom; We gave him wisdom and a decisive way of speaking' (Sad 38:20).
> JESUS: 'He will teach him (Jesus) the Scripture and wisdom, the Torah and the Gospel' (Al-Imran 3:48). 'Then God will say "Jesus, son of Mary! Remember my favour to you and to your mother: How I strengthened you with the Holy Spirit, so that you spoke to people in your infancy and as a grown man: How I taught you the scripture and wisdom, the Torah and the Gospel"' (Maide 5:110). 'When Jesus came with clear signs he said, "I have brought you wisdom: I have come to clear up some of your differences for you. Be mindful of God and obey me"' (Zuhruf 43:63).

MUHAMMAD: 'Just as We have sent among you a messenger of your own to recite Our revelations to you, purify you and teach you the Scripture, wisdom, and (other) things you did not know' (Bakara 2:151). 'God has been truly gracious to the believers in sending them a Messenger from among their own, to recite His revelations to them, to make them grow in purity, and to teach them the Scripture and wisdom – before that they were clearly astray' (Al-Imran 3:161).

Hikmah is the foundation of moral behaviour, and the purpose and the meaning of life. The Qur'an gives Luqman as an example of one who internalized *hikmah* in this sense: 'We endowed Luqman with wisdom: Be thankful to God: whoever gives thanks benefits his own soul, and as for those who are thankless – God is self-sufficient, worthy of all praise' (Luqman 31:12).

In the Qur'an, the term *hikmah* has a close affiliation with the concepts of knowledge, gnosis, intellect, heart, and comprehension. *Hikmah* does not contain only intellectual cognizance, however; it also consists of 'being' and 'producing value'. According to Islamic scholars, *hikmah* is the most prestigious success that a human being can obtain, independently of any kind of cultural and religious background. It goes beyond conceptual boundaries, tracing a direction of intellectual and ethical progress, and opening a way for an empathetic relation with the cosmos. It is to do the best word and deed, to be aware of what should happen and to grasp reality with science and reason. In their view hikmah is not a matter of rational 'knowing' only, but also of existential 'being' (Öztürk, 1991, 182–183; Tan, 2000, 250).

Hikmah has not been confined to Islam: it is the common name of all the creative-awareness powers in all the divine books. The Qur'an presents this view: 'He will teach him the Book, the *hikmah*, the Torah and the Gospel' (Al-Imran 3:48; Maide, 5:110).

To pronounce on the principles of religious education based on *hikmah*, or to defend them adequately, would exceed the limits of this chapter. What I want to do here is to introduce *hikmah* as a theological basis for individualized religion. This basis comprises knowledge, good deeds, and reason-based understanding.

What I am talking about is the possibility of an approach to the question of how I should live with my knowledge, in the learning which religious education provides, in order to feed my recognition of the whole self, of creativity, and of emotional and mental maturity. This is a matter of interpretation and a matter of theological perception.

Islamic pedagogy needs a theological framework for the relationship between the individual and Allah, the relationship between the individual and the substances in the cosmos, and rights and freedoms. I will put forward here a proposal based on the Qur'an for teachers of religious education. This is obviously not a solution to the challenge brought about by an individualistic perception of religion. However, my aim is to deepen the perception of this individualistic religious conception.

I presume that the process of learning that portrays the dimensions of creed, worship, and morality in Islam might be actualized in the light of the Qur'an's Meccan verses. Through my proposal, I believe not only that religious education might benefit most by this means from the modalities of education; but it will also produce a positive contribution to the whole development of students and bring forward the essence of religion.

The call of Muhammad's egalitarian and universal original religion, which put the *tawhid* creed in the centre, appeared as a form of religion during the Meccan period, concerned only with the creed, worship, and morality. As a matter of fact, studies on the Qur'an's Meccan chapters recognize that the verses revealed at that period mostly emphasized the topics of the existence and unity of Allah, resurrection, the hereafter, judgement, creed, and doing useful deeds for humanity. In the Meccan verses persistent emphasis was placed on the creed and morality, and illustrations of *ghayb*, paradise, and hell appear very often. Fables also have a significant place in the Meccan verses.

Within the framework of such a call, religious and moral responsibility has been primarily placed upon the individual, who has already been addressed as the target group as 'O human beings!' In this period the strongest attribution is 'pious-ones, the mindful, the righteous' (*al-muttakûn*): 'It is the one who brings the truth and the one who accepts it as true who are mindful of God' (Zümer 39:33). 'The righteous will live securely among gardens and rivers' (Kamer 54:54). 'But would We treat those who believe and do good deeds and those who spread corruption on earth as equal? Would We treat those who are aware of God and those who recklessly break all bounds in the same way' (Sad 38:28).

The term 'pious-ones' was used for those who have an awareness of responsibility. It deserves comprehensive study from the standpoint of religious education.

My own studies on the Qur'anic Meccan verses, which constitute sixty to seventy per cent of the Qur'an, allows me to say that these verses provide the theological framework for religious education in Islam as a religion of conscience based on individualistic choice and responsibility.

In the dichotomy of individual-society while the priority had been with the individual, in the Madinan period the priority shifted to society. When we look at the Madanise verses, alongside the principles of creed and morality, we find expressions dealing with social order and politics. These verses handle concrete social topics.

The bewilderment of Islamic pedagogy results from the clash between the traditional approach and the needs of modern society; it faces considerable difficulties in providing a balance in the relationships among the triad of religion-individual-society. Hesitations and contradictions are both to be found among religious educators with regard to deciding what the limits of Islam should be in the lives of both individuals and society.

My thesis is that a pedagogy based on a theological conception which has been shaped by the principles of creed, worship, and morality in Islam, will provide a strong epistemological framework for individualized religion.[3]

References

Abdel Haleem, M. A. S. (2005). *The Qur'an*. New York: Oxford University Press.
Altaş, N. (2004). *Gençlik döneminde din olgusu ve liselerde din öğretimi (The phenomenon of religion in adolescence and RE in secondary schools)*. Ankara: Nobel.

---

3   The translations of the Qur'anic verses are from Abdel Haleem, 2005.

Hatiboğlu, M. S. (1986). Kur'ân-ı kerim'de mahalli hükümler meselesi (Locally-bounded legislation in the Qur'an). *İslamiyat, 1* (7), 7-12.

Hatiboğlu, M. S. (2004). *Müslüman kültürü üzerine (On Muslim culture)*. Ankara: Kitabiyat.

Özarslan, S. (1994). *14-18 yaş lise gençlerinde kader inancı (Belief in predestination in adolescents aged 14-18)*. Unpublished Master's thesis. Ankara: Ankara Üniversitesi Sosyal Bilimler Enstitüsü. Ankara.

Öztürk, Y. N. (1995). *Kur'an'in Temel Kavramlari (Basic Concepts of the Qur'an)*. Istanbul: Yeni Boyut.

Selçuk, M. (1998). Din öğretimi özgürleştiren bir süreç olabilir mi? (Can RE be a liberating process?). *İslamiyat, 1,* 73-87.

Selçuk, M. (2007). The contribution of RE to democratic culture: challenges and opportunities – Religion, spirituality and character. Unpublished conference paper. Cambridge, England: St Edmund's College.

Tan, B. (2000). *Kur'an'da hikmet kavramı (The concept of hikmah in the Qur'an)*. Istanbul: Pinar Yayinlari.

Yaman, H. (2008). *The concept of hikmah in early Islamic thought: A thesis submitted to the Department of Near Eastern Languages and Civilizations*. Unpublished doctoral thesis. Cambridge, Massachusetts: Harvard University.

RECAI DOĞAN

7 An Ottoman Example of the Perception of Other Religions in Islamic Thought

Introduction

The developments in science and technology that have occurred over the last two centuries have provided experiences equivalent to a human adventure spanning hundreds of thousands of years. Thanks to science and technology, human beings have discovered unprecedented things and surpassed so-called unsurpassable thresholds. However, human science and technology has also threatened the future of humanity. Modern science and technology warn us what humanity will encounter when it ignores the reality of human being ('man') and the laws of creation.

Human beings are not wholly independent of nature. From the scientific and technological perspective, nature is an object to be used, consumed, and constantly exploited. The environmental pollution that threatens the future of humanity is the inevitable consequence of this approach. Excessive individualism drags humanity along with a meaninglessness and loneliness that daily increases.

In addition, globalization, as well as bringing positive progress through increased knowledge of other cultures and beliefs, has also brought some negative consequences. Some dispute the negative consequence of excessive secularization. However, violence and terror has now achieved a global dimension that threatens the future of all humanity. To address this, we must start by strengthening people's moral conscience, giving them a greater awareness of the claims and benefits of moral values, and in this way promote the formation of a character shaped by self-control, rather than by egoism. If we fail at this, we shall have no effective criterion for defining what is right and what is wrong, and we shall slip towards annihilation. Undoubtedly, we do not need to *reinvent* these moral values. These are the values that exist within the three great religions: Judaism, Christianity, and Islam. These all bring with them principles that need to be accommodated by secular society as well (Onat, 2007, 6).

Violence and terror have no part in religion. In its essence, no religion encourages them. The common ground of religions is to provide security for life and property, and to encourage goodness and righteousness. The problem does not lie in the religions, but in the perception of some religious people about their religion. Hence our ability to overcome religious terror on a global scale depends primarily on our achieving sound knowledge of the religions. All religions are on the side of humanity. Religion is not itself a goal. Religions are a means of contributing to the humane improvement of humanity.

If we focus on the heart of Judaism, Christianity, Islam, Buddhism, and Hinduism, we may summarize their common moral values as righteousness, purity, goodness and charity, reverence for the elderly, and not harming others. Unlawful murder is banned in all religions. All religions are against theft. False testimony is not tolerated by any of them. These core benefits are held in common by all religions, and must be brought to prominence through sound knowledge. This will prevent people viewing the followers of other religions negatively in the name of religion. In order to overcome our global spiritual crisis, we must base our lives on a new balance.

It is time to recognize that the spiritual dimension of life is of equal importance to its material dimension. It became obvious in the twentieth century that we had to say once again, 'never again'. If humanity is to take its destiny into its own hands within a harmonious world, it is inevitable that it must put moral rules at the centre (Brzezinski, 1999, 71–72).

As a result of globalization, we live in a multicultural world where individuals from different cultural, religious, economic, political, and ethnic origins live together. These differences can be seen in every sphere of life, starting from the areas of religion, politics, economics, and etiquette. Although we know that some in the past have lived together amicably with members of different religions, the great majority of them lived their lives in the limited world that they inherited from their own past. Factors such as developments in technology and communication, which allow us to receive knowledge produced in any other part of the world in a very short time, have not only accelerated contact between different communities but have also made this inevitable. This new situation brought about the problem of 'the other': the problem of knowing, accepting, and living together with the other. We mean by 'the other' here an individual or citizen who differs from us by his or her clothes, behaviour, eating and drinking, language and opinions; but who could be our closest neighbour in a world that has now become a global village.

Humanity is passing through a difficult and stormy period. In this period, humanity does not only need political programmes and activities. It also needs a vision to allow peoples, ethnic and moral groups, and religions to live together on our planet in peace, with common responsibility: a broad vision that requires these hopes, goals, ideals, and values (Küng and Kuschel, 1995, 15).

At this stage in the globalized world, the question arises as to how a believer perceives and relates to members of a different religion. This question necessarily forces all religious people into real conceptual crisis. In addition, religions have sometimes adopted the same, and at other times different approaches to how we should perceive and relate to the other. These different approaches can sometimes be seen among members of the same religion. The problem of how to perceive and relate to the other has become an important topic. It is one about which Muslim thinkers have always been concerned.

In general, attitudes towards the other can be placed in one of three categories: exclusive, inclusive, and pluralistic. According to the exclusivists, the truth can be obtained only by their own religion. There is, therefore, only one truth and one (their own) path to salvation. As there is no salvation outside their religion, all people must be invited to the salvation offered by this particular religion. According to inclusivists, however, truth may be found in different religions, though it might also be absent. But as the most excellent religion is their own, absolute truth is only to be found in their own religion. The best guide to salvation is therefore the way of their own religion. According to the pluralists, most religions – even all of them – are ways that offer a guide to truth. And none among them is superior.

At this point, the question inevitably arises as to which of these three categories represents the attitude of Islam towards the other. It is impossible to respond to this question with only one, permanently valid answer. This is also not possible for the other religions, because attitudes can change according to time, place, and other conditions. Our concern is to find an answer to the question whether or not Islam can ever present a pluralistic worldview. The answer here depends on what may be understood by the concept of pluralism. If we understand it in terms of the presence of social, political, economic, and cultural variety, Islam is pluralistic in the sense that the religion first came into being and later spread in this way. No religious movement ever arose and spread in isolation. Islam, Buddhism, Hinduism, Christianity, and Judaism are all pluralistic in the sense that all of them were born, developed, and became world religions in societies in which different religions existed.

If, however, we understand pluralism as a theory that proposes that every religion is the same and that all of them lead to the same truth, so that Islam is viewed as relative and just like other religions, then Islam would not accept this understanding. Of course, there are many common points within the essence of the religions. But it is important to accept the differences as they are, and to tolerate them.

If pluralism is defined as difference in essence coupled with peaceful coexistence, and as a worldview in which the rights of the other are guaranteed, then many Muslims will agree that, in this sense, Islam is a pluralistic religion on such an understanding. The Muslim community accepts itself as one community among other communities created by Allah. There are many examples in Islamic history which show the acceptance of this understanding. One of the first important examples of this is the Constitution of Madina, executed by the Prophet Muhammad. The Constitution put Muslims and Jews together under a conscious unity that defined the rights of the other in both theory and practice, and presented ways of being united. Another example is the tolerance of Muslims toward Hindus in India. According to Islam, Hindus are not accepted as people of the book (*ahl-i kitap*), but they nevertheless enjoyed the same rights, and were accepted and respected as citizens.

Today we see that tradition has a definite role in how a member of one religion perceives the other. Certainly, there are negative ways of perceiving the other in the traditions of almost all religions. Such traditions are transmitted to later generations through education. If negative perceptions and examples in the tradition are highlighted through education, then education will be one of the factors that plays a negative role in the perception of a member of one religion by another.

New interpretations and improvements about the perception of the other that occurred under new conditions at certain times, places, and circumstances are also important. The responsibilities of education involve not only that of transmitting the tradition to new generations, but also that of raising individuals who can improve this understanding. There is therefore an important role for education in reviewing the tradition that is inherited from the past. But, in order to make a positive change about the perception of the other through education, education needs to be improved in terms of its goals, contents, and methods.

In this chapter, an analysis is undertaken of two different paradigms as representative of Islamic perception by reference to the madrasas and takkas of the Ottomans, as an example of how we may make use of the tradition to progress a positive approach to 'the other' in the curricula of Islamic religious education.

The conception of Madrasa Islam is generally viewed in the history of Islamic thought as a theory which utilized mostly historical and traditional methodologies. The madrasa by losing its initial dynamism, especially as a result of political and social conflicts experienced after the Abbasid Dynasty, gradually became more literal and paid less significance to the rational sciences as compared to earlier periods. The sects (*madhhabs*) shaped the existing products, instead of their methodology, resulting in ponderous rather than prolific madrasa. This situation has been transmitted to the Ottoman Empire.

The concept of Takka Islam represents the perspective of mystical religion. The main characteristics of this perspective are: contemplation of the metaphysical world; acceptance of one resource for all beings; love and tolerance to all creatures, but primarily to human beings; esoteric interpretation; a concern for art and music; individualism; and an emphasis on moral values (Kutlu, 2001, 17–18).

The concept of Madrasa Islam

The Ottoman state is marked by an organized political authority and state tradition, legislative and executive bodies, and institutions and rules. Ottoman society was formed of administrators, scholars, military men, vocational groups, clergy, and other social classes. Business, agriculture, art, and scientific activities have all been of vital importance. In their lands, different religions and ethnic groups lived alongside one another. Among the Ottomans, religion played a very significant role in the political and administrative formation of the state. This formation was managed with the help of madrasa scholars. The scriptural and formalistic Madrasa conception of Islam, based on *fiqh*, has dominated the formation of the political and administrative structure of the Ottoman state. Its legal system was created by madrasa scholars who based their jurisprudence on interpretations of religious texts. Behaviour towards members of other religions living in Ottoman lands was prescribed within the juristic interpretation formed by these ulama.

These interpretations are as follows. Within Islamic law there are Muslims and non-Muslims. The non-Muslims, politically, are divided into two categories: *Ahl al-Harb* (those who are at war with Muslims) and *Ahl al-'Ahd* (those who have a treaty with Muslims). The *Ahl al-'Ahd* have been divided into three categories: (1) *Ahl al-Dhimma* (those who accepted the protection of the Islamic state), (2) the *Mu'āhad* (those with whom a peace treaty has been made), and (3) the *Musta'min* (those to whom assurance of security has been granted) (Şener, 1983, 41). The Islamic jurists classified non-Muslims into two categories, in accordance with their religion and beliefs: (1) *Ahl al-Kitab* (those to whom a divine scripture has been sent), and (2) those who are not *Ahl al-Kitab* (the pagan Mushriks and the Magians are in this category).

In Islamic law, non-Muslims possessed different statutes according to their position. As citizenship has been defined as 'the political and legal bond' between the individual and the state, all who permanently live in an Islamic country are the citizens of that country, regardless of whether they are Muslim or non-Muslim. The non-Muslim *Ahl al-Kitab*, as long as they agree to live under the sovereignty of the Islamic state, are given the 'protection (*dhimma*) of Allah and His Messenger', and are therefore called *dhimmî* (protected). (*Dhimma* means protection and providing safety.) The Islamic state pledges to the *dhimmis*, on behalf of Allah, to protect them against any possible internal or external dangers, and gives assurance as to their life, property, chastity, and their religious life and places of worship. According to this provision, the *dhimmis*, as long as they do not revolt against the state, have the same rights and responsibilities as Muslim citizens enjoy. Thus they have the right of marriage and being overseers to their children; and they have the right to appoint trustees, receive alimony, and obtain inheritance, and to obtain property and estates. They may practise their rituals as they wish. They may open places of worship. They are free with respect to their teaching and education (Şener, 1983, 42–48).

In the Ottoman state, the conception of official religion and state religion provided a scriptural interpretation of what it is to live together with the followers of other beliefs living on the same land, and implemented this. A social agreement was constituted as a way of living together. The Ottoman order was an order based on diversities: although 'sameness' or 'similarity' was essential, rather than 'diversity'. This body was formulated in accordance with differences in belief, and protected by laws. Plurality, in the fullest meaning of the term, has been perceived as protecting and sustaining diversity, and has been implemented. On this model, the various religious and cultural factions of the public realm come together; but they never become other than themselves. Each group maintains its own religion, language, thoughts, and form of life. They live together under the Ottoman political system, but have never been assimilated.

A different conception of Madrasa Islam conforms to its scripturality and formalism. This conception formed the legal foundations of living together with followers of other beliefs in the same land. However, this conception, based on *fiqh*, has partially eroded with the disappearance of the madrasa, due to changes witnessed by the social structure from the nineteenth century onwards. Some important aspects of Madrasa Islam regarding perception of the other can be beneficial today, guaranteeing the rights of others in terms of law. Living together today is not possible, however, solely through legal arrangements. But it may be possible by people's mutual willingness to live together, irrespective of the cultural, religious, and ethnic differences between them.

The concept of Takka Islam

The foundation of Takka Islam lies in *sufi* thought. The institutionalized state of sufi thought is designated '*tarîqa*' (the sufi order). The place where sufi education is given is the '*takka*'. The sufi orders that emerged in the Islamic world may be classified in two groups. The first developed mostly under the impact of Platonism. For example, the concept of *wahdat al-wucûd* rejects sources of knowledge other than intuition, and asserts that intuition is universal and the sole source of knowledge. It cannot be claimed that this conception has been generally accepted. The second group is shaped by Turkish people. Treating human existence as central, this sufi conception gives priority to training in morality and of the self, based on repentance, endurance, generosity, gratitude, love and fear of God, glorification, submission, sincerity, and so forth. Favoured by the public, it became widespread. Within this framework, in the foundation of Ottoman Takka Islam, are to be found the sufi orders such as Yasawism, whose formation started at the end of the eleventh century, and later Mawlawism and Baktashism, which developed around Yasawism.

The concept of 'other' in the Takka Islam of the Ottomans, in contrast to that of Madrasa Islam, does not rest only upon formal and legal regulations. In Takka Islam, there is empathy, respect, love, and tolerance towards the 'other'. Takka Islam is individualistic, morality-based, and love-founded. It originated from the Islamic concepts of existence and morality. According to sufi thought, existence is divided into two categories: Allah and others. Hence humanity as a whole is equal, as being human and being created. There is no difference among them in being human. Apparent differences only lie in the mundane, temporary things that will no longer exist when this universe perishes. Therefore, arrogance and fury should not be shown to human beings. It is necessary, rather, to practise and disseminate the culture of tolerance. Not breaking hearts is possible by restoring them. Respect and love shown to humanity is – in a way – also shown to the Creator. This has been put into words in the poetry of Yunus Emre, who expressed the understanding of Ottoman Takka Islam in this manner:

> Tolerate the created
> for the sake of the Creator.
>   The heart is the throne of God.
>   Thus God looks at the heart ...
>   If you break a true believer's heart once,
>   This obeisance is no prayer to God.
>   All of the world's seventy-two nations
>   Cannot wash the dirt off your hands and face.
>   (Aksakal, 2005, 13)

The sufi who practised these principles comprehended the mysteries of the beings. There is no darkness for him. His eyes have been opened. Wherever he looks, he will see the same reality. He will know that everything has been created by Allah. He will perceive that the being-world has been created for a purpose, and that human beings have been sent to this earth for a reason. There is a masterpiece from Allah in every human being, for Allah had breathed into him His Spirit. For this reason, human beings should not injure other humans, but should behave towards them with tolerance. Plurality is part of the manifest world, and is the reflection of the One. The main thing is love. And the best love is the divine love shown to the real being: that is, to Allah.

In the foundation of Takka Islam there resides good morality, the attributes of which include tolerance, sympathy, absolution, forgiveness, humility, gratefulness to Allah for the blessings He has given (no matter how little or bountiful), constancy, keeping an open table, ignoring the faults of other people, not having rancour or jealousy, being knowledgeable, exchanging greetings, enjoining the good and prohibiting the bad, seeing everybody as equal, patience, contentment, and honesty. Within these moral principles, it is necessary to show virtue towards the followers of other beliefs. For example, in the Ottoman period we find these statements about the approach to 'the others' from sufis who were influential on Takka Islam: 'It is sunnah of the Prophet not to hurt a human being, even though he or she may be an unbeliever. Allah does not accept the callous who hurts a heart' (Yasawî, 1992, 57). 'Never blame any nation or human being. Never forget that even your enemy is a human being' (Haji Baktash, 1971, 82).

> Supine is our name,
> Rancour is our enemy,
> We are never to be rancorous to anybody,
> All people are the same to us.
>   (Aksakal, 2005, 84)

This concept of Takka Islam in the history of Islamic thought provides us with an attitude for today for admitting and accepting members of different religions as they are, which makes living together possible.

Conclusion

The interpretations of Madrasa and Takka Islam in their approach to 'the other' originated from the Qur'an and the hadiths, the basic sources of Islam. However, they are only interpretations; they do not represent the religion itself. By highlighting human rights and freedoms, however, and showing respect for diversity, it is formalistic and *fiqh* based, due to its influence on the ideology of state enforcement. The Madrasa Islam conception goes beyond recognizing 'the other', and establishes what the legal relationship between the other and the state should be. Madrasa Islam is also an approach that gives priority to the teaching of moral values by placing the individual and human being at the centre. Therefore, even though the Takka and Zaviyahs were closed down in Turkey, they maintained their influence through various channels. In Turkey today, the sufi interpretations of Yasawism, Mawlavism, and Baktashism are still being adopted in an effective form.

In order to create a culture of compromise, tolerance, and trustworthiness, Turkey today aims at teaching a common basis of Islamic conceptions for those who define themselves as Muslims, through classes in religious culture and ethics that basically adopt a non-sectarian approach. This common ground is formed from the universal values in the Qur'an. It also seeks to develop tolerance towards the beliefs of the followers of all religions in the world, on the basis of knowledge of their religion through the educational curriculum. It aims at teaching them, not an approach to other religions, but how they should define themselves. In order to realize the aforementioned aims, in the curriculum of the religious culture and ethics classes, special reference has been made to the Turkish-sufi tradition. This development in the curriculum of Islamic religion classes in Turkey is a small, but most significant, step in solving the problems that the world faces, to benefit from the positive contributions of religion.

References

Aksakal, A. A. (ed.). (2005). *Yunus Emre'den Altın Öğütler*. Istanbul: Koza Publications.
Brzezinski, Z. (1999). Esnek Bati'nin Zayif Surlari. In N. Gardels (ed.), *Yüzyilin Sonu* (pp. 65–78). (B. Çorak, trans.). Istanbul: Remzi Publications.
Haji Baktash, Walî (1971). *Maqâlât*. E. Coşan (ed.). Ankara: Ensar Publications.
Küng, H., and Kuschel, K. J. (1995). *Evrensel Bir Ahlaka Doğru*. (N. Aşikoğlu, C. Tosun, R. Doğan, trans.). Ankara: Gün Publications.

Kutlu, S. (2001). İslam Düşüncesinde Tarihsel Din Söylemleri. *İslamiyat Dergisi, 4* (4), 15–36.
Onat, H. (2007). Küresel Şiddet ve Terörü Önlemede Dinin Rolü. *Global Strateji, 11*, 3–16.
Şener, A. (1983). İslam Hukukunda Gayr-i Müslimler. In *Türk Tarihinde Ermeniler Sempozyumu-Tebliğler ve Panel Konuşmaları* (pp. 41–52). İzmir: Safak Publications.
Yasawî, A. (1992). *Divan-i Hikmet*. Istanbul: Government Publications.

Z. ŞEYMA ARSLAN

8 A Holistic Approach in Education from the Perspective of the Islamic Understanding of Human Beings

In a sense, every educational thought or idea is based on a human image. When this begins to form its intellectual parameters it poses the question: 'How will this give meaning to human existence?' For it is the way in which humans see themselves, how they understand and accept themselves, that gives direction to all their other convictions and opinions. A short look at the history of educational thought reveals that different approaches to education have their roots in different approaches to human beings. The human being is the main subject of the process of education. The aim, contents, and methods of education are all shaped in relation to this human image.

The idea of holistic education, which has been frequently emphasized in the field of education over the past thirty years, also possesses an underlying human image. The idea of holistic education is based on the idea of the wholeness of the human entity. However, the interpretation of 'wholeness' may lead to different views of holistic education.

This chapter interprets the wholeness of the human being in an Islamic context, focusing on the concept of *fitrah*, which is the particular Islamic concept of human nature, and evaluating how this holistic view leads to a holistic perspective in education. Some main premises of this study are: that the concept of what a human is plays a core role in all aspects of educational thought; that Islamic thought has a special understanding of the human being which can be analysed under the concept of *fitrah*; and that this understanding of humanity exists within a holistic worldview frame, and can be used to create a holistic perspective in education.

In this study the first methodological decision must be how, and from where, to define the Islamic understanding of human nature. We have one and a half thousand years of accumulated thought behind us. But, of course, the main text for this worldview, the Holy Qur'an, is the basis for all this literature. With its detailed story of human existence and other indications, the Holy Book has been taken as the basis for analysis in this study. I have tried to pick out all the verses of the Qur'an relating to human nature and have categorized this compilation. Three categories have been identified as comprising the scope and content of the concept of *fitrah*. These categories have then been interpreted in terms of their effects on education. Through this procedure, a more concrete framework for the relationship between human nature and education has been targeted.

A second question which must be asked at the outset is what we mean by education, and which aspects of it will be considered in referring to the effects mentioned above. We use the word 'education' here in the widest sense that enables us to talk about educational theory. Accordingly, education is every type of process that shapes a human being. In its technical sense, however, education is the process by which society deliberately transmits what it has learned from one generation to another. When we talk about any educational theory in a general sense, we have to talk about at least three main elements: the aims, contents, and methods of education. These three elements ask and answer the basic questions about why, what, and how we educate. And, as sub-categories, they may help us to find a more concrete base for associating human nature with the theory of education.

Holistic education

The roots of holistic education, in the modern sense, go back well before the second half of the twentieth century. As a serious intellectual movement it is grounded in a synthesis of several philosophical and pedagogical perspectives. As pointed out by Miller (2005), holistic thinkers often draw on the work of theorists from the early and mid twentieth century, including Alfred North Whitehead (process philosophy), Carl Jung (archetypal psychology), Sri Aurobindo (integral philosophy), Gregory Bateson (cybernetics), and Ludwig von Bertalanffy (systems theory). The idea of wholeness in holistic education comes from the idea of the wholeness of the universe. Holism asserts that the universe is an undivided, interconnected whole, and that this whole embodies an all-encompassing creative source through many layers or contexts. In *The Wholeness Principle*, Lemkow (1990) identifies the fundamental beliefs of this worldview as: the oneness and unity of all life, the all-pervasiveness of ultimate Reality or the Absolute, and the multidimensional or hierarchical character of existence. Spirituality is at the heart of holistic education; it is, above all, education for the *soul* – for the essence – of the human being, not only for the social and psychological surface of the personality (Miller, 2005). Thus, holistic education reflects an attitude, a philosophy, and a worldview that challenges the fragmented, reductionist, mechanistic, and nationalistic assumptions of mainstream culture and education (Clark, 1990).

Holistic education, on the other hand, runs parallel to the theory of 'multiple intelligences' (Gardner, 1993) that highlights the diversity and complexity of the ways the human mind comes to know the world. It acknowledges that intelligence is multidimensional and can be expressed and assessed in a variety of ways according to personal differences (Clark, 1993). The holistic perspective also reflects an ecological awareness. This awareness is not simply a sensitivity towards nature and the environment, but sees a harmony and integrity between human beings and nature rather than a conflict, and correlates the basis of ecological awareness with existential wholeness. Eventually the person educated in this way comes to regard himself/herself as fully implicated in the existence of those beings around him/her, human and non-human, and to care deeply about them.

Stemming from this background, holistic education regards as arbitrary the boundaries which divide the sacred from the secular, the spiritual from the material, mind from matter, and so on (Clark, 1990).

An analysis of the concept of *fitrah*

The term *fitrah* literally means 'creation'; it comes from the verb *fatara* which means 'to crack or to split'. Related to this primary meaning, *fatara* also means causing a thing to exist for the first time, to start to invent something, to unfold and reveal. Consequently, the noun form *fitrah* is 'creation', having a certain talent or predisposition attributed at the very first moment of creation, the natural constitution of something before being exposed to external effects (al-Cevheri, 1979, 2: 781; Ibn al-Esir, 1963, 3: 457; al-Isfahani, 2002, 640). The *fitrah* of a human is his nature, that is to say the concept of *fitrah* states 'what the human is'.

Although it is possible to talk about the natural constitution, namely the *fitrah*, of anything, the word is used in the Qur'an only once and with reference to human creation, which relates this natural disposition to religious believers.

> So set thou thy face truly to the religion being upright; the nature in which Allah has made mankind: no change (there is) in the work (wrought) by Allah. (The Romans Ar-Rûm, 30/30)

When examining the true nature of something, the question of what it is has two meanings: the first one aims to describe its type of existence, and the second aims to describe its features. The question of what the human is also includes the question of what the human being is as a living creature in existential space, and what the human being is, in terms of his features. This question of the features of the human being has aspects within itself that relate to the entirety of this being, whilst at the same time including its individual components (members). Consequently, it is possible to ascertain the category of being and the features as sub-categories in order to analyse the concept of *fitrah* as it signifies the specific creation of a human being.

These aspects are identified below, using a deductive approach.

A Holistic Approach in Education from an Islamic Perspective

(i) The first aspect is that of human nature, namely a human being as a living creature in existential space.
(ii) The second is the characteristic feature(s) of this being (i.e., its potentials or incapabilities).
(iii) The third includes the personal natures of the members of this being (i.e., individual differences).

The following sections examine these categories and relate them to educational reflections.

Fitrah as the nature of the human being as a living creature in existential space

The nature of the human being as a living creature in existential space is its existence among other creatures, and the difference between him and the others, and his position among them. This has to be the first step in attempting to understand human nature (*fitrah*), because we cannot talk about the features of the human being without establishing or clarifying this first step. If *fitrah* is a thing that belongs to human being and is peculiar to it, its first meaning is 'what does it mean to be human?' This aspect of *fitrah* is concerned with human nature if it is a developed member among other living creatures on earth, or the sublime creature on earth with distinguishing features. In this respect, the first meaning of *fitrah* is being human; not animal or angel, or any other thing. This aspect also includes the aim of a person's life, the source of his existence, his position on earth, and his destiny.

The explanation in the Qur'an of the existence of human being states that the human has been created by God: his existence has a planned design, and is not one based on chance. The verses of the Qur'an tell us that the creation of the first member of the human race (Adam) began with God's announcement of his wish to create a vicegerent (caliph) on earth:

> Behold, thy Lord said to the angels: 'I will create a vicegerent on earth.' They said: 'Wilt Thou place therein one who will make mischief therein and shed blood? – whilst we do celebrate Thy praises and glorify Thy holy (name)?' He said: 'I know what ye know not.' (The Heifer/al-Baqarah, 2/30)

We also learn that the human was created from clay, and when God breathed his spirit into him, the angels respected him and fell prostrate before him:

> Behold! thy Lord said to the angels: 'I am about to create man, from sounding clay from mud moulded into shape; when I have fashioned him (in due proportion) and breathed into him of My spirit, fall ye down in obeisance unto him.' So the angels prostrated themselves, all of them together: not so Iblis: he refused to be among those who prostrated themselves ... (The Rocky Tract/al-Hijr, 15/ 28–43)

The aim of human existence is declared within the concepts of vicegerency (caliphate), confirmation of God, worship, and entrustment. Man accepted the burden of trust (amanah) which none in creation but he dared accept.

> We did indeed offer the Trust to the Heavens and the Earth and the Mountains; but they refused to undertake it, being afraid thereof: but man undertook it; He was indeed unjust and ignorant. (The Confederates/al-Ahzáb, 33/72)

According to classical interpretations, this is a commitment (al-Razi, 1990), an acceptance of freedom, and also of the responsibility towards both God and all other creatures. This means that human beings are able to transcend all degrees of existence, even that of the angels, and reach the divine presence. But along with this freedom come the possibility of rebellion and the negation of the very reality in whose image the human being was made. The difference, and the superiority, of this new creation is his being which enables this test to be carried out.

The educational inference of this frame is related to the ultimate aim of education. Education is for what the human being is for. That is to say, education exists for the sake of the human being, and its purpose is in relation to the ultimate purpose of human life on earth. The aim of education is seen within the aim of life itself and takes its meaning from this, as does the process of humanization. Therefore the aim of education varies in respect to the aim of life.

The concept of *fitrah* includes the definition of human being, the maker, and the aim of making. If there is a particular state of being at the moment of creation, it says that this is a given structure, the first and genuine character. The maker is God, and *fitrah* includes the notion of God in understanding human being.

In this respect, the nature of human being is in a way his destiny. It is the plan ordained at the moment of creation. Our nature is our destiny, just as the nature given to an apple tree is to be an apple tree. Knowing and worshipping God is also present in the structure and destiny of a human being. When the human being performs this, he also realizes his existence. Humanization, in essence, coincides with this recognition. Within the frame of the concept of *fitrah*, the ontological reality of humankind is based on the concepts of trust, faith, worship, and the caliphate. As human existence gets its meaning within God, the human being itself is the meaning of the world. When the human being disappears, the meaning of the world will also disappear. Since God has created the universe for the human being, and the human being for a particular purpose, the human being is therefore at the centre of the inward existence of the universe.

Since education is an activity relying on human nature, its aim is the realization of humanity in these terms. Because the human is a vicegerent in the world, a part of natural existence with responsibilities towards it, education should be channelled through this natural interconnectedness. I feel it necessary to emphasize briefly the difference of the above statement from the proclamation that the aim of education is 'maturation', either individually as self-realization, or socially as harmony and adjustment with society.

Fitrah as the characteristic features of a human being

Pursuing the threefold meaning of human nature, the second category is its characteristic features. Here we are concerned with the human features which exist wherever the human is: the phenomena in the concept of 'human' that we may call the conditions of human existence – to be the one who knows, acts, believes, speaks, performs, etc. All these features are the consequences of the elements or potential that form the human being, and of the relationship between the elements of this composition. This category is also about the inner wholeness of human being.

The Qur'anic revelation about the structure of human being states some interior constituents and dynamics that are difficult to distinguish one from the other, and which form the whole human existence: namely body, spirit (*ruh*), intellect (*aql*), heart (*qalb*), and the ego-self or soul (*nafs*). The first two (body and spirit) were mentioned above within the context of the creation story, when God speaks about a new creature made up originally from clay but which gained its real form after God blew his spirit into it (see also, for the body, Jonah/Yunus, 10/92; The Prophets/al-Anbiyáa, 21/8; The Letter/Sád, 38/34; and, for the spirit, The Prostration/as-Sajdah, 32/9; The Letter/Sád, 38/72; The Night Journey/Al-Isrá, 17/85).

As for the intellect, it is mentioned in the Qur'an always in verbal form (not in the noun form referring to its essential being), expressing a human activity like understanding, thinking, remembering, or contemplating. It is also always mentioned as a positive situation – we cannot talk about a bad intellect, but of not using it, 'not to understand' or 'not to think' (see The Heifer/Al-Baqarah, 2/171–172, 242; Jonah/Yunus, 10/100; The Criterion/al-Furqán, 25/44; The Dominion/al-Mulk, 67/10; The Family of 'Imran/al-Imrán, 3/190; Bowing the Knee/al-Játhiya, 45/5).

Conversely, heart (*qalb*) is used in so many forms in accordance with its literal meaning of change, which ranges from the one who is sound, receives revelation, understands, thinks, sees, believes, is beautified by faith, is placed in contentment, finds satisfaction in the remembrance of Allah, trembles upon mentioning God, is satisfied, is opened to receive God's message, is upright, is given strength, is softened by the remembrance of Allah, and is reconciled; to the one who grows hard, is severe, harsh, is sealed, is blind, diseased, in confused ignorance, is divided, is in doubt or agitation (see The Poets/Ash-Shuàráa, 26/89, 193; Victory/al-Fath, 48/4; The Inner Apartments/al-Hujurát, 49/7; Victory/al-Fath, 48/4; The Thunder/al-Ràd, 13/28; The Pilgrimage/al-Hajj, 22/35, 46; The Heifer/al-Baqarah, 2/260; Iron/al-Hadíd, 57/16, 27; Mutual Loss and Gain/at-Tagábun, 64/11; The

Cave/al-Kahf, 18/14; The Groups/az-Zumar, 39/23; The Family Of Imrán/al-Imrán, 3/103, 159; The Table Spread/al-Máída, 5/13; Bowing the Knee/al-Játhiya, 45/23; The Believer/al-Mümin, 40/35; Light/an-Nûr, 24/50; The Believers/al-Müminün, 23/63; The Gathering/al-Hashr, 59/14; Repentance/al-Tauba, 9/45; Those Who Tear Out/an-Náziàát, 79/8).

While there are fixed, unchangeable natural facts for the intellect – believing in God is among them – the heart receives distortion in itself. However, the distortion afterwards seems like an illness; conversely, it is in the remembrance of Allah that hearts find satisfaction (The Thunder/al-Ràd, 13/28).

Finally, the ego-self or the soul (*nafs*) is the self of the person and the structure arising from the gratification and the survival of the body. It may be called the inner personality of the body. It may sometimes incite to evil, and so should be subjugated and restrained from indulging in low desires. It can also experience self-reproach, or complete rest and satisfaction (Qáf, 50/16; The Resurrection/al-Qiyámah, 75/2; The Dawn/al-Fajr, 89/27, 28; Joseph/Yusuf, 12/53; Those Who Tear Out/an-Náziàát, 79/40).

While the heart is pure in its essence, the ego-self/soul has natural inclinations that need to be controlled. It has a structure open to maturation:

> By the Soul, and the proportion and order given to it; and its inspiration as to its wrong and its right; truly he succeeds that purifies it, and he fails that corrupts it! (The Sun/ash-Shams, 91/7–10)

The changeability, tendencies, and weaknesses of humanity are included within the concept of being human. These are the other features that make up a human – unless we are talking about angels, not humans. Human being is one of the creatures on earth, made up from the same items, surrounded with the same conditions, undertaking a similar struggle for survival. This part is also meaningful in the schema of its ultimate aim, the test.

This structure makes the human both theomorphic and terrestrial. Its potential, possibilities, natural faculties, and inabilities are all related to these elements: his/her will and freedom, the idea of reality, the idea of ethics and aesthetics, the sense of love, the faculty of using language and construing culture, and the weaknesses or desires of the mortal human.

Intelligence is the main attribute of human existence directed towards the realization of the purpose of the creation and therefore acting positively; the ego-self/soul is the structure arising from the needs and desires of the body as a worldly creature; the heart is the deepest centre of feeling and understanding, over which the intellect and the ego-self try to gain ascendancy. These potentials are the dynamics of maturation and perfection through the experience of a number of relationships with the environment.

The educational inference of this conceptualization is related mainly to the content of education, since the faculties and capabilities of human nature constitute the subject-matter for education. Each of the elements of the human constitution (body-spirit-heart-intellect-self) is a subject for improvement.

'Education is the development of all aspects of the individual.' This, of course, is a generally accepted opinion; but how are we to understand 'all aspects'? Referring to the framework mentioned above, we can say that education should concern itself not only with the instruction and training of the mind and the transmission of knowledge, but also with the education of the whole being, including the heart or ego-self. This issue is also one of the most criticized aspects of modern education, but again how we understand the heart and ego-self is important. Here we may remember that the first category of *fitrah* is the premise for understanding and explaining the ones that follow.

When we say that the content of education should promote the full development of human potential, we will consequently be talking about an education that comprises both spiritual and material aspects. The theomorphic and terrestrial dimensions of human life require it. The loss of the transcendent dimension may make terrestrial life itself precarious. Since there is an underlying unity between all the human faculties, this unity needs to be reflected in an integrated and holistic curriculum that does not draw rigid lines between different subjects and disciplines. One of the most problematic dichotomies of our time is the one between the religious and secular spheres of knowledge, to which our modern minds are highly accustomed. Owing to the presence of this compartmentalization, religious education can only exist in our time as one subject among others in schools, in a situation purified from the claims of mindset and character formation.

Fitrah as personal differences between individual human beings

A third category of human nature comprises the personal features of the members of this species. What is meant by this category is that, as well as all individuals representing the general characteristics of the human race, there are also specific patterns having their own personal natures (i.e., individual differences). Being individually different is a part of being human. This aspect of human nature is a successive and natural result of the former two categories; because taking on individual responsibility for free choice is needed to perform and fulfil the aim of life. Some of the verses concerned with differences between people are as follows:

> 'And among His Signs is the creation of the heavens and the earth, and the variations in your languages and your colors: verily in that are Signs for those who know' (The Romans/ar-Rûm, 30/22); 'Say: "Everyone acts according to his own disposition: But your Lord knows best who it is that is best guided on the Way"' (The Night Journey/al-Isrá, 17/84); 'It is He Who hath made you the inheritors of the earth: He hath raised you in ranks, some above others: that He may try you in the gifts He hath given you' (The Cattle/al-Anàam, 6/165); 'On no soul do We place a burden greater than it can bear' (The Believers/al-Mùminûn, 23/62).

We may infer that personal differences (natural or induced) are the normal practice of Allah (sunnah), a part of His eternal system. As the source of the differences among people is God's creating creatures that are different, or are able to be different, we understand that no kind of difference has a value attributable to itself. But how the difference is employed makes up the individual stories.

Here, we must admit the difficulty of distinguishing between inborn personal features and later acquisitions. Generally we make a distinction between character and temperament; but because the potential for difference comes to operate at the very beginning of life, we can hardly define their relative proportions. The important thing here for us is the natural ability we have through being and becoming different.

The educational implications of this conceptualization can be seen especially in relation to the methods of education. Education should provide a milieu for the total development of every student in every sphere of learning: spiritual, moral, imaginative, intellectual, cultural, aesthetic, emotional, and physical. Research on differences in learning styles, school achievement, the design of learning material, and teaching strategies show that there is a certain correlation between them. Modern education has evidently achieved success in ascertaining learning styles, and developing suitable teaching methods and materials to cater for these learning styles (Smith and Ragan, 1999). Acknowledging the role of personal differences in education affects almost every decision-making process and practice of education.

The achievements of modern education in addressing personal differences in education are a result of the predominance of the ideal of self-realization in education, which stems from the stress in modernism on individualism. But in the holistic view, whose framework we have attempted to draw above, an educational theory will be deficient if it neglects the abstract ideal of humankind. The self-knowledge and self-realization processes in education can only take on their true and proper value when they are considered in relation to the source of existence. Results reached from experiences and consequences show that it is doubtful whether human-centered thought has brought human beings the desired freedom, or the opportunity to establish themselves in their surroundings. The emphasis on mere individualism and self-realization engenders selfishness, alienation, and loneliness; reminding one of the words: 'Do not be like those who forgot God, those He made forget themselves' (The Gathering/al-Hashr, 59/19).

'I' cognition starts with the breathing-in of the spirit, when the human being stands at the centre of the universe as the 'choosing creature' and the one who accepts the burden of trust. This conceptualization should not be seen as a barrier to self-realization, but as a justification for and explanation of it.

Conclusion

Focusing on the concept of *fitrah*, we tried to interpret the wholeness of the human being and how this holistic view leads to a holistic perspective in education. We examined human nature in three consecutive categories: in the broadest sense it refers to human nature in terms of the genus of human being, then the characteristic features of this human creature, and finally the inborn individual differences of its members. Education can also be compartmentalized into the aims, the contents, and the methods of education.

We should first say that all these categories lie in relation with one another. But the first step in understanding human nature is most significantly related to the ultimate aims of education, such as the ultimate meaning of human existence. The second category relates to the content of education, and how and in which aspects the human being can be improved. The third category indicates a methodological perspective that should be considered in planning and engaging in educational processes.

I would argue that this categorization may allow us to think systematically about the relationship between human nature and education, enabling us to form a broad and balanced system of education based on an understanding of the full potential of the human being. We may also find some similarities with recent holistic education movements: such as, unity of all life, stress on other aspects of humanity like spirituality, a special emphasis on personal differences, and the multidimensional character of intelligence.

This is certainly not the first time that a holistic perspective in education referring to the basic Islamic resources has been put forward. To claim this would be to reveal an ignorance of a great historical tradition, especially that of sufistic literature, which offers a philosophy of life based on spiritual maturation. Here, as in the modern holistic education movement, there is a new attempt at thinking within a new conceptual framework and language. The holism of the title of this study may be understood in these terms.

References

al-Cevheri, Ebu Nasr Ismail (1979). *Tac al-lugat ve sihah al-Arabiyye*. Beirut: Dar al-Ilm li al-Melayin (7 volumes).

al-Isfahani, al-Raghib (2002). *Mufradat alfaz al-Qur'an*. S. Adnan Davudi (ed.). Beirut: Dar es-Shamiye.

al-Razi, Fahr al-Din (1990). *al-Mefatih al-gayb*. Beirut: Dar al-Fikr (32 volumes).

Clark, E. T. (1990). A search for wholeness in education. *The Education Digest, 56* (4), 47–50.

Clark, E. T. (1993). Guidelines for designing a holistic school. In C. L. Flake (ed.), *Holistic education: Principles, perspectives and practices* (pp. 80–86). Brandon: Holistic Education Press.

Gardner, H. (1993). *Frames of mind*. New York: Basic Books.

Ibn al-Esir (1963). *en-Nihaye fi garib al-hadis ve al-eser*. T. Ahmed Zavi and M. Muhammed Tanahi (eds). Cairo: Dar al-Ihya al-Kutub al-Arabiyye (5 volumes).

Lemkow, A. (1990). *The wholeness principle: Dynamics of unity within science, religion, and society*. Wheaton, Illinois: Quest Books.

Miller, R. (2005). Bütüncül eğitimin felsefi kaynakları (Philosophical sources of holistic education). *Journal of Values Education, 3* (10), 33–40.

Smith, P. L., and Ragan, T. J. (1999). *Instructional design*. New York: John Wiley & Sons.

PART III

Empirical and Pedagogical Studies

ELISABETH ARWECK AND ELEANOR NESBITT

9   The Interaction of the Major Religions
    at Microcosmic Level:
    Religiously-Mixed Families in the UK

The mixed-faith families project

'Investigating the religious identity formation of young people in mixed-faith families' was a three-year ethnographic study (June 2006–September 2009) in the Warwick Religions and Education Research Unit (WRERU) at the University of Warwick, UK, funded by the Arts and Humanities Research Council (AHRC). Fieldwork, mainly involving interviews with individual parents and young people, extended over a period of eighteen months (Autumn 2006–Spring 2008).

The stated aim of the project was to identify and explore processes in the religious identity formation of young people in mixed-faith families. The objectives were threefold: (a) to identify differences and commonalties between children's identity formation and parents' expectations and perceptions of this; (b) to assess the impact of religious socialization (formal and informal) and religious education on young people's religious identity and their responses; (c) to inform theoretical debate in religious studies and religious education on the representation of 'faith communities'/'religions' in syllabuses.

The research questions explored the importance of a range of factors, including gender, parents' commitment, education, socioeconomic status, locality, religious calendars, and perceptions of faith in young people's faith development, and how these were represented by them and their parents.

For the purpose of this study, the term 'mixed-faith families' referred to combinations between four faiths: Christianity, Hinduism, Islam, and Sikhism. The terminology used in the literature to denote the notion of 'mixed' in families and couples ranges widely and includes contested concepts, as Rodriguéz Garcia (2006) points out (see Arweck and Nesbitt, 2010b, 2). Our review of the relevant literature concluded that authors tend to take the terms they employ at face value, rather than discussing their usage of terms. The choice of the four faiths in our study was based on a number of reasons, including numerical preponderance in the UK (Census 2001), increase in intermarriages crossing all these boundaries, research experience in WRERU, and the analytical advantage of comparing two Semitic with two Indic faith communities. National surveys in this country and elsewhere (see, e.g., Census 2001; ARIS 2001) show an increase in the number of mixed families and the number of (especially young) people with dual heritage.

The project built on the experience and previous research within WRERU, especially empirical investigation of religious socialization and identity formation (e.g. Jackson and Nesbitt, 1993; Nesbitt, 2000; Nesbitt, 2007; Gent, 2005); but also on other research, such as studies of mothers' influence on children's religious identity (e.g. Pearce and Axinn, 1998), intercultural parenting in multifaith Britain (Becher, 2005), and intermarriage involving other religions (e.g., Romain, 1996) and in other countries (Ata, 2000; Ata, 2003).

The project's theoretical framework was guided by Ricoeur's 'narrative identity' (1992), Østberg's 'integrated plural identity' (2003), and Jackson's 'interpretive approach' for religious education (1997). Romain's typology of parental options (1996, 126–127) and parental patterns of allegiance (1996, 169), augmented by the typologies by Speelman (1997) and Furlong and Ata (2006), informed the analysis of the parents' approach; and Ricucci's typology (2007) informed the analysis of the young people's responses. The research aimed to contribute to understanding the notion of 'community' (Baumann, 1996) and children's agency (James and Prout, 1997) in 'choosing' a faith.

Regarding research methods, semi-structured interviews were conducted with young people and parents. Originally, we planned to focus on eight- to thirteen-year-olds and to involve families where a sibling pair of either gender in the specified age range was available. Our sample was to comprise five families of each possible combination between the four faiths, resulting in thirty families. However, we needed to adjust the age range of the young people and to work with a rolling sample. We also moderated the requirement of having a sibling pair in each family. (Further details about the challenges we faced during fieldwork are recorded in Nesbitt and Arweck, 2010.) We left it to parents to identify themselves as Christian, Hindu, Sikh, or Muslim, exploring varying levels of 'commitment' in the interviews.

Another aspect of the project was participant observation of occasions when children learn about religion or celebrate festivals or go through rites of passage, in the family, community, or school context. This was intended to complement the interviews, but opportunities to carry out participant observation did not arise. Further, we planned to combine 'traditional' or 'conventional' ethnography with the use of the Internet in order to identify, contact, and interact with potential families. However, this approach did not prove to be very successful (see Nesbitt and Arweck, 2010 for further details).

Given the involvement of young people and the potential sensitivity of these issues, careful consideration was given to ethical aspects of the study: including issues of consent, negotiating access to families, contact with young children, confidentiality, and data management.

The data gathered during fieldwork comprise 185 interviews (112 with adults, 73 with young people). On average, four or five interviews were conducted with each person, the length ranging from twenty minutes to over an hour. Most interviews were conducted in person (110), the rest by phone. Participants could choose which method they preferred. This also accounts for the negligible number of e-mail exchanges: very few participants opted to communicate in this way and none of these completed the process. The number of interviews relates to twenty-eight families (see Nesbitt and Arweck, 2010 for further details about the notion of 'families' in our study). The sample comprises two Hindu–Sikh, ten Hindu–Christian, six Christian–Sikh, and ten Christian–Muslim families. There are no families with the combination Hindu–Muslim or Muslim–Sikh.

An example of a mixed-faith family and its strategy

Having provided an outline of the project, we use the example of a mixed-faith family portrayed in the film *East is East* (1999) to illustrate aspects of interaction taking place between family members. One of the parents who participated in our study, Jiti, who had a Punjabi Sikh background, indicated that the film had captured the facets of his own upbringing and family life, commenting that the script writer must have had first-hand experience.[1] Although the film is billed as a comedy, it points to the problematic nature of mixed-faith families, such as the clash of parental attitudes and expectations regarding religion and culture, which is often an underlying theme in the wider literature. The film is set in Salford, a town in Northern England, in the 1970s. It opens with a religious procession in a street (showing Roman Catholic iconography), with a white British woman standing at a street corner, looking out for someone. This turns out to be her children, who are part of the procession, carrying religious icons and banners. When she spots them, her message to them is, 'George is back early from the mosque!' On hearing this, the young people dive into a side street, in order to avoid 'George', who turns out to be their Pakistani Muslim father; he is standing at another street corner watching the procession. The viewer realizes immediately that the father must not see his children taking part in a Christian festival and that Christianity is evidently the mother's religion. With this opening sequence, the scene is set for the viewer: here is a Pakistani Muslim married to a Christian white woman of Irish descent. However, the viewer never learns how they became a couple.

As the film progresses, it becomes clear that the husband feels strongly about Islam and Pakistani culture. He wants his children (six sons and one daughter, ranging in age from early to late teens) to embrace *his* values, beliefs, and cultural customs. Thus the 'mosque van' calls every week to take the children to *madrasa* where they learn the Qur'an by rote, but they really only go because their father requires them to do so. Only one of the

---

[1] All names relating to participants in our study are pseudonyms.

sons takes religion seriously. We see him observe prayer times and wear 'eastern' clothes outside work. The other children have adopted western life and dress styles. The daughter is shown playing football – enthusiastically – with other children in the street. Other scenes highlight the disparity between the values of father and children, such as the preparations for the oldest son's wedding. It becomes obvious that this is an arranged marriage; but, at the very last moment, the son pulls out, leaving his father feeling disgraced.

One of the most striking aspects about this family is that nothing is discussed – either between the parents, or between the parents and their children. There are no conversations over meals or cups of tea. We do not see the couple discuss anything related to their respective traditions. Family members seem to live their own lives, with the children doing things behind their father's back and with their mother's connivance: they eat bacon and sausages (hiding the smell, as father returns home early), and the older sons climb out of the back window to go to the disco or night club. The clash of cultures comes to a head when the father makes arrangements to marry two other sons and it all ends in disarray.

Given the lack of discussion between the parents, there is no indication about any agreement between them as to how the children should grow up. It is clear that the father wants to perpetuate the Pakistani Muslim way of life, with religion and culture interwoven, but the procession at the beginning of the film suggests the mother's socializing influence on the children. For the children, the father's attitudes and approach have no regard for their own aspirations or feelings, or for the fact that they are growing up in 'modern' Britain.

Mixed-faith couples' strategies

Looking at mixed-faith marriages, in particular Muslim-Christian marriages, in terms of interfaith dialogue, Gé Speelman (1997) devised a typology of strategies used by mixed-faith couples to deal with faith issues concerning them and their children. The typology comprises four approaches: annexation, yielding, ignoring, negotiating. The first two strategies – annexation and yielding – are, Speelman states, complementary. When one partner holds particularly strong religious convictions, s/he tries to convert the partner to his/her faith and way of life. In Speelman's view, it is mostly men who try to do this; because, she points out, men have more difficulties in dealing with what is different. The partner may respond by attempting to annexe her/his partner in turn – in which case, Speelman indicates, the marriage is not likely to last long – or by gradually yielding to all the demands.

Ignoring is a policy with which both partners, tacitly or otherwise, try to deal with their differences. This may work for a time, Speelman states, but leads to unexpected surprises when there are family crises. Such crises may be painful, such as the death of close family members or unemployment; or joyful, such as the birth of a child. However, such crises bring real and existing differences to the fore and force couples to stop ignoring them. In Speelman's view, the fourth strategy – negotiation – is difficult and uncertain, because it is like an open-ended story. Partners, she points out, keep promising each other things, going back on their promises, and bringing their resources into play in order to get the upper hand.

Applying Speelman's typology to the case of the couple in *East is East*, we can see that it falls into the third category (ignoring), but that there are also signs of the first two strategies (annexing and yielding). One partner (the father) has strong religious and cultural convictions and tries to align family life to his faith and way of life. The other partner (the mother) appears to yield to the demands, while at the same time adhering to her own tradition and values. However, the couple in the film mainly adopt the policy of ignoring: they avoid dealing with their differences. As the film shows, and as Speelman predicts, this works for a time but leads to unexpected surprises when the family faces crises – in this case, when the children are of marriageable age and decisions need to be made about their future. At this point, neither father nor mother can ignore existing differences.

Applying Speelman's typology to the couples in our project, we are clear that they are all in the fourth category, having opted for negotiation. While it may be true that they found at times that this is, as Speelman states, a difficult and uncertain approach, her description of this strategy as a 'power struggle' in no way reflects the situation in the families who participated in our study (see further below). The reference to a 'power struggle' reflects the underlying assumption in much of the literature that mixed-faith families are problematic and fraught with difficulties (see also Romain, 1996, 167–168).

In their article, 'Observing Different Faiths, Learning About Ourselves', Mark Furlong and Abe Ata (2006) offer six patterns of adaptation to mixed-faith marriage, again with a focus on Muslim–Christian couples. Using data from Ata's study on Christian–Muslim intermarriage in Australia (Ata, 2003), the authors developed these categories with a view to exploring the implications for casework practice, thus again reflecting the perceived 'pathology' of mixed-faith families which permeates much of the literature. Although Furlong and Ata refer to Speelman's typology of strategies, they do not indicate to what extent they built on it. However, there is some overlap between the two sets of classifications.

Furlong and Ata's categories are: (1) conversion or annexation, (2) ignoring or withdrawing, (3) active policy espousing a plurality of faiths, (4) compromising and negotiating, (5) pastoral/ecumenical yielding, (6) respect for 'otherness'. The first, conversion and annexation, involves one party converting to the faith of the other. Participants in Ata's study reported this as either a positive and progressive choice or as a type of co-option, an annexation. The second, ignoring or withdrawing, means that both parties withdrew from discussion of religious matters and enacted a *de facto* policy of ignoring (not speaking about) the question of religious difference. Although participants reported this as having some initial advantages, this style of adaptation was found to produce difficulties in the longer term. In the third pattern, the active policy espousing a plurality of faiths, some couples had adopted an explicit policy of religious pluralism, with both attending services in turn or adopting a pattern of joint membership and participation. In the words of one participant, 'it is a case of creating healthy boundaries ... of ensuring peaceful coexistence.' The fourth, compromising and negotiating, is a radical pattern: both parties leave their religion of origin and take up an 'in-between' allegiance. Although, Furlong and Ata state, this appeared to be the way in which approximately 30 per cent of their sample responded, participants found it difficult to discuss this openly in the interviews. Regarding the fifth pattern, pastoral/ecumenical yielding, some participants reported that they actively attempted to merge the rites and practices of their different faiths in their home. This was done to a greater or lesser extent and could forge a common ground, even if problems were encountered with respect to questions of coherence. Finally, respect for 'otherness' is in some ways similar to the previous pattern (pastoral/ecumenical yielding) in that some couples chose to individualize religious observations, with each partaking in his/her religious life and respecting the other's difference without co-opting or minimising the difference. As well as the expected advantages, some participants suggested that this approach risked companionship and was confusing to children (Furlong and Ata, 2006, 253–254; see also Ata, 2003, 70–73).

Applying Furlong and Ata's typology to the families in our project, some can be said to follow the third pattern, the active policy of espousing a plurality of faiths, as both attended acts of worship in both traditions or adopted some pattern of joint participation. Other families in our project can be described in terms of Furlong and Ata's fifth pattern, the pastoral/ecumenical yielding, as they gave space to some rites and practices of their faiths in their homes. As Furlong and Ata state, the degree to which this was done could vary, but it reinforced common ground for the families in our project (rather than forged it). However, none of our participants reported problems with respect to questions of coherence. Further, the overlap between the fifth and sixth pattern in Furlong and Ata's typology means that some families in our study also practised respect for 'otherness'. In some cases, individuals chose to observe religious practices on their own and respected the other's difference. This could, as Furlong and Ata suggest, affect companionship, but there was no indication in our study that is was confusing to children.

Jonathan Romain suggests ten types of mixed-faith marriage (1996, 169): (1) dual faith harmonious: both partners have their own strong faith, respect each other's religious needs and are mutually supportive;

(2) dual faith conflicting: both partners have their own faith, but find it a source of tension and rivalry; (3) single faith harmonious: one partner has a strong faith and the other does not, but is happy to be supportive; (4) single faith conflicting: one partner has a strong faith, while the other does not and thus resents the intrusion of religion in the marriage; (5) merged faith: both partners decide to merge their two faiths into a set of beliefs and way of life that they can share; (6) alternative faith: both partners agree to adopt a third faith to which they can both belong and feel at ease; (7) lapsed faith: neither partner values his/her religious tradition; (8) converted same-faith: one partner has converted to the faith of the other, whether before or after the marriage, but still carries vestiges of the former faith; (9) re-emerged mixed-faith: one partner, usually previously lapsed, feels a re-emergence of his/her religious roots and thereby changes the religious balance of the marriage; (10) confused faith: both partners have religious traditions of their own, but are not sure what they believe – they go through periods of making an effort, jointly or separately, then give up again.

It is hard to accommodate the couples in our project to Romain's typology, as their approaches to their respective faith traditions do not really fit his descriptions. Only the type in which one partner feels strongly about his/her faith and the spouse is supportive (the single faith harmonious) could be applied to our sample of parents. However, such couples formed a very small minority (see below).

Therefore, the conclusion from the application of the three typologies is that they are helpful to some extent in identifying patterns of responses in mixed-faith families, but none of the families in our study presented clear-cut examples of any given pattern. The following provides further details of our parent sample.

The majority of parents with whom we had contact were born in the UK. Some were the children of immigrants and some of them had been brought up in the cultural and religious traditions of their parents. However, being brought up in a western country and thus being exposed to cultural and social influences other than those of the parental tradition, led them to follow paths away from the one ostensibly mapped out for them. Some considered themselves as rebels or 'pioneers' (as Bobby, a father from a Punjabi Sikh background, put it), realizing that they had gradually distanced themselves from their respective traditions and crossed from its bounds into something different. The 'something different' was a combination of what they wanted to preserve from their upbringing and family background and elements of the 'modern' western lifestyle; they chose such elements according to what they saw to be appropriate or attractive for their lives and for their lives in Britain.

Equally, those parents born and raised within the British indigenous tradition, which often included a Christian background, tended to have drifted away from their religious roots, leaving residual connections and/or agnostic or atheist attitudes. Thus when individuals chose a spouse with a different faith background, they were fairly relaxed about their own and their partner's faith background and/or practice, or they were prepared to negotiate and compromise. Therefore, it would not be appropriate to classify them as 'lapsed', as in Romain's category of 'lapsed faith', because they still valued elements of their respective traditions. When this attitude was in place, it did not matter if one faith dominated or appeared to dominate in the lives of the children. Conversely, where parents felt strongly about their religion, they wanted to transmit this to the children. This required negotiation and concession or – as Sue, a mother from a Christian Punjabi background married to a Punjabi Sikh, put it – love and understanding and support. Parents like this mother formed a very small minority in our sample. As indicated earlier, parents like Sue could be considered, in terms of Romain's typology, 'single faith harmonious'; although from her point of view, being a mixed-faith family was not ideal.

Most parents wanted their children to have the choice of which religion to embrace and did not want to impose any religion on them, whatever their own stance and whatever their personal wishes regarding their children's choice. However – as Mina, a mother from a Punjabi Hindu background married to a British Christian, pointed out – 'how can they [the children] make a choice, if they don't know?' In this mother's view, saying that the children would decide later was avoiding the issue. She was clear that she wanted to pass on to her nine-year-old daughter Nikita what was important to herself. However, Mina also pointed out that a lot of what the family practised in terms of traditional customs was part of everyday life. This involved things that had always been done in the family and had been passed on to her – for example, putting oil on the steps outside the house to welcome visitors. In other words, there was no deliberate effort or instructive intention involved in these practices.

Most parents wanted their children to be raised with an awareness of both traditions, but the way they fostered this awareness differed. Some engaged in conscious acts of religious nurture (see Arweck and Nesbitt, 2010a) by initiating their children in, or introducing them to, experiences within their respective traditions: for example, by having a christening *and* a Hindu naming ceremony, by celebrating Christmas *and* Divali, by choosing a Christian *and* a Hindu name, or by making visits to a *mandir and* a church. For some families, their geographical location limited their opportunities of giving equal attention to both faith traditions, in terms of activities or practices linked to the wider faith community. For example, considerable distance from the nearest *gurdwara* precluded, while the close proximity of a church allowed for, frequent visits. However, some couples relied on the kind of religious nurture that is fostered by contact with the wider community, such as the school (religious education, school ethos, composition of the school, collective worship) and the extended family, as well as their children's own initiative in finding out about religious matters (see also Arweck and Nesbitt, 2010a).

It is important to note that the parents' positions and views were changing over time, thus encouraging a continuous dialogue between spouses and also between parents and children. This ties in with Speelman's comment that the strategy of negotiation is like an 'open-ended story'. While some couples in our study had discussed beforehand how they might bring up their children, the majority opted to deal with the issues as they arose. Yet most parents stated that they had started their families with a fundamental understanding between them, including shared views about religious matters, and this formed the solid ground on which their married life and their family life rested.

Young people's response to growing up in mixed-faith families

In order to describe the way the young people in our project responded to the presence of two different faith backgrounds in their family, we shall use Roberta Ricucci's study (2007) on adolescent immigrants in Italy, and the types of attitudes and the levels of integration she identified in the host society. Ricucci saw them divided into four groups: (1) the tightrope walker, (2) the marginal, (3) the indifferent, and (4) the involved (see also Ricucci, 2010).

Ricucci describes 'the tightrope walker' as an individual who attends a place of worship for cultural rather than for strictly religious reasons. Attendance is an opportunity to keep some contact with others, to maintain a link with the community, and to satisfy parents. Among some ethnic groups, parents see religion as a protection of the second generation against the 'immoral' influences of the host culture. However, the young people mix well with, and are more likely to adapt to the lifestyle and habits of, the local youth. They are able to share values and to play different roles in different settings.

'The marginal' on the other hand do not speak the language of the host country, as they joined their family during adolescence, and do not attend school, mixing only with peers of their own background and attending religious events and participating in community activities. Attending religious events provides a sense of integration in the new context.

'The indifferent', according to Ricucci, generally do not attend any place of worship and do not speak the heritage language. Sometimes they celebrate religious events. They were born in the host country, into a family which has a long history of residence in the host country; their parents have a large cultural capital and mix only with peers from the host country. The parents are aware that re-creating the original ethnic way of life in the host country is neither practically feasible nor desirable. Thus everything that pertains to the original way of life (language, traditions, culture, etc.) is rejected. This also involves a change of name and other modifications, causing individuals to forget and lose their cultural individuality.

Finally, 'the involved' in Ricucci's study displayed a much higher degree of attachment to their values and standards of morality. They stressed the mother's role as the main source of religious influence (thereby confirming previous research pointing to the stronger influence of the mother in religious socialization; see above), but contrary to existing research, 'the involved' also saw other family members as key agents in their religious socialization. They were well integrated in the host society, had clear ideas about their future (go to university, acquire citizenship, marry a fellow country(wo)man), were involved in religious associations, and wanted to promote integration and equality of rights for all of the second generation. Interestingly, their religiousness was also linked to (non)identification as citizens of the world or of Europe, depending on their specific ethnicity.

If we apply Ricucci's typology to the children in *East is East*, they can be situated somewhere between the category of 'tightrope walker' and 'indifferent'. As tightrope walkers, they attended mosque and *madrasa* to satisfy their father's requirements. For the father, religion (Islam) protected the second generation against the 'immoral' influences of the British culture. As 'tightrope walkers', the children also mixed well with their British peers and adapted to the lifestyle and habits of the local youth. They were also able to play different roles as required by the different contexts they found themselves in, displaying 'multiple cultural competence' (see Jackson and Nesbitt, 1993). As 'indifferent', they would rather not have gone to *madrasa*, although they sometimes celebrated religious events, such as the procession. They generally rejected whatever was connected with their father's origins (language, traditions, culture).

In contrast to the young people in Ricucci's study, but like the children in *East is East*, all bar one of the young people in our project were born in the UK and saw their Britishness as an important part of their identity. Thus they do not fall neatly into any of Ricucci's categories, as they display elements of each category, except that of 'the marginal'. The very fact that they had parents from different faith backgrounds made them aware of different life worlds, even when they did not move much between them. However, as stated above, most parents wanted their children to be exposed to both traditions, and experiencing these could be interpreted as a 'tightrope walk'. In families where the difference in faith also involved differences in ethnic and cultural background, children were more likely to be aware of negotiating boundaries, especially when they had contact with both sets of grandparents and members of the extended family. This also ties in with Ricucci's participants ('the involved') who recognized the socializing influence of the wider family.

Some young people in our study showed different degrees of being involved, in Ricucci's sense, ranging from 'somewhat involved' to 'very involved'. The former could be represented by occasional visits to a place of worship and some knowledge of the faith traditions, while the latter consisted in regular attendance and full immersion in a tradition. And some, a small minority, could be described as 'indifferent', not noticeably interested in religious matters and celebrating religious festivals without any reference to their religious roots. For example, Easter was associated with chocolate eggs rather than with any religiously symbolic meaning of eggs.

We found that young people's attitudes towards religion were connected to their maturity, although age was not a reliable indicator of this. An obvious assumption is that the younger children are, the less formed is their insight into religious matters. James Fowler's model of progressive stages of faith development (1981) suggests distinct periods in which individuals advance in their understanding, advancing from early childhood to adolescence and adulthood. This implies a linear sequence of phases in which individuals mould their faith with a view to finding meaning in life, outside dependence on the traditions of particular religious communities (Fowler, 1981, 5 and 81). As a strict chronology, the conversations with young people in our study did not bear this out. Some eight- to twelve-year-olds seemed quite 'young', while others were very mature, and this was reflected in the way they spoke about religious matters. Those interested in and connected to religion had the vocabulary and linguistic versatility to express what they thought and felt about religious matters, while those who were not lacked such skills. Not surprisingly, the less versed related to non-religious aspects within religious settings, such as the social side of religious gatherings, the food, or the opportunity for dressing in glamorous clothes. When they used 'technical terms' they were often not able to explain their meaning. For example, when we discussed the nativity story and the presents which the three wise men brought with eight-year-old Margarita, she thought that frankincense was money and myrrh a rock.

As mentioned, most young people – whatever their age – saw their Britishness as an important part of themselves. Their dual heritage did not consist of two separate elements. The two were intertwined: one could not be isolated from the other. In the interviews, we asked the young people whether the metaphor of two pieces of fabric stitched together in a patchwork, or that of a mixture of water and sugar, described their situation. Most agreed. Two young children, a brother and a sister, eight-year-old Nathan and five-year-old Gloria – with a white British Christian mother and a Punjabi Hindu father – suggested that their dual heritage was like two sides of a coin. None of the young people saw their dual heritage or the 'mixedness' of their family in any way 'special' or out of the ordinary.

Interestingly, school had less of a formative influence than expected, although there were differences between those of primary and secondary school age. The young people tended to see religious education as a subject like science and mathematics. At worst, they found it boring; at best they saw it as a source of factual information about religion, a way of learning about the nuts and bolts of religious traditions. Younger children tended not to make the link between religious practice and religion as they learnt about it in school (see also Arweck and Nesbitt, 2011). For them, parents and grandparents had the stronger influence, while for teenagers (especially those in their mid-teens), the greater influence came from peers. There were, therefore, fluctuations in the way young people viewed (and practised) religion, as relationships in their lives strengthened and weakened. This was borne out by young people in their teens indicating changes in their affinity with a religion that had occurred prior to our interviews with them. Sixteen-year-old Jasmin (her mother was from an Asian Muslim background, her father from a white Christian British background) reported, for example, that she had identified strongly with Islam the year before we met her. Although she still classified herself as a 'Muslim' when we spoke to her, she indicated that her practice and belief had become attenuated.

By the time young people had reached their late teens and early twenties, they tended to have formed a stance towards religion. This could be either parent's tradition, or an agnostic or atheist viewpoint, with previous statistical evidence suggesting the greater likelihood of children from mixed-faith families opting to have no faith. We do not have sufficient data either to support or to refute such a view. However, even where individuals did not identify with a faith, they could still connect with either parent's cultural and religious background in some ways. An example would be Sean, who was in his early thirties, with a father who had a Middle Eastern Muslim background and a mother with a white British Christian background, who had learnt Arabic and visited Muslim countries where he followed, in a matter-of-fact manner, Muslim practice such as Ramadan.

Regarding the hypothesis that maternal influence is stronger than paternal influence (see, e.g., Pearce and Axinn, 1998), our data are not sufficiently conclusive to point either towards confirmation or refutation. They suggest that the respective parent's attitude towards his/her own faith background, and towards religion in general, is important. They also suggest that the influence from parents depends on whether the mother or father assume the main care responsibilities – such as dropping children off at, or picking them up from, school; or spending time with the children after school. Our participants reported conversations about religious matters at those times, regardless of whether it was the father or mother who was present. Further, the hypothesis of parental influence is predicated on one variable (mother's faith versus father's faith), but our data strongly point to the fact that the formation of young people's attitudes towards religion is linked to a cluster of variables (see Arweck and Nesbitt, 2010b for further details).

Conclusion

Apart from gaining insights into the religious socialization of young people in mixed-faith families, our study raises important issues about the notions of the family, identity, community, culture, and ethnicity and what they mean in twenty-first-century Britain. It does not support the negative stereotype that children from mixed-faith families are confused and under-achieving. Nor does it support the general assumption that mixed-faith families are inevitably problematic or vulnerable and thus doomed to failure, which is often an underlying theme in the literature. Further, despite the various attempts at devising types of mixed-faith families (see above), our data point to the diversity of such families which defies neat categorizations.

Our study also points to implications for the way in which religion is taught in school and the way in which educators approach young people. In the classroom, religions are often (re)presented in discrete categories, without regard for variation and range of interpretations: described as static entities rather than living and lived traditions, detached from what religious content and practice mean to adherents and unconnected (and thus not relevant) to young people's own lives. Further, teachers tend to make assumptions about young people and their backgrounds, 'categorizing' them by physical appearance or assuming a comprehensive knowledge in both faith traditions (see also Arweck and Nesbitt, 2011). Thus sixteen-year-old Jasmin reported that her teacher only wanted 'the real Muslim students' to sit the mock paper on Islam, ostensibly oblivious of the fact that Jasmin felt herself close to Islam. However, neither Jasmin's appearance nor dress gave any indication of this, which led the teacher to assume that she was white and Christian. Fourteen-year-old Monika – her father was from a white British Christian background, her mother from a Punjabi Sikh background – was dismayed when she was called on in class to explain aspects of Sikhism or Christianity. She pointed out that having parents from those backgrounds did not make her an expert in either tradition. Therefore, our study seeks to raise in the teaching community a greater awareness and sensitivity towards young people such as Jasmin and Monika, especially as young people of mixed heritage are predicted to form a significant part of future generations.

References

American Religious Identification Survey (ARIS) (2001). Mixed religion families among selected religious groups (section 6). ARIS website, <http://www.gc.cuny.edu/faculty/research_briefs/aris/key_findings.htm> (accessed 25 June 2006).

Arweck, E., and Nesbitt, E. (2010a). Young people's identity formation in mixed-faith families: Continuity or discontinuity of religious traditions? *Journal of Contemporary Religion, 25*, 67–87.

Arweck, E., and Nesbitt, E. (2010b). Plurality at close quarters: Mixed-faith families in the UK. *Journal of Religion in Europe, 3*, 1–28.

Arweck, E., and Nesbitt, E. (2011). Religious education in the experience of young people from mixed-faith families. *British Journal of Religious Education, 33* (1), 31–45.

Ata, A. (2000). *Intermarriage between Christians and Muslims: A West Bank study.* Melbourne: David Lovell.

Ata, A. (2003). *Christian and Muslim intermarriage in Australia.* Melbourne: David Lovell.

Baumann, G. (1996). *Contesting culture.* Cambridge: Cambridge University Press.

Becher, H. (2005). Family practices in South Asian Muslim families: Parenting in a multi-faith Britain. Unpublished PhD thesis. University of East Anglia: School of Social Work and Psychosocial Sciences.

Census (2001). Available at <http://census.ac.uk/casweb or http://www.statistics.gov.yuk/census2001/> (accessed 15 October 2009).

Fowler, J. W. (1981). *Stages of faith: The psychology of human development and the quest for meaning.* San Francisco: Harper & Row.

Furlong, M., and Ata, A. (2006). Observing different faiths, learning about ourselves: Practice with inter-married Muslims and Christians. *Australian Social Work, 59*, 250–264.

Gent, B. (2005). Intercultural learning: Education and Islam - a case study. In R. Jackson, and U. McKenna (eds), *Intercultural education and religious plurality* (pp. 43–52). Oslo: The Oslo Coalition on Freedom of Religion or Belief.

Jackson, R. (1997). *Religious education: An interpretive approach.* London: Hodder.

Jackson, R., and Nesbitt, E. (1993). *Hindu children in Britain.* Stoke-on-Trent: Trentham Books.

James, A., and Prout, A. (1997). *Constructing and reconstructing childhood.* London: Falmer.

Nesbitt, E. (2000). *The religious lives of Sikh children: A Coventry based study*. Leeds: Department of Theology and Religious Studies, University of Leeds.
Nesbitt, E. (2007). The contribution of nurture in a sampradaya to young British Hindus' understanding of their tradition. In J. R. Hinnells (ed.), *Religious reconstruction in the South Asian diasporas: From one generation to another* (pp. 51–73). Basingstoke: Palgrave Macmillan.
Nesbitt, E., and Arweck, E. (2010). Methodological issues in investigating the religious identity formation of young people in mixed-faith families. *Fieldwork in Religion*, 5 (1), 7–30.
Østberg, S. (2003). Norwegian–Pakistani adolescents: Negotiating religion, gender, ethnicity and social boundaries. *Young, 11*, 161–181.
Pearce, L. D., and Axinn, W. G. (1998). The impact of family religious life on the quality of mother-child relations. *American Sociological Review, 63*, 810–828.
Ricoeur, P. (1992). *Time and narrative, Vol. 3*. Chicago: University of Chicago Press.
Ricucci, R. (2007). Religion and the adolescent immigrants. Paper presented to the bi-annual conference of the International Society for the Sociology of Religion, Leipzig, July 2007.
Ricucci, R. (2010). Religion and adolescent immigrants in Italy: A case of identifying with or turning away from their communities? *Journal of Contemporary Religion, 25* (3), 419–436.
Rodriguéz Garcia, D. (2006). Mixed marriages and transnational families in the intercultural context: A case study of African/Spanish couples in Catalonia. *Journal of Ethnic and Migration Studies, 32* (3), 403–433.
Romain, J. (1996). *Till faith us do part*. London: Fount.
Speelman, G. (1997). Christian-Muslim marriages. *Journal of the Association of Interchurch Families* (England), <http://www.aifw.org> (accessed 14 September 2006).

HANS-GEORG ZIEBERTZ

10 The Catholic View on Religious Pluralism in Empirical Perspective

Introduction

There is no doubt that the Catholic Church thinks of itself as providing the strongest link with the roots of Christianity: that is, with Jesus and his disciples. This is expressed in the Catholic theology of office. The theory of apostolic succession claims that Jesus passed on responsibility for the young Christian community to Peter, and all the bishops of Rome who followed him received the power of attorney in a direct line from Peter. The successor of Peter in the office of the Bishop of Rome is the Pope. He is the first bishop in a collegium of bishops and – as with Peter – the Pope's authority is legitimized by Christ. Against the background of this theological understanding, the Catholic Church developed concepts through which it defined its relation to other Christian Churches and non-Christian religions.

In the first chapter of this book Gloria Durka describes the Catholic view of the theology of religions, and puts it in the multicultural and multireligious context of the United States of America. We may argue that multiculturalism in the US is more developed than in many European countries. Nevertheless, the European process of integration, complemented by the development of globalization, has contributed to a growing awareness of plurality among Europeans. A pluralist context is most challenging to theologies which (unlike religious studies) are denominationally-based. Catholic theology reflects on and explores its object of research not only according to academic standards, but also in a conceptual and normative relation to the teaching of the Catholic Church. However, theology is not simply reducible to a translator of the Church's doctrine; it is called to reflect critically on theoretical doctrinal concepts. Practical theology as a critical reflection on practice – including what people believe, and how they understand and explain their faith – is a complementary task. Practical theology focuses both on doctrine in its historical and current shape and on the living practice of faith. When religious education (as a practical-theological discipline) develops its curricula both perspectives are taken into account. Several activities are thereby connected. First, practical theology is involved in a hermeneutical process to interpret contextually the theology of the Church. Secondly, practical theology focuses on practice so as to understand and explain how believers construct their religious world. Both empirical and hermeneutical procedures are required for this. Thirdly, practical theology critically reflects the commonalities and differences between theory and practice. This approach differs from an earlier view of theology as clearly normative in the sense that it deduces its theory (theological ideas) and applies it to practice.

Although theology is normatively restricted, the modern theology of the twenty-first century must take into account its pluralist environment. Theology itself, therefore, reflects on faith in the knowledge that religious expression is pluralist because it arises from and within a pluralist context. Modern theology is thus a form of dialogical and discursive theology that interacts with other theologies. The 'theology of religions' can be understood as fundamental theology that fits with the challenges of the modern pluralist world for which religious truth is always 'something beyond'. For this type of theology an open mindset that looks for commonalities is more adequate to religious pluralism than a narrow mindset which focuses only on the in-group. However, an in-group perspective is typical of every religion. Traditional theology is naturally 'narrow' in the sense that it stands for a mono perspective of convictions and truth valid in a certain denomination. Therefore the key question is how religions deal with the spectrum from narrowness to openness. Religions are problematic not only from the perspective of other religions, but also from the perspective of secular society, if they do not present themselves to the public with an open mindset. How does Catholic theology navigate between narrowness and openness, and what role can it play in interreligious dialogue? The term 'catholic' may be understood as *holos* (Greek for 'whole', 'complete'), where *holos* is a concept that goes beyond any single tradition. Will the Roman Catholic Church define itself as part of the *holos* – or as the best expression of it?

Historically, the first great challenges to Christian doctrinal thinking were the schism of 1054, when the Latin and Byzantine branches separated, and the early sixteenth century when the Reformation took place. The concept of *religio vera* was developed serving both apologetics and contemporary self-consciousness. In this way pluralism emerged within the Christian world. But societal processes of modernity since the French revolution led to the Roman Catholic self-understanding that resistance was required as much against other religions as against the liberal 'Zeitgeist' and anti-religious worldviews (in the sense of non-conformity to Roman Catholic doctrine). The First Vatican Council (1869–70) made crucial decisions about the succession theology mentioned earlier, with decrees about the Pope's authority to speak *ex cathedra* in areas of faith and ethics. Its theology of other religions was clearly exclusivist: *extra ecclesiam nulla salus est* – outside the Church (the Roman Catholic Church) there is no path to salvation. The only recognized gateway was through Christ and the Catholic Church. This theology was maintained as valid until the Second Vatican Council (1962–65) and was strongly controlled by the Vatican.

The harshness of this exclusivist attitude against other religions was modified by Vatican II, which developed a theology usually described as inclusivist. Efforts were made to adopt rules of tolerance. The German theologian, Karl Rahner (1964, 1965, 1983), expanded on this inclusive understanding by arguing that authentic experiences of God are possible not *through* other religions, but *within* them. Whoever searches for God in other religions may find God if God stands for the universal Good that is also expressed in Catholic theology. The consequences of this thinking connect with Christian ecumenism and the dialogue with non-Christian religions. As far as Rahner was concerned, the fact that Jesus was sent by God to save humankind reveals that there is no other way to salvation than Jesus, the Christ. Because of the succession, the Catholic Church claims a distinctive access to this truth. The basic documents of Vatican II that reflect this approach are the decrees *Nostra aetate*, *Dignitatis humanae* and

Ad gentes. There is no doubt that for the Catholic Church of the 1960s and later, this change from exclusivism to inclusivism was more than a footnote. It represents a new frame of thinking. But our focus on Roman Catholic *theology* should not lead us to suppose that this type of thinking is typical of the Roman Catholic Church. Soft or even strong exclusivism was and is a widespread phenomenon. It is also present in other Christian denominations (including many of the Protestant Churches), and it is a guiding concept for many non-Christian religions.

Since the 1980s a growing number of scholars have treated Vatican II's 'inclusivism' as a form of 'soft exclusivism', and have searched for alternative frameworks for the development of a theology of religions (Ruokanen, 1992). These scholars are aware that the globalized world now looks very different from the world of the 1960s. They base their theories on their experience of pluralism, and seek to take seriously the challenge that there are many truth-claims (Clarke and Winter, 1991). As Durka points out in her chapter here, a 'replacement-' or 'fulfilment-model' cannot convince. At the same time, and from a theological perspective, the question of truth cannot be ignored; so the liberal 'acceptance-model' is unacceptable. For this reason, Durka endorses the 'mutuality-model', which can be called the model of interreligious dialogue. This claims (1) that truth is not embedded in one tradition, (2) that it is not unreasonable to talk about truth, but (3) that truth is something we must reach by a process of encounter, exploration, and rational argument. *If* this model implies that truth is an open question that is far beyond us, something that is probably not completely given in any one single tradition, then we may call this model 'pluralistic'. But *if* encounter and dialogue are used to find the truth which is already given, and given in only one tradition, this mutuality-model would still be inclusivist.

The question is increasingly asked whether the inclusivist position represents an end point in theological thinking, or whether it offers a perspective that not only legitimizes the removal of borders, but also treats this as the desirable position. Within Catholic theology, Paul Knitter has presented the most progressive proposal. He focuses on religious pluralism and stresses the need for theology to shift away from a Christocentric position to one that emphasizes a theocentric position. Only on this approach does the way become clear for a new (theological) understanding of religious pluralism (Knitter, 1985, 85–89). For Knitter it is theologically legitimate to take this step. His core concept is the message of the kingdom of God (Luke 11:20, 17:21). Jesus, in both his mission and person, is deeply aligned with God – although Jesus plays a special role, an emphasized eschatological function, in the realm of God. The turn towards Christ first arose during the development of the written texts of the New Testament. The New Testament makes the preacher into the one preached, and even the Christocentrically oriented Paul differentiates clearly between Christocentrism and theocentrism (1 Corinthians 3:23). With this new view, according to Knitter, Christianity is able to abandon some of the features that impede dialogue, such as concepts of 'plan', and of what is 'exclusive', 'final', and 'absolute', without becoming relativist. Christ and Christianity would not lose their uniqueness, although they may lose their absolute titles. Christians may admit and testify that Christ is unique, but they do not need to assume that this uniqueness must be understood as *exclusiveness*.

Knitter's position, like that of some other theologians who supported pluralism, provoked both contradiction and agreement. His thinking clearly goes far beyond the tradition of Roman Catholic doctrine. The Vatican therefore published several papers to place pluralist theology within what the Church regarded as an acceptable context. For the academic world, however, one effect is undeniable: these theological movements have stimulated a new dynamic within theology. With regard to epistemological thinking, they introduced a modification of the absolutist understanding of truth, which had thus far operated under the concept of 'either-or'. On that view, that which was once determined as 'true' must always remain true. Theologians such as Swidler (1992) regard truth as more relational, in conformity with a theoretical awareness of scientific development. Truth cannot be achieved through the exclusion of other perspectives; rather, one is in pursuit of truth, which can only be achieved through a connection of all perspectives. Each view represents only a fragment. Each truth has its 'place in life', which applies to a specific time. Historical understanding can only be transferred to other times to a limited extent, as our knowledge and understanding increase with the passage of time. Secondly, truths target practice and action, such that they are always oriented to the speaker. Thirdly, they are bound to a location, within which they must be interpreted. Fourthly, they are fragmentary, resulting from the limitation of language, which is incapable of speaking of 'absoluteness'. Fifthly, truth contains only interpreted knowledge, and cannot be an 'absolute understanding' of 'true' meaning. Finally, it has a dimension of dialogue, since truth is not simply received, it is *produced*. Applying relational theory to truth does not qualify truth; rather it considers its constitutive conditions, providing us with a standard against which to set human truth.

As we mentioned above, pluralist theologies stimulated theological reflection and theory building, but it also motivated the Catholic Church to refresh its official doctrine. That happened recently in the Vatican document *Dominus Jesus*, which was published on 6 August 2000 – thirty-five years after the Second Vatican Council. This text claims that

> the church's constant missionary proclamation is endangered today by relativistic theories which seek to justify religious pluralism, not only *de facto* but also *de jure* (or *in principle*). As a consequence, it is held that certain truths have been superseded ... (*Dominus Jesus*, 2000, 4)

The Pope does not only restrict himself to such a general statement, but goes into detail. A clear critique of the pluralist theology mentioned earlier is obvious in the following clarification:

> The roots of these problems are to be found in certain presuppositions of both a philosophical and theological nature, which hinder the understanding and acceptance of the revealed truth. Some of these can be mentioned: the conviction of the elusiveness and inexpressibility of divine truth, even by Christian revelation; relativistic attitudes toward truth itself, according to which what is true for some would not be true for others; the radical opposition posited between the logical mentality of the West and the symbolic mentality of the East; the subjectivism which, by regarding reason as the only source of knowledge, becomes incapable of raising its 'gaze to the heights, not daring to rise to the truth of being'; the difficulty in understanding and accepting the presence of definitive and eschatological events in history; the metaphysical emptying of the historical incarnation of the Eternal Logos, reduced to a mere appearing of God in history; the eclecticism of those who, in theological research, uncritically absorb ideas from a variety of philosophical and theological contexts without regard for consistency, systematic connection, or compatibility with Christian truth; finally, the tendency to read and to interpret Sacred Scripture outside the Tradition and Magisterium of the Church. (*Dominus Jesus*, 2000, 4)

What is brought into focus in this quotation is a relativistic mentality which is, according to the Pope, becoming ever more common. The declaration goes back to the New Testament and argues that these developments in theology are unacceptable. It also refers to earlier documents and encyclicals of the Church to claim that the truth the Church justifies and stands for is sacrosanct.

> Therefore, the theory of the limited, incomplete, or imperfect character of the revelation of Jesus Christ, which would be complementary to that found in other religions, is contrary to the Church's faith. ... Such a position is in radical contradiction with the forgoing statements of Catholic faith. (*Dominus Jesus*, 2000, 6)

The Pope underpins the distinction between theological faith which is the 'acceptance of the revealed truth', and belief in other religions which is understood as the 'sum of experiences that constitutes the human treasury of wisdom'. Sacred books of other religions 'receive from the mystery of Christ the elements of goodness and grace which they contain' (*Dominus Jesus*, 2000, 9). 'Jesus Christ has a significance and a value for the human race and its history, which are unique and singular, proper to him alone, exclusive, universal, and absolute' (*Dominus Jesus*, 2000, 15). In these reflections, pluralist theologies that constitute a dialogue about truth that goes beyond the doctrinal definition of truth in Christianity are fundamentally criticized.

When the declaration uses the term 'Christian' this is specified in an institutional context (*Dominus Jesus*, 2000, 16). Jesus Christ is seen as the constitutor of the Church as a salvific mystery: 'he himself is in the Church and the Church is in him.' The Church is defined as the 'single Catholic and apostolic Church'. The etymological roots of the term Catholic can be found in *catholicus* (Latin) and *katholicós* (Greek) which expresses wholeness (*holos*). But *holos* is not interpreted as the sum of Christian churches and denominations. To the contrary, *holos* is assigned to 'the' Church, the Church which possesses the full tradition of succession. The Church founded by Christ and the Catholic Church are synonymous terms. Therefore *Dominus Jesus* quotes the declaration *Lumen gentium* from Vatican II:

'This Church, constituted and organized as a society in the present world, subsists in [*subsistit in*] the Catholic Church, governed by the Successor of Peter and by the Bishops in communion with him.' With the expression *subsistit in*, the Second Vatican Council sought to harmonize two doctrinal statements: on the one hand, that the Church of Christ, despite the divisions which exist among Christians, continues to exist fully only in the Catholic Church, and on the other hand, that 'outside of her structure, many elements can be found of sanctification and truth', that is, in those Churches and ecclesial communities which are not yet in full communion with the Catholic Church. But with respect to these, it needs to be stated that 'they derive their efficacy from the very fullness of grace and truth entrusted to the Catholic Church'. (*Dominus Jesus*, 2000, 16)

To sum up, the official statement of the Catholic Church is still both exclusivist and inclusivist. It is more exclusivist towards non-Christian religions, and more inclusivist towards other Christian denominations. It was no surprise that many Protestant Churches reacted indignantly when this declaration was published. But is this result unusual, compared with other religions? Could we not find similar claims in Islam, Judaism, and also in Hinduism? Is it not inherent to a religion to think this way? We must probably conclude that religions are examples *par excellence* of exclusivist thinking.

However, this does not make the task of developing models of inter-religious learning easier. If our objective is within the public school, we cannot transfer doctrinal thinking directly into the curricula. The context is different if we talk about socialization into faith within church communities or teaching religion within a school setting. School curricula are not solely based on theological concerns, but also on educational principles. Theology comes into play when we think of confessional religious education, combined with pedagogical reasoning; but pedagogy is the discipline of reference if we are thinking of non-denominational religious education, combined with the study of religion or even theology. This distinction is not only derived from intellectual reasoning, but also from practice. In most European countries religious education is still organized confessionally (with variations); in a minority of countries, it follows a non-denominational, multifaith approach (Ziebertz and Riegel, 2009).

European countries hold in common that education has to avoid indoctrination. Education can make students familiar with faith (or faith traditions), but it has to respect the autonomy of the students. They may accept or reject religious directions for their life. It is therefore understandable that many scholars of religious education, although they refer to the in-group language of certain religions in their teaching, have adopted the more open-minded, pluralist approach. In this approach they identify a theological legitimization for a religious education approach to interreligious learning. The focus of religious education is on developing communication between religions, thereby increasing mutual understanding and the development of mutual tolerance. The concept of a dynamic relational truth helps to promote cooperation with other religions, especially in religiously-mixed classes. In a denominational setting, or in religiously-affiliated schools, one would add that religious education embraces the objective of students exploring and finding God together. This religious exploration has a dialogical dimension. Taken together, all religions can come closer to discover the truth of God. The process of finding God is not simply the transfer of theories. Religious encounter is a process that involves the meeting and swapping of perspectives, leading to a general progression in understanding. Interreligious learning presents pluralism in a way that does not neutralize the differences between religions. The religions and their differing claims to truth are not made equal, but are the actual subject of study. The aim is not to reach the lowest common denominator but to show the variety of religious claims, which can help students to understand other religions as well as their own traditions. As in Catholic teaching, doctrine can be taught in catechism lessons, but in religious education in public schools it has to be adapted to the conditions of school practice.

This empirical question arises for religious education: which 'theologies of religions' do students hold? In addition to any theological and theoretical considerations, we may turn to empirical investigation to help us towards an answer. The analyses below are based on findings from an international empirical research project.

Method

Before we explore its empirical results, the framework of the research project will be described in terms of its method (procedure and sample) and conceptualization and operationalization, as well as its research questions and assumptions.

Procedure

The present empirical enquiry is based on an international research project, 'Religion and Life-Perspectives of Youth in Europe' (Ziebertz and Kay, 2005, 2006; Ziebertz, Kay, and Riegel, 2009). A questionnaire with about 350 items was used, translated into the different languages of the participating countries. The fieldwork took place in 2002 and 2003. After being coded and checked, the analysis of data was carried out in the Department of Practical Theology of the University of Würzburg, using SPSS.

Sample

The total number of respondents within the entire project is N=9852. Altogether, ten countries took part in the study (Croatia, Finland, Germany, the UK, the Netherlands, Poland, Ireland, Sweden, Turkey, and Israel). Three preliminary decisions were made about the sample: (1) the study should focus on a specific group of young people, school pupils aged between sixteen and eighteen who attended good academic secondary schools, e.g. grammar schools (selective secondary schools) and Gymnasia (Germany). The pupils who participated were those in their penultimate year of school, with exam results that would enable them to study at university. (2) The survey was carried out in places considered as regional centres in the different countries, where the infrastructure is comparable. (3) With this focus, a homogenization of the respondents can be taken for granted, and therefore a number of stratifying variables like age, level of education, town/country could be omitted from the study of attitudes. However, it would be wrong to expect entirely homogenous answer patterns within the chosen group. Although the respondent group has a number of common characteristic features (such as age, level of education, urban location), the study concerns itself with unearthing individual and collective differences.

Conceptualization and operationalization

The research should not be seen as an attempt to analyse the breadth of the formation of theories regarding problem of religious plurality. Its goal is more modest. It draws on three arguments that serve as a platform for empirical study, seen as ideal types. A criterion for ideal types is that they can be clearly differentiated from one another, without it being claimed that (in their ideal-typical form) they reflect reality. One can react more or less positively or negatively to each ideal type so that, empirically speaking, a large variety of attitude patterns are possible for each one. Models of dealing with religious pluralism are conceptualized and operationalized in a scale developed in 1994 and often used in the past (cf. Ziebertz, 1993; van der Ven and Ziebertz, 1994; Vermeer and van der Ven, 2004). The ideal types are called *mono*religious, *multi*religious and *inter*religious (see table 10.1). These three models can be understood in reference to the theological discussion illustrated above. I will not repeat all the information about scale construction here; rather, I will summarize the main arguments.

Table 10.1 Concepts and items of the Scale of Religious Pluralism

Concept	Item
Mono-incl	My religion is the best way to salvation compared to other religions.
Mono-incl	Compared to my religion, other religions contain only part of the truth.
Mono-incl	Compared to other religions, my religion contains the supreme salvation.
Mono-incl	Compared to other religions, the deepest truth lies locked in my religion.
Mono-excl	Only in my religion do people have access to true redemption.
Mono-excl	Only in my religion can people attain true salvation.
Mono-excl	The only way to true salvation is revealed to mankind in my religion.
Mono-excl	My religion contains the one, true light of redemption.
Multi	Religions are equal to each other; they are all directed at the same truth.
Multi	All religions are equally valuable; they are different paths to the same salvation.
Multi	There is no difference between religions; they all stem from a longing for God.
Inter	The way to real salvation can only be found in a dialogue between the religions.
Inter	God may only be found in the meeting between religions.
Inter	The real truth can only be discovered in the communication between religions.
Inter	Before finding real redemption, religions must enter into dialogue with each other.

NOTE: AS = agree strongly; A = agree; NC = not certain; D = disagree; DS = disagree strongly; Cronbach's alpha: Mono .96; Multi .83; Inter .76

To avoid misunderstandings, the *monoreligious model* cannot be the full representation of the position of the Catholic Church. The operationalization of concepts in short understandable statements generates a construct that never captures the hermeneutical richness of a theoretical or theological discussion. More than this: if we take theological discussion into account we have to talk about a variety of concepts which overcomes a single type of theory. We may, however, add that if one were forced to say which principle of the operationalized models Catholic positions most closely represent, it would be the monoreligious model. Proponents of this model do not necessarily think that other religions are completely without justification or are wrong – or even that they are inferior, imperfect, incomplete, or temporary. Fundamentalist thinking tends toward such a view, which would be an exclusivist interpretation of the monoreligious model. In the inclusivist interpretation, it is inherent to the monoreligious model that one should take many different religions into account and consider that they actually communicate with one another. One should adopt a positive attitude towards members of other religions and approach them with an open mind, because their personal faith may contain stimulating ideas and elements of the Christian faith, even if they are not aware of them. The basic idea of the inclusivist approach of the monoreligious model recurs in Christology in the principle of the incarnation, in which Christ is universally present in everything that is considered valuable in this world. Self-reference is a very important indicator for the operationalization of the monoreligious model. (This model is not exclusively a religious one. We also find the mono principle in monocultural or monoethnic thinking.)

The *multireligious model* differs in many aspects from the monoreligious model. With respect to how to deal with religious plurality, the principles of the multireligious model are equality of religions and their truth-claims, the comparison of dimensions of different religions, and relativism. Both in the literature and in empirical studies, it is said that this thinking is widespread in modern societies. We can find this concept developed theoretically in both psychological and philosophical perspectives. The multireligious model is in conflict with theology, because theologies as religiously committed reflections do not recognize a model that is based on a distant relation and a certain degree of relativism. However, the model applies to the religious studies approach; and beyond this, multireligious thinking can be expected to be evidenced empirically. From the academic standpoint of reflecting the plurality of religions, the objective of the multireligious model is not religious truth (as it is in the monoreligious model), but comparison. It aims at neither diligence in the search for the truth, nor the search for real meaning. Its motive is curiosity and the pursuit of knowledge. Its aim is to receive cultural information about the religious experiences, feelings, and behaviour of believers, so as to understand the motivation of religious people to whom one may or may not feel personally attracted. The multireligious model may be seen as directly opposed to the monoreligious model.

The main principles of the *interreligious model* are relation, process, and changing perspectives. In a certain sense the interreligious model is a reaction against a monoreligious tradition that corresponds to the I-perspective of Christian believers. In that model little or no attention is given to the you-perspective of other religions, and little or no attention is given to coordination between the I and the you. The multireligious model, by contrast, is based on a neutral it-perspective, distancing itself from the religious involvement of the individual. The interreligious model, however, views the it-perspective as being just as much bound by situation and context as are the I-and you-perspectives. Theologically, the interreligious model seeks to overcome the narrowness of the monoreligious model, but takes the aspect of commitment into account. It also wants to overcome the neutrality-approach of the multireligious model, but acknowledges the aspect of 'the other(s)'. Thus, the interreligious model states that there are always I-perspectives and one or many you-perspective(s). The interreligious model describes a process of *interaction* that aims for the development of insight, and maintains a concept of truth based on relations and an assumption that humans cannot formulate the last word about truth. Theologically, the interreligious model implies the pursuit of mutual understanding, tolerance, and respect; but it also stands for reflection about oneself and for self-criticism.

These models are conceptualizations of different ways of dealing with religious plurality. They neither reflect three distinctive theological schools, nor function as boxes in which we can place real people. These are constructed ideal types to which every respondent can answer more or less positively or negatively. All items were operationalized by using the five-point Likert format.

Research questions and assumptions

The overall research question is which theology of religions do students espouse? We want to know what attitude they adopt with regard to religious truth-claims. We assume that the majority of students, especially in Western European countries, will reject exclusivist and inclusivist thinking as expressed in the monoreligious model. In these countries we expect the multireligious model to be valued positively. Because the interreligious model is based on religious commitment, this model should be evaluated positively in Western European countries that are regarded as less secularized. Among the Jewish sample in Israel and the Muslim sample in Turkey, the monoreligious approach should be highest valued because both religions share – in some sense – the Catholic type of reasoning.

We will first compare the mean values of the models by countries, then by the three religions (Christianity, Islam, and Judaism), and finally we shall compare four Christian denominations. Here our expectation is that Catholic youth will agree more closely than other young people with the monoreligious model, because it best expresses Catholic doctrinal thinking.

Results

Using the mono-, multi- and interreligious models in international comparative research during the last fifteen years shows that the three models are clearly distinguishable (Ziebertz, 1993; van der Ven and Ziebertz, 1994; Vermeer and van der Ven, 2004). Exclusivism and inclusivism undergird the monoreligious model, which includes the one truth expressed by one (one's own) religion. The multireligious model represents the reasoning that all religions are equal. This model can be understood as opposite to the monoreligious one, because questions of truth are neglected. The concept of equality does not derive from theological thinking, but it is included in our consideration because it is present in people's minds. The interreligious model elaborates a certain pluralist understanding. It deals with many truth-claims and perceives truth as a result of encounter with and exploration of religions.

We want first to analyse the students' attitudes towards the monoreligious model (see table 10.2). There is a wide range in mean values between the answers, varying from a mean of 1.59 up to a mean of 4.05. Students in some countries absolutely disagree with these statements, while students in other countries highly agree. There are seven significant subgroups. Table 10.2 shows that the monoreligious model is rejected by students in Northern and Western European countries. We find the strongest rejection among British students (mean = 1.59), followed by their peers in Germany (mean = 1.89). The mean values for both groups are below 2.0. The next three groups of students, representing Sweden, Finland, and the Netherlands, also disagree. Their mean values are around 2.3. The fourth significantly different group are students from Ireland. With a mean value of 2.62 they vote negatively, but they are less negative than other students in Northern and Western European countries. Ireland is traditionally a Catholic country. In the middle of the scale we find Croatia, with a mean of 2.97. Students in Croatia neither reject nor agree with monoreligious statements. Croatia is also mostly Catholic. Finally, three countries lie on the positive half of the scale. One group includes students from Poland and Israel with means of 3.22 and 3.40, which can be read as a moderate agreement. A significant step beyond these is made by Turkish students who vote with a mean of 4.05, representing a very positive view of the monoreligious model. We may conclude that the two non-Christian countries, Israel and Turkey, socialize students most strongly into the monoreligious attitude that one's own religion represents the true religion. A comparison of European countries supports our assumption that in less secularized countries the agreement with mono statements is higher. Secondly, there are students from three traditionally Catholic countries (Poland, Croatia, Ireland) who are significantly positive, compared with students from the Protestant Nordic countries and religiously-mixed countries such as the Netherlands and Germany.

Table 10.2 Monoreligious perspective (Scheffé-Procedure)

Country	N	\multicolumn{7}{c}{Subgroup for Alpha = .05}						
		1	2	3	4	5	6	7
UK	1012	1.590						
Germany	1912		1.890					
Sweden	736			2.310				
Finland	581			2.340				
Netherlands	804			2.370				
Ireland	1009				2.620			
Croatia	1048					2.970		
Poland	797						3.220	
Israel	757						3.400	
Turkey	901							4.050
Significance		1.000	1.000	.992	1.000	1.000	.087	1.000

Table 10.3 shows how respondents evaluated the multireligious model. The range of answers is much closer when compared with the monoreligious model, and there are only five significant subgroups. Students from Israel disagree most strongly with the multireligious model. For them the idea that religions could be understood as equal in their claims and dignity is not acceptable at all (mean = 2.54). Students from Britain show a similar negative response (mean = 2.65), followed by Turkish students with a mean of 2.79. Israel and Turkey represent Jewish and Muslim samples in this research. While Jews and Muslim were at the top of the mono-scale, they are at the bottom of the opposite model, the multi-scale. When we compare both groups with Christian students we may conclude that a monoreligious and anti multireligious attitude is most strongly expressed in Judaism and Islam. Both religions teach more successfully than does Christianity that their religion is superior, and that the different religions may not be viewed as equal. This does not mean that the multireligious model is broadly accepted within the Christian West. Students in four countries neither disagree nor agree with the multi-statements – Sweden, the Netherlands, Finland, and

Poland, whose means are between 3.04 and 3.13. A more positive attitude is expressed by German students (mean = 3.30), and the highest endorsement comes from youth in Ireland and Croatia (both mean = 3.42). To sum up, it is obvious that traditional Catholic countries have a positive image of the multireligious model: Croatia, Ireland, and Poland, together with the religiously-mixed Germany, lie at the top; Turkish and Israeli youth are at the bottom, together with young people from Britain.

Table 10.3 Multireligious perspective (Scheffé-Procedure)

Country	N	Subgroup for Alpha = .05				
		1	2	3	4	5
Israel	758	2.540				
UK	1021	2.650	2.650			
Turkey	901		2.790			
Sweden	734			3.040		
Netherlands	812			3.100		
Finland	582			3.120	3.120	
Poland	797			3.130	3.130	
Germany	1918				3.300	3.300
Ireland	1009					3.420
Croatia	1050					3.420
Significance		.783	.500	.943	.099	.680

The outcome of the interreligious model is demonstrated in table 10.4. There are also five significant differences with a range of means between 1.71 and 3.21. The means tell us that the rejection of the interreligious model is stronger than its acceptance. British youth are most negative (mean = 1.71). Overall, the results from the British sample are difficult to understand, because they reject all three concepts. Does this tell us anything about the religious landscape in Britain, or about the British concept of religious education? The interreligious model is also slightly negatively evaluated by students in Sweden, Israel, Finland, and the Netherlands (means between

2.53 and 2.68). In three countries students are neither positive nor negative about the interreligious statements: Turkey, Ireland, and Germany (means between 2.91 and 3.03). A slightly positive evaluation is visible among students from Croatia (mean = 3.12), and one that is more positive among Polish students (mean = 3.21). We may conclude that traditional Catholic countries support interreligious attitudes; whereas students from other countries, including Muslims from Turkey and Jews from Israel, are more critical of interreligious ideas.

Table 10.4 Interreligious perspective (Scheffé-Procedure)

Country	N	1	2	3	4	5
UK	1020	1.710				
Sweden	732		2.530			
Israel	758		2.590			
Finland	582		2.620			
Netherlands	810		2.680			
Turkey	901			2.910		
Ireland	1009			2.990	2.990	
Germany	1917			3.030	3.030	
Croatia	1049				3.120	3.120
Poland	797					3.210
Significance		1.000	.091	.588	.324	.898

Subgroup for Alpha = .05

Table 10.5 shows the hierarchy of models within the countries. With the exception of the British, who reject all three models, the multireligious models appears six times at the top of the list of preferences, and the monoreligious model three times. In four cases (the Netherlands, Sweden, Finland, and Ireland) the multireligious model is approved. Without a simultaneously positive assessment of the interreligious model, this finding reflects the attitude that religions should exist beside one another, without it being clear at the same time how plurality should be dealt with

– except that one leaves things as they are. Only in two cases (Turkey and Israel) is the monoreligious model valued positively. From a Western European perspective, the rejection of the two other models raises the question: How does this relate to pluralism? With the Poles, pluralism is dealt with by the integration of the three models: the emphasis on the claim of truth for one's own religion, the recognition in principle of other religions, and a readiness to communicate about controversial questions. Croatians and Germans place the principle of equal rights in first position and approve of interreligious dialogue. They reject an emphasis on one's own claim to truth. Against the background of different cultures and the social-historical conditions in these countries, this finding is comprehensible. The advantage of an open attitude to pluralism is that it allows the asking of systematic questions that help in the construction of self-portraits of religious communities. Further, an open attitude also allows religions to be made compatible with public welfare needs by preventing grounds for religiously-inspired social conflict.

Table 10.5 Mono, multi and interreligious perspectives in an international comparison

	UK	NL	SWE	FIN	IRE	GER	CRO	POL	TUR	ISR
Positive Evaluation		Multi	Multi	Multi	Multi	Multi Inter	Multi Inter	Mono Multi Inter	Mono	Mono
Negative Evaluation	Multi Inter Mono	Inter Mono	Inter Mono	Inter Mono	Inter Mono	Mono	Mono		Inter Multi	Inter Multi

To sum up, only Muslims from Turkey, Jews from Israel, and Catholic Christians from Poland support the monoreligious model. What do these students, these countries and these expressions of religious attitudes have in common? Is it the strength of social cohesion (which includes cultural, national, religious, and ideological patterns) that makes the difference?

What does the monoreligious model mean in this context, when Polish youth integrate the interreligious approach, whereas young people from Turkey and Israel reject these statements? (We may add that they also reject a multireligious approach.) Only in Germany, Croatia, and Poland are interreligious statements positively evaluated by students. In the Nordic countries, the Netherlands, and Ireland only the multireligious model is accepted. Except for Ireland, one interpretation could be that for the so-called secularized countries the multi approach seems adequate.

We now focus on religious differences. First, we compare respondents who belong to the Christian religion, to Judaism, and to Islam. It is obvious that these groups are not homogeneous. The item distinguishing the three religions is operationalized as religious belonging. 'Belonging' does not necessarily include religious commitment and religious practice. Especially within the Christian group there are several degrees of religiosity, and even agnosticism. Second, focusing on Christian respondents only, we compare Anglicans, Lutherans, and Roman Catholics. Again these groups are heterogeneous. From detailed analyses we know that Catholics in Poland and in Germany do not share identical attitudes. Nevertheless, religious belonging explains differences, although this item is not all-embracing.

In our previous analyses the following findings were already implicitly reported. It should be mentioned that the mean values can differ, for instance when we talk about Muslims and Jews. When we compared countries we talked about Turkey and Islam, and about Israel and Judaism. Here we talk about Muslims, which includes not only Muslims from Turkey but also Muslims who live in European countries. The number of Jews in our sample living outside Israel is small, but they are also included when we talk about Judaism. There were no Christians in the Israeli and Turkish samples, so Christians are only represented in the other eight national samples.

Table 10.6 shows the outcome of the monoreligious model. There are significant differences between all the three religions: Christians reject this model (mean = 2.42), while Jews agree (mean = 3.39), and Muslims strongly agree (mean = 3.89). Taking these average outcomes into account, we have to conclude that exclusivist and inclusivist thinking is represented most strongly in Islam and also in Judaism, but not in Christianity.

Table 10.6 Monoreligious by religion (Scheffé-Procedure)

| | N | \multicolumn{3}{c}{Subgroups for Alpha = .05} |
Religion		1	2	3
Christian	5663	2.420		
Jewish	762		3.390	
Muslim	1053			3.890
Significance		1.000	1.000	1.000

Table 10.7 concerns the multireligious model, and we find significant differences here too. Jewish respondents reject this model (mean = 2.54), Muslims reject it slightly (mean = 2.81), and Christians support it (mean = 3.26). Because the multireligious model can be understood as opposite to the monoreligious model, these findings are understandable.

Table 10.7 Multireligious by religion (Scheffé-Procedure)

| | N | \multicolumn{3}{c}{Subgroups for Alpha = .05} |
Religion		1	2	3
Jewish	763	2.540		
Muslim	1053		2.810	
Christian	5672			3.260
Significance		1.000	1.000	1.000

Table 10.8 refers to the interreligious model. Only two significant groups can be evaluated here, and the data show that all the groups reject this model. The strongest rejection exists among the Jews (mean = 2.59); Christians and Muslims disagree slightly (mean = 2.89 for both).

Table 10.8 Interreligious by religion (Scheffé-Procedure)

Religion	N	Subgroups for Alpha = .05	
		1	2
Jewish	763	2.590	
Christian	5667		2.880
Muslim	1053		2.890
Significance		1.000	.949

To sum up, the Jewish respondents show a clear preference: they have a monoreligious orientation and reject both the concept that all religions are equal, and the encounter approach represented by the interreligious model. Among Muslims we find the same tendency. They are stronger in supporting the monoreligious approach, but they are less strong in their rejection of the multireligious model and the interreligious model. Christians show the opposite position: they reject the monoreligious and interreligious models, and prefer the multireligious model. This tells us that both of the models that imply religious commitment are rejected, while the religiously distant model finds acceptance. This result is understandable in the context of mostly secular countries. These countries are culturally liberal and any fixed ideology, especially religiously-driven fundamentalism, evokes resistance. For the majority, it is not popular to be too committed to fixed ideas, with no openness to different approaches.

In the following section we focus on the Christians. We constructed three groups of Anglicans, Protestants (mostly Lutherans), and Roman Catholics. In all three analyses these groups differ to a significant degree.

Table 10.9 shows how Anglicans, Protestants, and Roman Catholics evaluate the monoreligious model. All groups show negative means. Having in mind the previous findings for British youth, it does not surprise us that Anglicans reject monoreligious statements most strongly (mean = 1.66). Between them and the Protestants there is a difference of 0.5 points on the five-point Likert scale. Protestants show their disagreement with the monoreligious model by a mean value of 2.12. But Catholics also disagree: their mean value is 2.55. As mentioned above, the notion of 'Christian' is here pluralist. Only when we select Polish Catholics is there agreement with the mono-model (mean = 3.22) which shows that for more detailed analyses the degree of religiosity must also be considered.

Table 10.9 Monoreligious by Christian denominations (Scheffé-Procedure)

Christian denomination	N	\multicolumn{3}{c}{Subgroups for Alpha = .05}		
		1	2	3
Church of England	306	1.660		
Protestant	1061		2.120	
Roman Catholic	4250			2.550
Significance		1.000	1.000	1.000

Table 10.10 refers to the multireligious model. Anglicans reject this model (mean = 2.64), despite the fact that they experience a multireligious approach in the British system of religious education. Protestants show agreement with the idea that religions should be seen as equal (mean = 3.14), but this agreement is still higher among Catholics (mean = 3.33). This is also valid for Polish Catholics, who value multireligious statements with a mean of 3.12.

Table 10.10 Multireligious by Christian denominations (Scheffé-Procedure)

Christian denomination	N	Subgroups for Alpha = .05		
		1	2	3
Church of England	306	2.640		
Protestant	1063		3.140	
Roman Catholic	4257			3.330
Significance		1.000	1.000	1.000

The Catholic View on Religious Pluralism in Empirical Perspective

Finally, the interreligious model is analysed in table 10.11, and shows the Anglicans strongly rejecting the model (mean = 1.69), followed by Protestants with a mean of 2.70. Between both groups there is a distance of 1.0 point on the five-point Likert scale. With a mean of 3.01, the Catholics are in the middle of the scale.

Table 10.11 Interreligious by Christian denominations (Scheffé-Procedure)

Christian denomination	N	Subgroups for Alpha = .05		
		1	2	3
Church of England	306	1.690		
Protestant	1061		2.700	
Roman Catholic	4254			3.010
Significance		1.000	1.000	1.000

Comparing the Christian denominations, we can conclude that Anglicans disagree with all three models. Protestants prefer the multireligious model and reject the alternatives. Catholics are most positive about the multireligious model, and are neither positive nor negative about the interreligious model. Among Christians generally, the monoreligious model is not an attractive option.

At the end of our analysis we return to our assumptions. First, we expected that the majority of students, especially those in Western European countries, will reject exclusivist and inclusivist thinking, and that the multireligious model will be valued positively. With some exceptions these assumptions are confirmed by our data. In our assumption about the interreligious model we voiced some reservations, because this model requires a positive religious commitment. Indeed this model is not at the top in any country, but it is positively evaluated in three (partly less secularized) European countries. We further expected that Jews and Muslims would be in favour of the monoreligious approach, and this is empirically confirmed. Finally, the assumption that Catholic youth would agree more than other Christians with the mono-model needs some correction. Catholics are only less negative than other Christians (Poles are an exception).

Discussion

Putting all our findings together, we cannot say that there is one 'theology of religions' possessed by all students. Their perspectives differ, depending on where they come from and to which religion they belong. The majority of respondents in the North and West of Europe have a moderate, liberal attitude. For them (too much) normativity or ideology seems to be out of order, and equality represents an appropriate approach within a pluralist society. The more that students see themselves as hardly religious or not religious at all, the more they fail to understand why it is necessary to talk about truth, or why one should encounter and explore religions. These students might say: Leave religions as they are, as long they behave peacefully and their members are not too vocal in public. With regard to the concepts discussed by Durka above, they follow the 'acceptance-model' whereas the 'mutuality-model' claims too much – this model is only acceptable for the religiously committed and interested students. But religiously committed students also favour the multireligious approach, although they connect it with the interreligious model. For them, it seems appropriate in a modern multireligious context not to give too much significance to religious diversity. Has empirical reality realized what Jean-Jacques Rousseau elaborated in his concept of religion, and Ephraim Lessing later pointed out in his parable of the rings? This surely does not correspond to the Roman Catholic doctrine, as we outlined it above. Faced with this situation, should we bemoan the loud endorsement of the confessional approach, or may we conclude that – in the perspective of most of the students – religious diversity no longer causes tension by seeking answers to the question: Who is right? This latter view makes it clear that the available theologies of religion are not readily usable as theories to be adopted in practice in religious education. Theological and philosophical debate has a different point of departure from the constructing of curricula for school learning. Theologies of religion can be understood as the subject-matter of multireligious and interreligious learning, but not as their normative frame.

Finding ways to expose students to plurality may be considered one of the elementary and indispensable tasks that all human beings must face today, in the same way that they must come to terms with political and religious institutions. It is evident that no particular opinion can be generalized and claimed to be valid. Pluralism, as the ordered configuration of plurality, has no Archimedean point at its disposal from which can be derived rules for life that can be shared by all. The pluralistic configuration of plurality must place personal interests and interests of the common good into relationship with each other, and negotiate an understanding between the two. In times of modernity (or postmodernity), these no longer have a quasi 'super-temporal' character. Rather, when they can be found they are temporary, and limited to specific sectors of plurality and never to plurality as a whole.

Religions are affected by these developments. As worldviews, they represent a specific particular interest *par excellence* that, in many different ways, connects with a claim of truth or even a claim of validity for all. Where this is the case, for example, in radical Islam or in fundamentalist groups in Judaism or Christianity, then tensions are apparent. It is easily discernible that it is difficult, especially for religions, to define their relationship to plurality. They must, out of the perspective of a worldview, bring their personal perspective into equilibrium with other personal perspectives, without hardening into fundamentalism or, at the other extreme, losing their profile entirely through modifying their own convictions.

In all western societies, with plurality growing ever more conscious, monopolistic worldviews become strained. The end of the meta-story, as expressed by Lyotard (1984), represents this issue very concretely. In a postmodern perspective, a return to such dominant ideologies is not only impossible, but also undesirable. In that sense, Lyotard proclaimed his programme of a 'war on totality'. The problem arises as to how understandings should be met in modern society if – in postmodern thinking – wholeness is neither possible nor desirable and the 'fragment' represents normality. Does one not come close to the well known adage of 'throwing the baby out with the bathwater', if one changes an ideologically uniform community into its opposite, regardless of whether it is politically or religiously motivated, where concepts such as wisdom are treated as if they are irrelevant? It appears that religious communities are faced with the problem of discovering every mode possible, in their search for understanding and in marking differences. Without living and working together, this becomes difficult in the conditions of globalization – if not altogether impossible. The secure, private, known, and trusted world is increasingly exposed as a fiction; and the global village is not yet a clear-cut, definable reality in the world of individual experience. Both exist, but the way in which lines of interaction should be drawn remains to be clarified on the micro-level, as well as on the macro-level.

The three mono-, multi-, and interreligious models handle this problem in their own ways. They stress the security of their own ideology (monoreligious), the equal validity of all positions (multireligious), or the perspective of interaction – where the greatest chance for individuals and the collective to reach a satisfactory working through of plurality (even pluralistically) exists in the active dispute with the different perspectives and in what changes (interreligious model). It is evident that this is a complex problem for Christian theology in general, and for the Catholic Church in particular. Practical theology cannot solve this problem, but it is its duty to identify a theory while practising the coping strategies that are available in lived religions regarding education in religion. If this project has made it clear that young people take no pleasure in the monoreligious perspective, then it is valid to judge these connections. The restriction to the personal perspective seems anti-modern, because it is not compatible with the composition of modern life, whose basic constant is plurality and the diversity of cultural and religious understandings. A religion that wants people to feel like they belong must express the sense that principally it has a positive commitment to modernity. It must affirm the diversity of the inner and the outer. It is both theologically and ecclesiastically clear that this does not mean approving every characteristic of diversity, but it can be seen as a duty to have dialogue with that which is valid. The danger is that a religious community that does not cultivate this competence will contribute to people ignoring the relativization of all claims. The empirical findings show that this process is already underway.

It may be recognized that we are moving towards the interreligious approach. The more that pressure grows on the individual to come to his or her own integration of differences in the context of diversity (including religious diversity), while at the same time the more people feel that a return to unity is out of the question (for the reasons stated above), the greater is the possibility of resorting to the multireligious model instead of the interreligious model. If the policy of the Church ignores this problem, the Church community of the future could become attractive only to those who need a closed and secure world, while pluralist believers will escape from it. If systematic theology ignores this problem, its theories will lose their empirical anchorage.

References

Dominus Jesus (2000), <http://www.vatican.va/roman_curia/congregations/cfaith/documents/>.

Clarke, D., and Winter, B. W. (eds). (1991). *One God, one Lord: Christianity in a world of religious pluralism*. Cambridge: Tyndale House.

Knitter, P. (1985). *No other name? A critical survey of Christian attitudes toward the world religions*. New York: Orbis.

Lyotard, J.-F. (1984). *The postmodern condition: A report on knowledge*. Minneapolis, Minnesota: University of Minneapolis Press.

Rahner, K. (1964). Das Christentum und die nichtchristlichen Religionen. In *Schriften zur Theologie, vol. V* (pp. 136–158). Einsiedeln: Benzinger.

Rahner, K. (1965). Die anonymen Christen. In *Schriften zur Theologie, vol. VI* (pp. 545–554). Einsiedeln: Benzinger.

Rahner, K. (1983). Über den Absolutheitsanspruch des Christentums. In *Schriften zur Theologie, vol. XV* (pp. 171–184). Einsiedeln: Benzinger.

Ruokanen, M. (1992). *The Catholic Doctrine of Non-Christian Religions*. Leiden: Brill.

Swidler, L. (1992). *Die Zukunft der Theologie: Im Dialog der Religionen und Weltanschauungen.* Regensburg: Pustet.

Van der Ven, J. A., and Ziebertz, H.-G. (eds). (1994). *Religiöser Pluralismus und Interreligiöses Lernen.* Weinheim and Kampen: Kok Pharos.

Vermeer, P., and van der Ven, J. A. (2004). Looking at the relationship between religions: An empirical study among secondary school students. *Journal of Empirical Theology, 17* (1), 36–59.

Ziebertz, H.-G. (1993). Religious pluralism and religious education. *Journal of Empirical Theology, 6* (1), 82–89.

Ziebertz, H.-G., and Kay, W. K. (eds). (2005). *Youth in Europe I: An international empirical study about life perspectives.* Münster: LIT-Verlag.

Ziebertz, H.-G., and Kay, W. K. (eds). (2006). *Youth in Europe II: An international empirical study about religiosity.* Münster: LIT-Verlag.

Ziebertz, H.-G., Kay, W. K., and Riegel, U. (eds). (2009). *Youth in Europe III: An international empirical study about the impact of religion on life orientation.* Münster: LIT-Verlag.

Ziebertz, H.-G., and Riegel, U. (2009). *How teachers in Europe teach religion: An empirical study in 16 countries.* Münster: LIT-Verlag.

MARIAN DE SOUZA

11 The Dual Role of Unconscious Learning in Engendering and Hindering Spiritual Growth: Implications for Religious Education in Pluralist Contexts

Introduction

The dying years of the twentieth century were witness to a world that had become, relatively speaking, a small place so that the movement of people across the globe was immense. Some were tourists exploring new habitats that were now more accessible; other moves were generated by career and/or study interests; and still others chose to move to another country in the hope that they would find a better life for themselves and their families. And then there were those who were the victims of natural disasters or devastating human actions, who found their lives uprooted and destroyed and who were forced to flee their homelands and seek refuge or asylum in a number of countries that were culturally, religiously, and linguistically different from their own. It is not surprising, then, that this movement of people has become a significant event for the first decade of the twenty-first century. More importantly, the differences between host and newcomer has given rise to 'them' and 'us' tensions, as diverse cultural and religious traditions have encountered and/or engaged with one another.

This has been particularly true in Australia where, from the seventies, people from non-European backgrounds and cultures started arriving to settle. With the economy in good shape and a government promoting the concept of multiculturalism, including funding to celebrate different aspects of cultural diversity and to help newcomers establish links into their own ethnic communities, Australians appeared to welcome the newcomer. However, Mackay (1993) identified what could be described as a certain level of superficiality in the apparent tolerance that Australians displayed to new arrivals. He suggested that for most Australians, migrants were welcome as long as they were prepared to become assimilated by embracing Australian social practices and values and being able to communicate easily in English. As well, Mackay noted the fact that in affluent times, when jobs were plentiful, there were few problems because Australians did not perceive any real threat to their employment or career opportunities. In general, then, migrants were welcomed providing they did not alter the Australian way of life. This summed up the attitude of many Australians so that, often, their engagement with the newcomers remained at the surface level of their lives.

If we accept Mackay's thesis, it is not surprising that, following in the wake of 9/11, global political tensions began to impact on local communities that included Australian Muslims. Indeed, this was a similar experience for Muslims in other western countries. Australia's subsequent involvement in the war against terrorism dismantled the façade of the buoyant and cohesive Australian society which had, to all intents and purposes, flowered in the seventies and eighties. This has in some part been due to what could be described as somewhat irresponsible media coverage which appeared, consciously or non-consciously, to encourage attitudes of 'them' and 'us' between Australian non-Muslims and Australian Muslims. At another level, it may be attributed to particular government thinking and policies of that time which fanned the flames of fear and insecurity – and, yes, intolerance and racism.

Writing from an Indigenous Australian perspective, Alexis Wright (Tsiolkas, Haigh, and Wright, 2008) aptly described the Australian experience of the turn of the century:

> The closing years of the last century and most of those of the first decade of the twenty-first century will be remembered in the history of Australia as the time when the country lost its image of innocent *carefreeness* and wellbeing – an image that had seemingly always represented *Australianness*.

Wright also joined in the 'them and us' discussion when she suggested that the war against terrorism was really about the government attempting to 'change other people and other countries into something that looked like us' (131–132). Certainly, such intentions were clearly identifiable in the early assimilation policies so that migrants, 'them', were inevitably encouraged to become more like 'us', the Anglo-Australian.

There was evidence of these fears and insecurities in the outpouring of public opinion in the media. It also led to publications such as Waleed Ali's *People like us* (2007) and the Sydney Pen Voices – The 3 Writers Project publication: *Tolerance, prejudice and fear* (2008) by Christos Tsiolkas, Gideon Haigh, and Alexis Wright. Ali (2007) describes himself as a Muslim, born and raised in the West (Australian society), whose experiences in the past several years have seen himself 'standing at the intersection of these two conceptual entities we very loosely call "Islam" and the "West"' (xii). In his introduction, he refers to the extensive discourse on these subjects offered by people from each side where each has attempted to discuss the other but, he argues, are driven by two distinct but related problems: egocentricity and dehumanization.

> By egocentricity I mean the inability to understand the world from the perspective of another. It is egocentricity that leads us to assume our own historical and social experiences are universal; to assume that the solutions to our problems are the solutions to everyone else's, even when the circumstances surrounding them are entirely different; to assume that the world would be so much better if only everyone was like us. (xiv)

Ali (2007) recognizes the arrogance in such a stance but also acknowledges that it is rarely a *conscious* one. Accordingly, if some of our attitudes and actions are generated by our non-conscious learning it is difficult to identify one's own egocentricity or, indeed, recognize that our worldviews are created and shaped *consciously* and *non-consciously* by our lived experiences and environments which call for particular responses and expressions. Further, he argues, 'the more we attempt to describe and analyse the other, the more we end up describing little but ourselves ... In spite of this, and more likely because of it, this discourse is often thoroughly dehumanizing.' He points out that the dehumanizing effect starts at the most basic level when the discussion is framed 'in terms of "Islam" or "the Muslim world" and "the West" as though each is a coherent singular entity' (xvi).

Another situation that reflects this dehumanizing effect is when people from the dominant culture reach out to a minority culture. The superiority that so often accompanies dominance is projected into their attitudes and actions, even though they have little consciousness about this. Therefore, while their conscious minds lead them to extend positive gestures towards the minority other, their non-conscious attitudes imprint their own ideas and concepts on the other. Thus, for the past fifteen or so years in Australia, when many Anglo-Australians have a raised consciousness about the plight of their indigenous people, it has become customary to acknowledge the indigenous people at the beginning of any formal event or celebration. Hence, these occasions are usually opened with lines about acknowledging the traditional owners of the land. However, the concept of ownership is distinctly not part of indigenous Australian culture so these instances, a product of the conscious mind, become very good examples of the non-consciously generated imposition of the values of the dominant culture on the minority one.

Ali's perspective on the effect of dehumanization bears some resemblance to Andrew Wright's argument that religious educators who focus on sameness to promote solidarity, instead of recognizing difference of belief and practice, may be perceived as committing a violent act since it reduces the other to 'the sameness of my treasured world-view' and it is triggered by an inclination to avoid the 'disruption that challenges me to look beyond myself towards a wealth of new horizons'. Instead, Wright provides an alternative approach which is based on the notion of hospitality, a guest-host relationship where 'the Other has a moral claim on me' which calls me to embrace the stranger precisely as a stranger with a sense of 'infinite care and ultimate responsibility' (Wright, 2007, 70). Wright's argument is that if a group is allowed to be different and is accepted and given respect, there is less chance that the group members will feel threatened and respond accordingly – that is, with violence.

Returning to Ali's contention, in essence he is describing a 'them and us' scenario that has become particularly relevant to Australian society during the first decade of this century where certain groups of people with different religious beliefs and cultures, most particularly European Muslims, have suddenly found themselves left without the sense of belonging within the communities where they have previously been able to live comfortably without attracting much attention. Many of these communities have changed in recent years to become pluralistic, with a visible presence of non-European cultures and religious beliefs. As a result, a large number of individuals are being exposed to the other who has a different worldview and associated values; and, sometimes, the differences in these worldviews appear to be unbridgeable, thereby creating tensions that can erupt into displays of hatred and violence. This has happened between some Muslim and non-Muslim Australians in the past few years.

It is without doubt that Ali's (2007) experiences of standing at the intersection of different cultures would possibly resonate with other new Australians. More importantly, this is not just about people who come from different religious groups but would also include people who share the same faith tradition, but whose cultural background is different: for instance, those who come from non-western Christian backgrounds where religious thinking, worldviews, and practices may look, sound, and feel different from the dominant Anglo-Christian religious culture. This is, certainly, the case for Anglo-Australian Catholics who have inherited Catholic practices that were generated by a nineteenth-century Irish Catholicism. Due to their relative isolation from the 'mother' country, as well as the level of marginalization that most Catholics experienced throughout the nineteenth and early twentieth century, they have retained a certain insularity which tends to generate amongst many from earlier generations a wariness of the other who is different, including other Catholics.

Accordingly, much work needs to be done so that social cohesion and community wellbeing may be restored within these societies where all individuals may experience acceptance and inclusion, and living conditions that allow them to worship freely and to grow and reach their potential. One way forward is through education about different religious and spiritual cultures and, certainly, there has been much research and practice directed to addressing and overcoming some of the associated problems. However, I believe there is an element that is frequently neglected in most educational programmes – the role of non-conscious learning.

Non-conscious learning

As Ali (2007) noted when he referred to the concept of egocentricity in relation to Australians, too often this is a non-conscious characteristic. This is one reason why non-conscious learning can be an impediment to nurturing the spiritual traits of connectedness, empathy, and compassion. If an individual has no awareness of their tendency to particular attitudes, biases, or hidden character traits which spring from their non-conscious minds, any opportunity to address them, modify them, or control them are most likely to be missed.

In this discussion on non-conscious learning, I will focus on the Australian context but I would suggest that the implications are relevant for many other countries that used to be monocultural and monoreligious but which have changed to becoming pluralistic in their structure and composition in more recent times. One difference between Australia and other countries is that the dominant culture in Australia which has been derived from an Anglo-Saxon/Celtic culture is a little over 200 years old. Therefore, it does not have the hidden depths that compose the cultural fabric of older countries. Thus, if the top layers are stripped away in older countries, there are other layers beneath which are composed of past versions of the culture. This is not present in a young country in quite the same way. In Australia, the layers peel away to reveal an indigenous culture, much of which has been lost both to its own people as well as to the migrant Australian who came to settle. A serious discussion of such a scenario would extend beyond the limits of this chapter. Therefore, for purposes of this chapter, I will focus on contemporary society which still bears features of an Anglo-Saxon/Celtic culture and examine the divisiveness that has become evident over the past decade through the settlement of the other who is different, and to discuss the implications for religious education programmes.

The positive implications of non-conscious information processing

I have previously discussed in detail the role of the intuition in the learning process which is triggered by, mostly, non-conscious learning (see, for instance, de Souza, 2006, 2008). One theorist who has discussed intuitive thinking in detail is Myers (2002) and, along with other theorists (for instance, Claxton, 2000; Eraut, 2000; Hogarth, 2001) he describes intuition as the knowledge we do not know we have. Moreover, we do not know how we got it, since much of it derives from non-conscious perceptions and sensations. Myers asserts that a vast amount of information is processed by the mind, much of it outside of consciousness and beyond language (Myers, 2002, 29). The mind sifts through this information at top speed and only releases into the conscious mind the specific information that is discerned to be relevant at a particular point in time. Myers describes this information processing as a parallel process which results in two ways of knowing, controlled (conscious) and automatic (non-conscious), and argues that much of the information that passes through the mind remains deeply submerged and out of sight of the conscious mind. When new learning takes place, therefore, time and silence are required for the absorption and merging of new and old learning. Time needs to be allowed for cogitation or the 'ruminating' process as described by Claxton (2000). Lucas and Claxton (2010) cite an intuition expert, Eugene Sadler-Smith, who says, 'Everyone has intuition. It is one of the hallmarks of how human beings think and behave. It's impossible for us to function effectively without using gut feeling' (80).

Intuitions in the learning process, then, provide the function of integration involving the inner and outer person and connecting new learning to previous learning. In other words, intuitions act like a unifying factor between perceptions, thoughts, and feelings with the potential to end in transformative learning. Unquestionably, intuitions are useful for problem-solving exercises and other imaginative and creative expressions and, as such, should be an essential consideration in the planning of educational experiences.

These are the positive aspects of non-conscious learning which can be used to nurture spirituality through self-awareness and self-knowledge, as well as to develop imagination, creativity, and a response to beauty and truth. It can also be used to help children think laterally so as to make connections and elicit meaning out of diverse bits of information. This is particularly relevant when educators desire to develop in their students an understanding of the different perspectives and worldviews about particular issues, events, and actions that stem from different cultural and religious experiences and traditions. It is only through such understandings that individuals may develop some empathy in their engagement with the other. Further, non-conscious learning through intuitive and imaginative thinking can help students transcend the ordinariness and routines of the everyday, and dream of or envision previously unrecognized possibilities. Consequently, what should be essential for learning today is for teachers to explore different strategies that may be used to assist students to retrieve and use more effectively the information that is stored in the non-conscious mind and to develop creative and alternative responses to situations, problems, and other learning tasks with which they engage.

The negative implications of non-conscious information processing

While non-conscious processing of information is a valuable trait of the human person which can enhance the learning experience, there are some less positive aspects. One characteristic that Myers (2002) identifies is the tendency to make generalizations and create stereotypes – 'we speedily, spontaneously and unintentionally infer others' traits' (40). This notion is supported by Wilson (2002) in his discussion of the human mind's dual processing of information. He refers to the non-conscious mind as the adaptive unconscious and argues that individuals 'might have learned to respond in prejudiced ways, on the basis of thousands of exposures to racist views in the media or exposure to role models such as one's parents' (190). Wilson argues that people often do not know themselves very well because much of what we want to know about ourselves is beyond the reach of our conscious awareness (4). In other words, we may have developed prejudicial attitudes towards others through non-conscious learning without actually being aware that we have them. He contends further that the adaptive unconscious absorbs information, interprets, and evaluates it, and sets goals in motion, quickly and efficiently; and all this occurs outside our conscious selves. In addition, we may make intuitive judgements and interpret situations in a way that has more to do with our sense of wellbeing rather than our desire for accuracy, as it is more important for us to maintain a worldview that makes us feel safe and comfortable. These responses occur at much greater speed than responses triggered by the rational mind. The rational mind moves in later when we start examining, explaining, or articulating the reasons for our responses.

It is this aspect of non-conscious learning that has relevance here. It is possible, for instance, that people in positions of power or authority can manipulate individuals through their non-conscious learning and lead them to believe that certain traits and characteristics of the other who is different are unhealthy, undesirable, and unwanted. This happened in Australia in the week prior to an election in 2001, when the then Prime Minister used a photograph of children being thrown overboard and declared, 'We don't want people like that.' The claim was that the asylum seekers were throwing children overboard in the hope of obtaining rescue and safe passage to Australia. After the election, the public learnt how the situation had been misrepresented and that children were being thrown into the water, with adults jumping in after them, because their boat was capsizing. However, a large number of Australians rallied to the Prime Minister's call precisely because he played on the fears of an island nation about being overrun by the arrival of 'boat people' on their shores. In this case, the fears were greater given the political tensions generated because the people who were arriving were, for the most part, fleeing from non-European Muslim countries. In other words, they were easily categorized as 'them'.

A further aspect of the fear that individuals may feel towards the other who is different is that humans tend to be drawn towards people who are like themselves in beliefs and practices, and certainly in physical appearance. Being with such people enhances our feelings of security and comfort. It promotes a certain sense of group superiority as well. Law (2006) argues this when he says:

> Human beings are peculiarly attracted to them-and-us thinking. By holding up the twisted looking-glass of tribalism, in which 'they' appear dirty, smelly, amoral and perhaps even less than fully human, while 'we' take on a noble countenance (we may even find ourselves reflected back as 'the chosen people' of 'the master race'), an Authority can foster still deeper feelings of loyalty to the group, its leadership and its beliefs, making it still more difficult for its members to question them. (Law, 2006, 30)

For instance, the group superiority element was clearly alive in the Cronulla riots of 2005.[1] Referring to the clash between Middle Eastern and other Australian youth, Tsiolkias (Tsiolkias, Haigh, and Wright, 2008) posed a pertinent question:

> I know that if I had been on that beach, how would the murderous mob, waving their flag, have known if I was one of them? In our swimmers, a Greek wog looks very much like a Lebo wog. This is what contemporary Australian nationalism does. It reminds us that there are the true Aussies and then there are the boons, the wogs, the slope-heads, the refos, chinks and niggers. Any protest, any dissent from such a view, any expression of intelligent engagement with Australian history is met with the arid, brain-numbing, immature response of 'you are being un-Australian'. (41)

The word 'un-Australian', introduced by Prime Minister John Howard in the early years of this century, clearly raised questions of identity. It is more than likely that the non-conscious processing of such a term in the political context of the time has encouraged in a new generation of Australian children a 'them and us' attitude, with a corresponding mindset and conduct. And while subsequent learning and education may lead them to recognize and adopt more appropriate attitudes towards others who are different, in moments of trial, stress, anxiety, or fear it is their non-conscious learning that will generate their feelings and actions.

---

[1] Cronulla is a popular beach in Sydney. For more information about the riots see (among other websites) <http://cts.hss.uts.edu.au/students06/Group%20Website%20Turning%20the%20Lights%20on/cronulla.html> .

I would like to offer a further consideration of how non-conscious learning may affect Anglo-Australian Catholics.[2] Those Catholics who grew up in some isolation because they were still subject to a degree of marginalization in the 1950s and 1960s would rarely have engaged with people who were different from themselves culturally and religiously, and most certainly, racially. This was due to the fact that, within the monocultural Christian context, community leaders still identified and maintained differences between their own communities and others so that Catholics and non-Catholics did not usually mix socially. Many Catholic children were segregated because of their attendance at Catholic schools, and their social and emotional support and connections came from within their own communities. As well, there were few non-European people living in Australia at that time, so their experience of other cultures and races were extremely limited. What they knew of Catholics situated in Asia and Africa was that that was where their missionaries went to spread the Christian message. No doubt they put their pennies into the Mission Boxes as their contribution towards saving those little black and brown babies from the dreadful fate reserved for pagans. This conscious learning is likely to have promoted non-conscious feelings of superiority towards people from these other countries.

It is possible, too, that the history of white/black relations for the past few hundred years, focused as it was on the supremacy of white people in every way – culture, intelligence, education, and worldviews – may have seared the human consciousness of the twentieth century, so that at a collective non-conscious level people from western countries, where the population has been predominantly white, may have unstated and unrecognized feelings of superiority towards their black/brown/yellow neighbours. In the latter years of the twentieth century, when Catholics from these other worlds have arrived to settle, have become members of parishes and attend Catholic schools, Australian Catholics who grew up in that monocultural

---

2   Although I am discussing the Australian Catholic context because this is one that I know and have experienced, it is possible that the same issues may be applied to the broader Christian context in Australia and other western countries.

world have found themselves having to engage at some level with Catholics whose expressions and practices of Catholic beliefs are sometimes quite different. As a result, for some, a rather patronizing attitude towards these new arrivals becomes a manifestation of their non-conscious learning from their earlier years. And further, for some, there is an underlying belief, although not always identified, that their contemporary educated Anglo-Celtic Catholic practices and expressions are somehow superior, and they may speak disparagingly of the rather 'devout' and 'devotional' practices of the newcomers. Once again, this situation is an example of 'them and us' attitudes which, potentially, divide a community and impede social cohesion and wellbeing.

A concrete example

To examine further how non-conscious learning, through a lack of understanding and empathy, may lead to a display of unacknowledged bias towards the other who is different, I would like to recount here a short incident from a television programme that was screened on national television in April 2006 in Australia. This incident took place during a show called 'Geoffrey Robertson's Hypothetical'. (Geoffrey Robertson was a well known presenter of such programmes.) The object of the show was to pose a question and then ask relevant questions of a panel of guests. The panel was made up of well known public figures, politicians, and so on. The incident I will describe has relevance for this chapter because it clearly shows the role of non-conscious learning. The social and political context is also relevant because it was in the aftermath of the 'war against terror' and other associated conflicts. It was a tension-filled time due to the overt and covert hostility that had become evident in society, driven by media reports which frequently and indiscriminately linked Muslims with terrorism, as well as by the pronouncements by certain politicians that reflected their prejudices about people who were 'not like us'.

The context

In 2005, the Federal Government in Australia, influenced by the actions taken in other countries, introduced new laws that impacted on individual freedom and liberties.[3] Effectively, it meant that the Australian Federal Police (AFP) were able to carry out what was termed preventative detention orders, effectively locking up people thought to be involved in or to have knowledge of a terrorist act. One response from the Law Council of Australia was to say that passing the proposed laws would push the nation closer to becoming a police state.[4]

Following the new legislation in late 2005, the Australian Federal Police led dawn raids against various Muslim men in two capital cities who were suspected of being involved in or supporting acts of terror. These were followed by arrests, court cases, and convictions. In addition, the newspapers frequently reported on acts of hostility and violence on Muslims by other members of the public. This included verbal and/or physical attacks on school children by other school children. In December 2005, things came to a head in Cronulla where Middle Eastern Australian and Anglo-European Australian youths clashed, leading to almost uncontrollable riots for a couple of days. In effect it was a clash of religious and ethnic cultures. Most Australians, cushioned as they were from such activities because of their relative isolation from the rest of the western world, were appalled that something like this could have taken place in what most believed was a safe, multicultural society.

---

3   See The Anti Terrorist Act (no 2) 2005: <http://www.ag.gov.au/agd/WWW/nationalsecurity.nsf/AllDocs/A41A86E81E52A0B2CA25710A001A7EEA?OpenDocument>.

4   See article 'Police state fears over terrorism laws': <http://www.smh.com.au/news/national/police-state-fears-over-terrorism-laws/2005/10/16/1129401135040.html>.

The incident

The following year, in April, the Hypothetical scenario was screened. It asked the question: 'How multicultural is Australia?' The presenter came from an Anglo-Australian background and was well known for his skill at asking tricky questions of politicians and other public figures. His career had also shown him to be a strong defender of human rights. Among the guests on his programme was a Muslim woman, easily identifiable by the hijab she wore. Well into the programme, after the presenter had asked difficult and awkward questions of several of his guests related to multiculturalism and tolerance, he turned to the Muslim woman and posed the following question which had oblique references to an actual incident that had occurred (this is my wording of the actual question): 'It is quite late one evening and an Imam arrives at your door seeking help. It is alleged that he has had dealings with terrorists and the Feds are looking for him. What would you do?' The woman quickly replied that she would not let him into her house but would point him to other people in the community who could help him Without a pause, the presenter turned to the Anglican Archbishop and posed the same question. The Archbishop's response was that he would open his cathedral doors to the fugitive. After all, that was the teaching of Jesus Christ. The message contained in his reponse, therefore, clearly implied that Christianity was distinctly more charitable than Islam.

Discussion

My own reaction to the posing of the question was strong. I felt the question was an unfair one to ask of the Muslim woman and it was equally unfair to juxtapose the same question to the Archbishop. But my real concern came later when this incident was being discussed by people around me, including my colleagues. Few of them shared my response. There was a general consensus that on such a programme one should expect to be asked tricky questions. I found these responses perplexing and I made an effort to communicate my discomfort about the whole situation.

As my lecture for that week with my undergraduates was on the topic of addressing religious diversity, I described the incident to them but got similar responses – with the exception of one mature-age student. She approached me at the end of class and said: 'I've been thinking about that woman you told us about and I've realized she was damned if she did and damned if she didn't!' These were my thoughts exactly. In the social and political climate of the times, this woman had no choice but to answer the way she did, even though it meant that she sounded quite uncharitable. Rather that, than have the audience see her as a supporter of a suspected terrorist, particularly given the new legislation which could have her held and detained for days with little communication with anyone if she was perceived to be such a person. The Archbishop, on the other hand, had no such quandary. He could make his sweeping statement without any fear that someone in the audience would point a finger at him as having any links with terrorists. After all, he was the Anglican Archbishop in a large city and, of course, he came from the dominant Anglo-Australian background, hardly a likely contender to support an act of terrorism. I felt that the attitudes of both the presenter and possibly the Archbishop reflected a bias drawn from their non-conscious learning about the other who was different from themselves, so that they were unable to have any real understanding or empathy with the woman. I felt, also, that perhaps it was the non-conscious learning of my colleagues, most of whom had grown up in a monocultural Australia, which prevented them from sensing the woman's dilemma, precisely because she wore a hijab which made her different. They failed to see the predicament in which she had been placed by the question.

The life experiences of the presenter, the Archbishop, and most of my colleagues placed them beyond the daily experiences of this woman given the tensions within Australian society caused by the actions of Muslim terrorists around the world, accompanied by the role played by the media and politicians in influencing the general public to believe that Muslim equals terrorist. As Tsiolkas (Tsiolkas, Haigh, and Wright, 2008) puts it:

> Those of us who do not fear deportation, starvation, the knock on the door from the police or the immigration officer, are going to experience liberation and opportunity differently to someone living in fear, living in poverty. (22)

Such a lived experience was confirmed for me a few weeks later when I attended a Values Education Forum as part of a large Government-funded research project where I briefly met the same Muslim woman. I asked her how she was going, the usual Australian greeting. She responded that she was having a bad day. She was a Principal of an Islamic school and she had just received a phone call to say that two of her male students had been picked up for questioning by the police. She then went on to say that this was a common experience for her students and she found the whole talk of values education rather hypocritical since her students' life experiences did not reflect the values we had been talking about. Further, she described for me an incident that took place two weeks before the Cronulla riots. She had been sitting in a café near the beach working at her laptop and a young male surfer came in. He stopped at her table, put his finger in her face and said 'you people should go back to where you came from!' Ironically, I learnt later that the woman was, in fact, an Australian who had converted to Islam when she married a Muslim. In other words, she was in her own country, the country of her birth.

This incident, I believe, presents a very good example of unacknowledged attitudes of bias that may be generated by non-conscious learning. And the only way such learning can be redressed is through sincere and real engagement with the other. It is only through such engagement that acceptance can move on to inclusion, empathy, and compassion.

Conclusion

These issues are all relevant to a discussion of non-conscious learning which can have both a positive and a negative impact on the relationality of the individual: that is, the connectedness that is an expression of human spirituality. As becomes apparent, this is of particular importance in any society, such as contemporary Australia, which has developed pluralistic traits in the space of only a few years. Education is needed for all members of the community, in order to promote understanding of and engagement with others whose religious culture and worldviews have been shaped and determined by a range of factors and conditions that bear little similarity to one another. In particular, religious education programmes in schools need to shift from the reductionistic and objective worldview that dominated twentieth-century education programmes, and become more responsive to the shifting paradigms that reflect the contemporary world: one where East and West learn from each other to create new knowledge and new understandings. Harman (1998) summed this up well when he argued that humans have created their knowledge-systems to reflect and shape their societies, and these systems continue to be sustained because they satisfy the tests that are put to them: that is, they are confirmed by lived human experience in the society in which they originated. In other words, western philosophical and scientific thought is what it is because of the particular nature of the society in which it was developed, and other knowledge-systems (for instance, in the East) differ from it because they reflect the characteristics that were valued in the particular societies where they evolved. In noting the implications that arise from this contention, Harman suggests that while the West has assumed a certain confidence and superiority that their scientific view of reality is essentially correct and all other views are wrong, there is a need to consider that other views may perceive reality through different cultural windows which emphasize other aspects of the total human experience. This would make them complementary rather than wrong.

To be sure, this thinking and understanding needs to be applied to the discipline of Christian religious education in Australia and other pluralistic societies. Scholars and researchers, curriculum planners, educational leaders, and practitioners in religious education need to become more knowledgeable about the historical and cultural influences on religious expressions and practices; and they need to do this through more than book learning and dialogue. They need genuinely to engage with the other so that they find ways to include them in different areas of their communal and familial lives.

As well, they need to be more inclusive of leadership levels of Christians from non-western countries so that new and alternative perspectives are brought to light which, potentially, may enhance understanding and learning experiences in the discipline.

Finally, leaders, policy makers, and religious educators need to recognize and identify the unstated prejudices and beliefs that stem from their own non-conscious learning towards others whose cultural and religious practices seem foreign. They need to consider how they can use strategies to further assist students to engage with difference, to think outside traditional patterns, and to develop accepting and inclusive dispositions towards the other. These are holistic elements which reflect the spiritual dimension of education (de Souza, 2003, 2004), where teaching for meaning and connectedness with the other provides the foundational base for the development of learning programmes and environments. In particular, they need to recognize the incompatibility for the contemporary world of the thinking and practices of an education system that was born in a previous century. Instead, they need to discover approaches to learning in religious education that moves away from compartmentalization to one that recognizes and addresses the complementarity of the intellectual, emotional, and spiritual aspects of the human person and which, potentially, will enhance their ability to live cohesively in the pluralist context of contemporary society.

References

Ali, W. (2007). *People like us: How arrogance is dividing Islam and the West.* Sydney: Picador.
Claxton, G. (2000). The anatomy of intuition. In T. Atkinson and G. Claxton (eds), *The intuitive practitioner: On the value of not always knowing what one is doing* (pp. 32–52). Buckingham and Philadelphia: Open University Press.
de Souza, M. (2003). Contemporary influences on the spirituality of young people: Implications for education. *International Journal of Children's Spirituality, 8* (3), 269–279.

de Souza, M. (2004). Teaching for effective learning in religious education: A discussion of the perceiving, thinking, feeling and intuiting elements in the learning process. *Journal of Religious Education*, *52* (3), 22–30.

de Souza, M. (2006). Rediscovering the spiritual dimension in education: Promoting a sense of self and place, meaning and purpose in learning. In M. de Souza, K. Engebretson, G. Durka, R. Jackson, and A. McGrady (eds), *International Handbook of the Religious, Moral and Spiritual Dimensions of Education, Part 2* (pp. 1127–1139). Dordrecht, The Netherlands: Springer Academic Publishers.

de Souza, M. (2008). Spirituality in education: Addressing the inner and outer lives of students to promote meaning and connectedness in learning. *Interface: A forum for theology in the world* (Australian Theological Forum), 98–118.

Eraut, M. (2000). The intuitive practitioner: A critical overview. In T. Atkinson and G. Claxton (eds), *The intuitive practitioner: On the value of not always knowing what one is doing* (pp 255–268). Buckingham and Philadelphia: Open University Press.

Harman, W. (1998). *Global mind change: The promise of the twenty-first century*. San Francisco: Berett-Koehler Publishers, Inc.

Hogarth, R. M. (2001). *Educating intuition*. Chicago and London: The University of Chicago Press.

Law, S. (2006). *The war for children's minds*. Abingdon: Routledge.

Lucas, B., and Claxton, G. (2010). *New kinds of smart: How the science of learnable intelligence is changing education*. Berkshire: McGraw-Hill Education/Open University Press.

Mackay, H. (1993). *Reinventing Australia: The mind and mood of Australia in the 90s*. Pymble, New South Wales: CollinsAngus & Robertson Publishers.

Myers, D. G. (2002). *Intuition: Its powers and perils*. New Haven and London: Yale University Press.

Tsiolkas, C., Haigh, G., and Wright, A. (2008). *Tolerance, prejudice and fear: Sydney pen voices – the three writers project*. Crows Nest, New South Wales: Allen & Unwin.

Wilson, T. (2002). *Strangers to ourselves: Discovering the adaptive unconscious*. Cambridge, Massachusetts and London: The Belknap Press/Harvard University Press.

Wright, A. (2007). Hospitality and the voice of the other: Confronting the economy of violence through religious education. In J. Astley, L. J. Francis, and M. Robbins (eds), *Peace or Violence: The ends of religion and education?* (pp. 64–80). Cardiff: University of Wales Press.

LESLIE J. FRANCIS AND MANDY ROBBINS

12 The Theology of Religions and Psychological Type: An Empirical Enquiry among Participants at the Parliament of the World's Religions

Introduction

Even in the twenty-first century religion remains a matter of considerable importance in world politics and in the public sphere (see Francis and Ziebertz, 2010). The importance of religion is both complex and paradoxical. Wellman and Tokuno (2004, 291) capture the paradox succinctly: 'Religion brings war. Religion brings peace'. In twenty-first century world politics religion seems, on the one hand, to be fuelling conflict, oppression, and terrorism; and, on the other hand, to be motivating reconciliation, liberation, and humanitarian aid.

Whether religion emerges as a power for good or as a force for evil may not be an arbitrary accident. The religious educator may yet hold a formative role. For the role to be realized the religious educator needs to understand the distinguishing characteristics of different self-understandings of religious people. The thesis of the present chapter is that the theology of religions is central to appreciating different self-understandings of religious people, and that different approaches to the theology of religions can be traced (at least in part) to fundamental psychological differences among religious adherents. This thesis is tested and supported by an empirical enquiry among the participants to the Parliament of the World's Religions in Barcelona, Spain, during 2004.

Theology of religions

The theology of religions is concerned with the way in which religions understand and evaluate claims to special revelation and to truth within their own tradition, and the way in which religions understand and evaluate claims to special revelation and to truth within other traditions. The issue is not simply to do with how one religion (say Christianity) views another religion (say Islam), but also with how one strand within a religion (say Roman Catholicism) views another strand within the same religion (say Anglicanism). If, for example, Christianity keeps tightly to the claim that Jesus holds the sole key to salvation, it might be argued that the Islamic tradition may be null and void. If, for example, Roman Catholicism keeps tightly to the claim that the Petrine Successor holds the sole key to salvation, it might be argued that the Anglican tradition may be null and void.

In a series of studies, Ziebertz (1993, 1995, 1996, 2003, 2005, 2007) has distinguished between four positions that characterize the ways in which religious traditions may view one another. He describes these positions as exclusivism, inclusivism, multireligiosity, and interreligiosity (see also van der Ven, 1994; Vermeer and van der Ven, 2004). Exclusivism is based on the conviction that God can only be experienced in, and salvation can only be accessed through, one's own religious tradition. Other traditions have no access to God. Inclusivism is also based on the assumption that God can only be fully experienced and salvation can only be fully accessed through one's own tradition, but accepts the idea that other traditions may have partial access to God. Multireligiosity accepts all religions as equal and does not see the difference between them as being of real importance. Here is a syncretistic model. Interreligiosity also sees all religions as equal, but takes the differences between religions seriously. Here is a pluralistic model that seeks to find the truth in the dialogue among the religions.

Parliament of the World's Religions

The Parliament of the World's Religions offers an interesting context in which to explore a variety of positions within the theologies of religion.

The first Parliament of the World's Religions was held in Chicago in 1893, and the centennial was marked by another Parliament in Chicago in 1993 (Seager, 1996). Subsequent Parliaments were held in 1999 (Cape Town, South Africa), in 2004 (Barcelona, Spain), and in 2009 (Melbourne, Australia). According to the 1993 Executive Summary, that Parliament was attended by around 5,500 individuals, representing a total of 55 nations and 60 religions (Parliament, 1993a).

The ethos of the Parliament is summed up in two documents that emerged from the 1993 and 1999 meetings: *Toward a global ethic* (an initial declaration) (Parliament, 1993b) and *A call to our guiding institutions* (Parliament, 1999). The 1993 document made the following claim.

> We affirm that a common set of core values is found in the teachings of religions, and that these form the basis of a global ethic ... There already exist ancient guidelines for human behaviour which are found in the teachings of the religions of the world and which are the condition for a sustainable world order. (Parliament, 1993b, 2)

The 1993 document proceeded to identify four 'irrevocable directives' that emerge from 'most' of the world's religions:

> Commitment to a culture of non-violence and respect for life; commitment to a culture of solidarity and a just economic order; commitment to a culture of tolerance and a life of truthfulness; commitment to a culture of equal rights and partnership between men and women. (Parliament, 1993b, 8)

Following the Chicago Parliament of 1993, Teasdale and Cairns (1996) edited a collection of essays that provide a valuable record of that event, containing major addresses and reflections as well as short evocations of the spirit of the Parliament. In the opening chapter, His Holiness the Dalai Lama, XIV, one of the twenty-four presidents of the Parliament's Assembly, offered the following aspiration.

> The Parliament of the World's Religions encourages us to meet in an atmosphere of mutual respect to exchange our experiences and learn from each other. It is my prayer that by doing so we shall all contribute to a genuinely more peaceful and amicable world. (21)

It is this expressed openness to the dialogue between religions that suggests that a study among participants at the Parliament may provide a good context in which to sample a range of positions within theologies of religions and to test the association between different theological positions and different psychological types.

In a preliminary analysis of the views of participants at Barcelona, 2004, Francis, Robbins, and Cargas (2010) found a wide range of positions represented. For example, 15 per cent said that their own religious tradition is the only true source for truth; 27 per cent said that knowledge of God is most fully achieved through their own religious tradition; and 74 per cent said that knowledge of God should be sought through many religious traditions.

Psychological type

Psychological type theory has its origins in the pioneering work of Carl Jung (see Jung, 1971) and has been operationalized in ways appropriate for empirical research within the individual differences tradition of psychology through instruments such as the Myers-Brigg Type Indicator (Myers and McCaulley, 1985), the Kiersey Temperament Sorter (Keirsey and Bates, 1978), and the Francis Psychological Type Scales (Francis, 2005). In essence psychological type theory distinguishes between two orientations (styled introversion and extraversion), two perceiving processes (styled sensing and intuition), two judging processes (styled thinking and feeling), and two attitudes toward the outer world (styled judging and perceiving).

Within the broad field of the empirical psychology of religion, psychological type theory has been used in two creative ways. First, it has been used to profile religious professionals and religious communities. Pioneering work among religious professionals was published in such studies as Cabral (1984), Harbaugh (1984), Holsworth (1984), and Bigelow, Fitzgerald, Bask, Girault, and Avis (1988). More recent studies have been reported by Francis, Payne, and Jones (2001), Craig, Duncan and Francis (2006), Francis, Craig, Whinney, Tilley, and Slater (2007), and Burton, Francis, and Robbins (2010). These studies have demonstrated some highly significant type differences between religious professionals and the population norms. Pioneering work among church congregations was published in studies by Gerhardt (1983), Delis-Bulhoes (1990), and Ross (1993, 1995). More recent studies have been reported by Francis, Duncan, Craig, and Luffman (2004), Francis, Robbins, Williams, and Williams (2007), and Francis, Robbins, and Craig (under review). These studies have demonstrated both some highly significant differences between church congregations and the population from which they are drawn, and between church congregations and the religious professionals who lead them.

Second, psychological type theory has been used to explore the association between personality and different ways of expressing religious commitment and religious belief (see Francis, 2009). Two examples of this kind of enquiry have focused on two forms of religious experience: charismatic experience and mystical experience. Research on psychological type and charismatic experience has been published by Francis and Jones (1997), and Jones, Francis, and Craig (2005). Charismatic experience tends to be higher among extraverts, thinkers, and perceivers. Research on psychological type and mystical experience has been published by Francis and Louden (2000), Francis (2002), and Francis, Village, Robbins, and Ineson (2007). The most secure conclusion to emerge from these studies is that mystical experience is associated with the perceiving process: intuitive types are more open than sensing types to mystical orientation.

Research hypothesis

Against the background of previous research exploring the association between psychological type and individual differences in religious commitment and religious belief, specific hypotheses can be advanced regarding the ways in which an exclusivist position within the theology of religions may be related to psychological type.

First, the perceiving process (sensing and intuition) has been identified by Francis and Ross (1997) as the core psychological construct in shaping differences in religious expression. According to the theory, sensing types tend to focus on specific details rather than on the overall picture. They are concerned with the practical and tend to be down to earth and matter of fact. They are fond of the traditional and the conventional. They may tend to be conservative. Intuitive types focus on the overall picture rather than on specific facts. They follow their inspirations with enthusiasm and aspire to bring innovative change to established conventions. The first hypothesis is that intuitive types will be more willing than sensing types to challenge and to overthrow the exclusivism of traditional religious expression.

Second, the judging process (thinking and feeling) has been identified by Francis and Jones (1998) as the core psychological construct in shaping differences in religious belief. According to the theory, thinking types make decisions by using objective, analytical logic. They consider conforming to principles to be of more importance than cultivating harmony. They are often good at making difficult decisions about systems because they give more priority to the integrity of the system than to its impact on people. Feeling types make decisions by using subjective, personal values. They are more concerned to promote harmony than to adhere to abstract principles. They may be thought of as 'people persons', as they take into account other people's feelings and values in their own decision-making and problem-solving. They may find it difficult to criticize others, even when it is necessary. The second hypothesis is that feeling types will be more willing than thinking types to re-evaluate their own belief-systems in order to accommodate people of other faith persuasions.

Third, the attitude toward the outer world (judging and perceiving) identifies which of these two processes individuals prefer to use in the outer world. According to the theory, judging types enjoy routine and established patterns. They like their outer world to be systematic and ordered. They find it difficult to deal with unexpected interruptions to their plans. They are inclined to be resistant to changes to established methods. Perceiving types present a spontaneous and explorative attitude toward the outer world. They may find plans and schedules restrictive and tend to be easy-going about issues such as punctuality, deadlines, and tidiness. They may welcome change and variety, as routine bores them. The third hypothesis is that perceiving types will be more willing than judging types to take a flexible and open view of the relations between religions and less likely to hold on to an exclusivist position.

Fourth, the orientation (introversion and extraversion) identifies a person's preferred energy source. Extraverts focus their energy on and gain their energy from the outside world of people and things. They enjoy communicating and thrive in stimulating and exciting environments. They prefer to act in a situation rather than to reflect on it. They may wish to talk issues through with others rather than to think them through privately. Introverts focus their energy on and gain their energy from their inner world of ideas and reflections. They may feel drained by events and people around them and they prefer to reflect on a situation rather than to act on it. They enjoy solitude, silence, and contemplation. They may prefer to have a small circle of friends rather than many acquaintances. Since there is no *prima facie* reason for linking the orientations with theological beliefs, the fourth hypothesis is that extraverts and introverts will hold similar levels of attachment to the exclusivist position.

Within the context of psychological type theory, these hypotheses can be tested in two ways. The first step takes each of the four components of psychological type separately and explores the levels of attachment to the exclusivist position between introverts and extraverts, between sensing types and intuitive types, between thinking types and feeling types, and between judging types and perceiving types. The second step draws on Jung's theory of type dynamics to identify the role of the dominant and auxiliary functions (see Francis, 2005). The theory of type dynamics suggests that each individual develops one of the four functions (sensing, intuition, thinking, or feeling) more strongly than the others. This is the *dominant* function that does much to shape the individual's personality. Dominant sensing is seen in the practical person; dominant intuition is seen in the imaginative person; dominant thinking is seen in the logical person; dominant feeling is seen in the humane person. The dominant function is then supported by the *auxiliary* function, the individual's second most developed function. The auxiliary function complements the dominant function from the other process (judging, perceiving). If Francis and Ross (1997) were correct in identifying the perceiving process (the sensing function and the intuitive function) as the core psychological construct in shaping differences in religious expression, the fifth hypothesis is that the key distinction in levels of attachment to the exclusivist position should be reflected in the distinction between sensing and intuition in both the dominant and auxiliary positions.

Method

Procedure

A substantial questionnaire was distributed to participants attending the 2004 convention of the Parliament of the World's Religions convened in Barcelona by representatives of the International Interfaith Centre at Oxford (IIC). Participants were assured of complete confidentiality and anonymity, and invited to approach the team at the IIC table in the exhibition hall if they had questions about the project. Those who returned completed questionnaires to the IIC table received a free rucksack. A total of 580 questionnaires were returned that included no missing data for the variables under consideration.

Sample

The 580 respondents comprised: 229 men, 342 women, and 9 individuals of undisclosed sex; 29 individuals under the age of twenty, 102 in their twenties, 64 in their thirties, 98 in their forties, 145 in their fifties, 108 in their sixties, 31 aged seventy or over, and 3 of undisclosed age. Of the ten religious traditions listed in the questionnaire, 284 individuals self-identified as Christians, 37 as Hindus, 35 as Buddhists, 22 as Muslims, 21 as Sikhs, 21 as Pagans, 19 as Baha'is, 14 as Jews, 5 as Jains, and 4 as Zoroastrians. Nearly half of the participants in the survey were born in the USA (273); with the next largest group coming from Spain, the host nation (60), UK (44), Canada (27), and India (29). The remaining participants identified a total of sixty other countries.

Measures

Psychological type was assessed by the Francis Psychological Type Scales (FPTS: Francis, 2005). This forty-item instrument comprises four sets of ten forced-choice items related to each of the four components of psychological type: orientation (extraversion or introversion), perceiving process (sensing or intuition), judging process (thinking or feeling), and attitude toward the outer world (judging or perceiving). Recent studies have demonstrated this instrument to function well in church-related contexts. For example, Francis, Craig, and Hall (2008) reported alpha coefficients of .83 for the EI scale, .76 for the SN scale, .73 for the TF scale, and .79 for the JP scale.

Theology of religions was assessed by an eleven-item scale designed for the present study (see table 12.2). Each item was assessed on a five-point Likert scale: agree strongly, agree, not certain, disagree, and disagree strongly. The scale, coded so that a high score reflected an exclusivist position, was named the Francis Index of Theological Exclusivism (FITE).

Analysis

The data were analysed by the SPSS statistical package employing the following routines: frequencies, correlations, reliabilities, t-test, and ANOVA.

Results

All four scales of the Francis Psychological Type Scales recorded satisfactory levels of internal consistency reliability, generating the following alpha coefficients (Cronbach, 1951): EI .79; SN .65; TF .64; JP .71. Table 12.1 presents the frequencies of the sixteen complete types as recorded by the Francis Psychological Type Scales. These data demonstrate that, overall, participants at the Parliament for the World's Religions tend to prefer introversion (54 per cent) over extraversion (46 per cent), intuition (57 per cent) over sensing (43 per cent), feeling (62 per cent) over thinking (38 per cent), and judging (73 per cent) over perceiving (27 per cent).

Table 12.1 The sixteen complete psychological types

Introvert types	N	%	Extravert types	N	%
ISTJ	57	9.8	ESTP	4	0.7
ISFJ	45	7.8	ESFP	16	2.8
INFJ	69	11.9	ENFP	50	8.6
INTJ	66	11.4	ENTP	11	1.9
ISTP	7	1.2	ESTJ	36	6.2
ISFP	11	1.9	ESFJ	73	12.6
INFP	45	7.8	ENFJ	53	9.1
INTP	15	2.6	ENTJ	22	3.8

Table 12.2 presents the eleven-item Francis Index of Theological Exclusivism (FITE), together with the correlation between each item and the sum total of the remaining ten items, and the percentage endorsement (as the sum of the agree and agree strongly responses). The internal consistency reliability of this instrument was supported by an alpha coefficient of .82. These data demonstrate that a sufficient number of participants at the Parliament of the World's Religions endorsed the exclusivist items to ensure that a full range of theological opinion was expressed by the sample.

Table 12.2 The Francis Index of Theological Exclusivism (FITE): correlation coefficients for each item with the rest of test and item endorsement

	r	%
My religious/spiritual tradition is the only true source for Truth/Enlightenment	.61	15
My religious/spiritual tradition is the only true source for knowledge about God	.67	7
My religious/spiritual tradition is the ultimate source for knowledge about God	.64	16
Other religious/spiritual traditions are inferior to my own	.53	8
Knowledge of God is most fully achieved through my religious/spiritual tradition	.44	26
Many religions/spiritual traditions can lead people to Truth/Enlightenment*	.43	87
Many religious/spiritual traditions have valuable knowledge about God*	.46	89
Many religious/spiritual traditions can lead people to union with God*	.53	82
Truth/Enlightenment should be sought through many religious/spiritual traditions*	.30	68
Knowledge about God should be sought through many religious/spiritual traditions*	.34	72
God reveals truth in more than one religious/spiritual tradition*	.51	83

NOTE: * These items were reverse coded to calculate the correlation coefficient.

Table 12.3 presents the mean scores recorded on the Francis Index of Theological Exclusivism according to the dichotomous psychological type preferences recorded by the participants. These data demonstrate that higher levels of theological exclusivism are expressed by sensing types than by intuitive types, by judging types than by perceiving types, and by thinking types than by feeling types. On the other hand, no significant differences in scores distinguish between introverts and extraverts.

Table 12.3 Mean FITE scores by dichotomous type preferences

Comparisons	N	Mean	SD	F	p <
Extraversion	365	21.8	7.1		
Introversion	315	20.8	6.7	1.8	NS
Sensing	249	23.1	7.3		
Intuition	331	19.9	6.2	5.7	.001
Thinking	218	22.1	6.9		
Feeling	362	20.7	6.8	2.3	.050
Judging	421	22.0	7.0		
Perceiving	159	19.2	6.0	4.4	.001

Table 12.4 takes the analysis one step further by examining the mean scores recorded on the Francis Index of Theological Exclusivism according to the dominant type preferences recorded by the participants. These data demonstrate that the highest scores of theological exclusivism are recorded by dominant sensing types and the lowest scores are recorded by dominant intuitive types.

Table 12.4 Mean FITE scores by dominant type preferences

Dominants	N	Mean	SD	F	p <
Thinking	80	22.0	7.3		
Feeling	182	21.4	7.0		
Sensing	122	22.6	7.0		
Intuition	196	19.9	6.4	4.7	.01

Table 12.5 completes the analysis by examining the mean scores recorded on the Francis Index of Theological Exclusivism according to the dominant and auxiliary type preferences. These data demonstrate that

the range of scores is somewhat wider than when the dominant type preference was discussed in isolation. According to table 12.5, the four highest mean scores are all associated with sensing, either in the dominant or the auxiliary position. The two lowest mean scores are both associated with feeling and intuition, either in the dominant or the auxiliary position. The type least likely to endorse the exclusivist position is dominant intuition with auxiliary feeling.

Table 12.5 Mean FITE scores by dominant and auxiliary type preferences

Comparisons	N	Mean	SD	F	$p <$
Dominant feeling with sensing	84	23.7	7.6		
Dominant thinking with sensing	43	23.2	7.5		
Dominant sensing with thinking	61	22.6	6.9		
Dominant sensing with feeling	61	22.6	7.1		
Dominant intuition with thinking	77	21.7	6.6		
Dominant thinking with intuition	37	20.7	6.9		
Dominant feeling with intuition	98	19.5	5.8		
Dominant intuition with feeling	119	18.7	6.0	6.3	.001

Conclusion

The present study set out to test the thesis that the particular position adopted by individuals on the theology of religions was related (to some extent) to their individual psychological type profile. More specifically, four hypotheses were advanced that commitment to the exclusivist position would be:

- higher among sensing types than among intuitive types;
- higher among thinking types than among feeling types;
- higher among judging types than among perceiving types;
- equal among introverts and among extraverts.

The thesis was tested on data provided by 580 participants at the Parliament of the World's Religions in Barcelona in 2004, who completed the Francis Psychological Type Scales and the Francis Index of Theological Exclusivism. The data supported each of the four hypotheses. Higher exclusivism scores were recorded by sensing types than by intuitive types. Higher exclusivism scores were recorded by thinking types than by feeling types. Higher exclusivism scores were recorded by judging types than by perceiving types. No significant differences were found between the exclusivism scores recorded by extraverts and by introverts.

Going beyond the binary type preferences the data also highlighted some of the particular combinations of type components associated with higher and with lower exclusivism scores. In particular, higher exclusivism scores were associated with the sensing preferences in either the dominant or auxiliary function. Lower exclusivism scores were associated with the combination of feeling and intuition: either as dominant feeling with auxiliary intuition or as dominant intuition with auxiliary feeling.

Two main conclusions can be drawn from these finding. The first is that some of the variance in individual differences in positions taken on the theology of religions can be attributed to more basic psychological factors. What appears initially to be presented as a theological issue needs to be reconceptualized (at least in part) as a personality issue. When theological educators are challenging individuals to rethink their positions on exclusivity they may anticipate greater reluctance and greater resistance on the part of some psychological types than on the part of other psychological types. They may be attacking a more fundamental psychological structure than is first apparent.

The second conclusion concerns the broader value of psychological type theory within the empirical psychology of religion. The present study has provided one further example of the way in which psychological type theory is able to generate well-grounded and testable hypotheses regarding the expression of individual differences in religious beliefs. Moreover, the empirical data supported the hypotheses.

The present study is, nonetheless, vulnerable to four criticisms which in turn may lead to further research. The first criticism is that specific claims have been made about the association between theological exclusivism and psychological type among participants at the Parliament of the World's Religions based on just one sample survey concluded in 2004. This criticism can be addressed by replicating the research among participants at the subsequent meetings of the Parliament.

The second criticism is that the Parliament of the World's Religions may provide a highly distinctive group of people and that the findings could not be generalized to other constituencies. This criticism can be addressed by replicating the research among other groups, say the membership of the International Seminar on Religious Education and Values.

The third criticism is that the sample was highly diverse in terms of both national identity and of religious identity, and that the analysis did not check the association between psychological type profile and either national origins or religious affiliation. The data set was not large enough to allow such analyses to be meaningful. This criticism could be addressed by accumulating data at the Parliament of the World's Religions over a number of years.

The fourth criticism concerns the way in which the thesis was tested by just one instrument focusing on one specific perspective within the spectrum of theologies of religions, namely the exclusivist position. This criticism could be addressed by the careful development of a more sophisticated and better nuanced battery of scales. Here is a visionary objective for a much more detailed research project that would require substantial funding.

References

Bigelow, E. D., Fitzgerald, R., Busk, P., Girault, E., and Avis, J. (1988). Psychological characteristics of Catholic sisters: Relationships between the MBTI and other measures. *Journal of Psychological Type, 14*, 32–36.

Burton, L., Francis, L. J., and Robbins, M. (2010). Psychological type profile of Methodist circuit ministers in Britain: Similarities with and differences from Anglican clergy. *Journal of Empirical Theology, 23*, 64–81.

Cabral, G. (1984). Psychological types in a Catholic convent: Applications to community living and congregational data. *Journal of Psychological Type, 8*, 16–22.

Craig, C. L., Duncan, B., and Francis, L. J. (2006). Psychological type preferences of Roman Catholic priests in the United Kingdom. *Journal of Beliefs and Values, 27*, 157–164.

Cronbach, L. J. (1951). Coefficient alpha and the internal structure of tests. *Psychometrika, 16*, 297–334.

Delis-Bulhoes, V. (1990). Jungian psychological types and Christian belief in active church members. *Journal of Psychological Type, 20*, 25–33.

Francis, L. J. (2002). Psychological type and mystical orientation: Anticipating individual differences within congregational life. *Pastoral Sciences, 21*, 77–99.

Francis, L. J. (2005). *Faith and psychology: Personality, religion and the individual*. London: Darton, Longman and Todd.

Francis, L. J. (2009). Psychological type theory and religious and spiritual experience. In M. de Souza, L. J. Francis, J. O'Higgins-Norman, and D. G. Scott (eds), *International handbook of education for spirituality, care and wellbeing* (pp. 125–146). Dordrecht: Springer.

Francis, L. J., Craig, C. L., and Hall, G. (2008). Psychological type and attitude toward Celtic Christianity among committed churchgoers in the United Kingdom: An empirical study. *Journal of Contemporary Religion, 23*, 181–191.

Francis, L. J., Craig, C. L., Whinney, M., Tilley, D., and Slater, P. (2007). Psychological profiling of Anglican clergy in England: Employing Jungian typology to interpret diversity, strengths, and potential weaknesses in ministry. *International Journal of Practical Theology, 11*, 266–284.

Francis, L. J., Duncan, B., Craig, C. L., and Luffman, G. (2004). Type patterns among Anglican congregations in England. *Journal of Adult Theological Education, 1*, 66–77.

Francis, L. J., and Jones, S. H. (1997). Personality and charismatic experience among adult Christians. *Pastoral Psychology, 45*, 421–428.

Francis, L. J., and Jones, S. H. (1998). Personality and Christian belief among adult churchgoers. *Journal of Psychological Type, 47*, 5–11.

Francis, L. J., and Louden, S. H. (2000). Mystical orientation and psychological type: A study among student and adult churchgoers. *Transpersonal Psychology Review, 4* (1), 36–42.

Francis, L. J., Payne, V. J., and Jones, S. H. (2001). Psychological types of male Anglican clergy in Wales. *Journal of Psychological Type, 56*, 19–23.

Francis, L. J., Robbins, M., and Cargas, S. (2010). The Parliament of the World's Religions, who goes and why? An empirical study of Barcelona 2004. *Journal of Beliefs and Values, 31*, 143–153.

Francis, L. J., Robbins, M., and Craig, C. L. (under review). The psychological type profile of Anglican churchgoers in England: Compatible or incompatible with their clergy?

Francis, L. J., Robbins, M., Williams, A., and Williams, R. (2007). All types are called, but some are more likely to respond: The psychological profile of rural Anglican churchgoers in Wales. *Rural Theology, 5*, 23–30.

Francis, L. J., and Ross, C. F. J. (1997). The perceiving function and Christian spirituality: Distinguishing between sensing and intuition. *Pastoral Sciences, 16*, 93–103.

Francis, L. J., Village, A., Robbins, M., and Ineson, K. (2007). Mystical orientation and psychological type: An empirical study among guests staying at a Benedictine Abbey. *Studies in Spirituality, 17*, 207–223.

Francis, L. J., and Zierbetz, H-G. (2010). *The public significance of religion*. Leiden: Brill.

Gerhardt, R. (1983). Liberal religion and personality type. *Research in Psychological Type, 6*, 47–53.

Harbaugh, G. L. (1984). The person in ministry: Psychological type and the seminary. *Journal of Psychological Type, 8*, 23–32.

Holsworth, T. E. (1984). Type preferences among Roman Catholic seminarians. *Journal of Psychological Type, 8*, 33–35.

Jones, S. H., Francis, L. J., and Craig, C. L. (2005). Charismatic experience and psychological type: An empirical enquiry. *Journal of the European Pentecostal Theological Association, 25*, 39–53.

Jung, C. G. (1971). *Psychological types: The collected works*. Vol. 6. London: Routledge and Kegan Paul.

Keirsey, D., and Bates, M. (1978). *Please understand me*. Del Mar, California: Prometheus Nemesis.

Myers, I. B., and McCaulley, M. H. (1985). *Manual: A guide to the development and use of the Myers-Briggs Type Indicator*. Palo Alto, California: Consulting Psychologists Press.

Parliament (1993a). *Executive summary: 1993 Parliament of the World's Religions*. Chicago, Illinios: Council for the Parliament of the World's Religions.

Parliament (1993b). *Toward a global ethic: An initial declaration*. Chicago, Illinois: Council for the Parliament of the World's Religions.

Parliament (1999). *A call to our guiding institutions*. Chicago, Illinios: Council for the Parliament of the World's Religions.

Ross, C. F. J. (1993). Type patterns among active members of the Anglican church: Comparisons with Catholics, Evangelicals and clergy. *Journal of Psychological Type, 26*, 28–35.

Ross, C. F. J. (1995). Type patterns among Catholics: Four Anglophone congregations compared with Protestants, Francophone Catholics and priests. *Journal of Psychological Type, 33*, 33–41.

Seager, R. H. (1996). The two Parliaments, the 1893 original and the centennial of 1993: A historian's view. In W. Teasdale and G. Cairns (eds). *The community of religions: Voices and images of the Parliament of the World's Religions* (pp. 22–33). New York: Continuum.

Teasdale, W., and Cairns, G. G. (eds). (1996). *The community of religions: Voices and images of the Parliament of the World's Religions*. New York: Continuum.

van der Ven, J. (1994). Religious values in the interreligious dialogue. *Religion and Theology, 1*, 244–260.

Vermeer, P., and Van der Ven, J. (2004). Looking at the relationship between religions: An empirical study among secondary school students. *Journal of Empirical Theology, 17*, 36–59.

Wellman, J. K., Jr., and Tokuno, K. (2004). Is religious violence inevitable? *Journal for the Scientific Study of Religion, 43*, 291–296.

Ziebertz, H.-G. (1993). Religious pluralism and religious education. *Journal of Empirical Theology, 6*, 82–99.

Ziebertz, H.-G. (1995). Jugendliche in mulitkulturellem und multireligiösem Kontext. SchülerInnen zu Modellen interreligiöser Kommunikation – ein deutsch-niederländischer Vergleich. *Religionspädagogische Beiträge, 35*, 151–167.

Ziebertz, H.-G. (1996). Religion in religious education. *Panorama: International journal of comparative religious education and values, 8*, 135–145.

Ziebertz, H.-G. (2003). Religion im Plural. Empirische Befunde zu Einstellungen Jugendlicher. In Th. Franz, and H. Sauer (eds), *Glaube in der Welt von heute. Theologie und Kirche nach dem zweiten Vatikanischen Konzil. Band 1: Profilierungen* (pp. 380–414). Würzburg: Echter.

Ziebertz, H.-G. (2005). Models of inter-religious learning: An empirical study in Germany. In L. J. Francis, M. Robbins, and J. Astley (eds), *Religion, education and adolescence: International empirical perspectives.* (pp. 204–221). Cardiff: University of Wales Press.

Ziebertz, H.-G. (2007). A move to multi? Empirical research concerning the attitudes of youth toward pluralism and religion's claims of truth. In D. Pollefeyt (ed.), *Interreligious Learning* (pp. 3–24). Leuven: Peeters.

ÜZEYIR OK

13 How Open is Muslim Youth to People of Other Faiths?

Introduction

Religious particularism connotes belief in the exclusive authenticity of one's own religious tradition. 'Religious particularists are likely to believe that salvation is confined to rather narrowly defined groups of believers' (Jelen, 2010). Accordingly, one set of religious values is seen as superior to another (Becker, 1977). The concept of religious exclusivism, which refers to more or less the same phenomenon, denotes that the adherents of a particular faith will be redeemed, whilst the rest of humanity will be deprived of such salvation or divine reward.

The opposite pole to the particularism/exclusivism position attracts labels such as interreligious pluralism (Gennerich and Huber, 2006), interreligious dialogue, or religious openness. Religious pluralists see all faiths as equal in terms of truth and none of them is seen as superior over the others. Similarly, proponents of religious dialogue emphasize the constructive power of establishing relations between members of different faiths without devaluing them. People who possess the mindset of religious openness are open to the contributions of other faiths to their own understanding of the world, and show a sincere respect for the wisdom and uniqueness of other faiths. 'They welcome the claim that truth is many sided and complex ... [and] take into account many divergent views in making difficult decisions' (Astley and Francis, 2002). As John Hick stresses, religious openness requires us to go beyond the dominant self-understanding of each tradition by de-emphasizing each religion's own absolute and exclusive claim, and seeing one's belief as one among many (Hick, 1989). An equivalent conceptualization is xenosophia (Streib and Klein, 2010). Streib argued that this is more than religious pluralism and involves 'appreciation for the creative surplus of the encounter with the alien'.

Religious exclusivism is not a social-psychological concept. However, related concepts within social psychology include prejudice, stereotyping, in-group/out-group distinction, discrimination, intolerance of ambiguity, cognitive complexity, open- versus closed-mindedness, and authoritarianism. A religiously exclusivist person could be assumed to be prejudiced against people of other faiths, closed-minded, not enjoying cognitive complexity, emphasizing the in-group/out-group distinction, and behaving in a discriminating way. Similarly, authoritarians are characterized by aggression towards minority groups, whether religious or ethnic.

Interreligious exclusion can be seen as the result of our human motivation towards being part of a social group, which creates an 'us' versus 'them' division. It is possible to speculate about its likely causes. Behind the exclusivistic attitude may lie what is called *intergroup anxiety*: that is, feeling discomfort in interaction with those who do not belong to one's own faith group. This may be a projection of perceived generalization about out-groups stemming from the illusion of seeing out-groups as homogenous, either all-good or all-bad. In addition, people often exaggerate the differences between the values of their own group and those of others (Stephan and Stephan, 2007). Another factor could be a strong need for belonging to one's own group or a salient internalization of its norms, which may lead people to see out-groups as inferior compared with in-groups, a phenomenon called 'in-group bias'. Through excluding others, people benefit from holding resources or rewards for themselves, in which case the reward could be seen as the blessing of God or as redemption. Furthermore, religious exclusivism provides the excluding group with a positive distinctiveness that 'may enhance the social identity and self-esteem of in-group members' (Spears, 2007).

Through religious exclusivism an exclusivist would feel protected from the evil of other faiths by belonging to a distinguished and superior group. Existential anxiety can be eliminated by strengthened group ties. 'The act of excluding can strengthen the perceived cohesiveness and power of the group. Acts of exclusion provide an immediate sense of power, control, and cohesiveness.' Theologically, by holding the monopoly of God's bountiful resources, a person may guarantee eternal redemption and be saved from personal dissonance; whereas acknowledging other faiths would mean the relativization of their own. As a result, the more insecure a person feels, and the more s/he needs to belong, the more exclusivist s/he may become. The next step in expressing an exclusive attitude is probably the act of discrimination, which may subsequently lead to aggression (Williams, Wesselman, and Chen, 2007). In contrast, those who are exposed to ostracism (being ignored and excluded) suffer from a loss of belonging, low self-esteem, lack of control, and existential meaninglessness. They may be motivated to reduce these feelings by conforming to the norms of their group, or by joining a new group (Williams and Carter-Sowell, 2007).

Religion's role with regard to tolerance and prejudice has been discussed for centuries in religious disciplines. Are religious people more prejudiced or more exclusivist than less religious or non-religious people? Religion is often found to be positively related to prejudice (Argyle, 2000; Batson, Schoenrade, and Ventis, 1993; Jacobson, 1998). In a study with a Christian sample several religiosity scales, including image of God as judge, image of God as redeemer, the schema of truth of texts and teachings, and mystical experience are positively linked to Islamophobia (Streib and Klein, 2010). In the same study men were found to be more Islamophobic than women. The relation between religion and prejudice or exclusivism is often explained, not by the content of a certain religion, but by the way religion is held by individuals. The ways in which religious exclusivism is fostered is mediated by such psychological traits as right-wing authoritarianism, closed-mindedness, dogmatism, and the need for closure (Saroglou, 2002). People with an authoritarian personality, for example, may hold antagonistic feelings to other religious minority groups (Nelson, 2007). Hunsberger maintains that it is an oversimplification to posit a clear connection between religion and prejudice. However, he acknowledges that some aspects of religion may contribute to prejudice and discrimination. This happens by religions: claiming absolute truth; teaching (at least indirectly) that other groups are inferior; stimulating nationalism; encouraging authoritarianism and in-group/out-group stereotyping; and fostering dogmatism (Hunsberger, 1995). In contrast, religiosity, in the form of orthodoxy or intrinsic religiosity, seems to show no link to openness (see Astley and Francis, 2002).

Although almost all religious groups espouse tolerance and empathy towards the members of other faiths, the world is far from experiencing interreligious peace. This inconsistency between the positive idea expressed in pencil and paper tests and the more negative overt behaviour is best explained by the factor of social desirability – the motivation to 'look good' towards others in the tests. Furthermore, the positive side of religions is expressed not as facts but as desired ideas (as a result of idealistic inspiration derived from self-selected religious texts). These are put forward mostly by intellectual religious elites, and often do not reflect the position of a wider public. Religious texts are so flexible and diverse that it is possible to find both references that support peace and tolerance towards 'others', and references that enhance intolerance, discrimination, and even war against 'enemies'. This oscillation in interpretation is determined by the different needs of people in different situations seeking different meanings.

Particularly after the US intervention in Afghanistan and other events subsequent to 9/11, there have been campaigns against Muslims across Europe and North America. Referring to the Qur'an, Islamic faith was blamed as a faith of brutality and aggression, and their societies or lifestyles scorned. On some occasions, these campaigns led to physical aggression. The concept of Islamophobia came into common parlance, and relationships with Muslims viewed with close scrutiny. In the context of such a global climate, it is worth investigating how Muslim youth sees people of other faiths: with tolerance and dialogue, or with prejudice and discrimination?

There are relatively few studies on how Muslims see non-Muslims. In one study done with University students in Turkey, both Jews and Christians were seen as heretics by 24 per cent of Muslim students, and 28–35 per cent refused to live in proximity to a Jewish or a Christian family (Yapici, 2004). In the same study, religiosity and dogmatism were found to be linked to exclusivism. Yapici and Kayiklik (2005) found a relatively high positive correlation between religious orientation and religious particularism ($.45, p < .001$). Similarly, negative correlations were found between religious orientation and proximity to Christians and to Jews ($-.52$ and $-.56, p < .001$). A positive correlation between religiosity and exclusivism was also reported in a secondary school sample (Özdemir, 2004) and a university sample (Ok, 2006).

In another large sample (n=1644), it was reported that, while 88 per cent of young adults are against restricting freedom of religious belief, 9 per cent proposed that this right should be restricted when required (Yilmaz, 2005). Similarly, while 71 per cent are against forcing others to believe and practise religion in the same way as they do themselves, 10 per cent are in favour of such enforcement. This shows that around 9–10 per cent are in favour of restricting religious freedom when required, and/or forcing others to believe in the same way as they do themselves. This act of enforcement could be seen as expressing the extreme edge of exclusivism. In brief, religiosity in its conventional form is often positively correlated with religious exclusivism in both Christian and Muslim samples. This is obviously not consistent with the peaceful messages of these religious traditions, as claimed by many of their adherents.

The aim of the present study is to investigate the extent of both interreligious exclusivism and dialogue among Muslim adolescents in Turkey, and their relation to religiosity. What is the extent of religious exclusivism and interreligious dialogue among Muslim youths? What is the relation between religiosity and interreligious attitudes?

Method

Research tools

This study is part of a survey which was originally designed for the study of human rights and religiosity in an intercultural and international project run by Hans van der Ven of Radboud University in Nijmegen, The Netherlands. The survey was translated into Turkish from its English version by the project team, and the translation was revised and modified, where required, by the author and one of his colleagues.

For the purposes of this study, the survey contained scales on interreligious attitudes: namely, interreligious pluralism, interreligious dialogue, and interreligious exclusivism. Religiosity variables included scales of religious saliency, religious openness, and religious stress (uncertainty and contradiction). The last two scales were added to the instrument by the author (see Tables 13.2 and 13.4 for the items). The Religious Saliency Scale included items related to the effect of religion as a whole on one's life, and items related to one's relation to God and one's belief in Muhammad as God's messenger. The Religious Openness Scale was constructed with four items from Streib's Religious Schema Scale (RSS) (see Streib, Hood, and Klein, 2010) and one item from the initial item pool of RSS. A Religious Stress Scale was built from a set of selected items from the religious conflict scale developed by Funk (1967).

The survey also contained Eysenck's well known model of personality with four scales: i.e., psychoticism, neuroticism, extraversion, and the lie scale (Eysenck and Eysenck, 1991). However, because of the low alpha scores, the psychoticism and lie scales were dropped from the analysis. Demographic variables included gender and age.

All scales were constructed as Likert scales with five options ranging from strongly disagree to strongly agree, except for the personality scales which used the options of yes and no.

Participants and procedure

The survey was distributed to 422 students in two secondary schools in a rural Turkish city. They were invited to contribute to the survey in group sessions in their classrooms, and were told to feel free not to participate if they did not want to do so. Few withdrew. The survey was distributed to the students and after around forty-five minutes collected after the session. The ages of the respondents ranged from thirteen to eighteen (the average age was 15.41, sd=1.18). Around 52 per cent of the respondents were male (n=220) and 48 per cent female (n=201).

Results

Intercorrelation of the dependent and independent variables and their descriptive statistics can be seen in Table 13.1.

The Cronbach Alpha reliability scores of the scales are more or less satisfactory in light of the number of items (numbers in brackets). As may be seen from both mean scores and positive mean percentage scores, Religious Saliency was found to be highest with a mean of 4.46 followed by Interreligious Exclusivism (m=3.76). Religious Openness took third place, followed by Interreligious Dialogue.

Religious Saliency negatively correlated with Interreligious Pluralism ($-.25, p < .001$) and did not correlate with Interreligious Dialogue. It was positively and strongly linked to Interreligious Exclusivism ($.55, p < .001$). By contrast, Religious Openness was positively correlated with Interreligious Pluralism (.31) and Interreligious Dialogue (.49); it showed no correlation to Interreligious Exclusivism. Religious Stress showed a positive correlation to Interreligious Pluralism (.33) and Interreligious Dialogue (.12), and a negative correlation to Interreligious Exclusivism (-.33). Finally, Neuroticism was weakly but positively correlated with Religious Openness. To give a rough idea of the distribution of responses to the items of interreligious attitudes, the percentages of the responses to the items of interreligious attitudes were introduced in Table 13.2.

Table 13.2 shows that the percentages of positive answers given to the items of Interreligious Exclusivism is rather high, ranging from 58 to 74, while the percentage of responses to Interreligious Pluralism is rather low, ranging from 13 to 21. In contrast, the affirmative responses given to Interreligious Dialogue is somewhat below the halfway mark, namely around 43 to 44.

Table 13.1 Correlational matrix of variables

	M	SD	Alpha	%*	Saliency	Openness	Stress	Pluralism	Dialogue	Exclusivism	Neuroticism
Religious Saliency	4.46	0.56	.86(8)	93.4							
Religious Openness	3.54	0.59	.62(5)	51.4	.01						
Religious Stress	1.94	0.81	.83(6)	05.7	-.41**	.19**					
Interreligious Pluralism	2.39	0.89	.78(3)	11.1	-.25**	.31**	.33**				
Interreligious Dialogue	3.23	0.88	.81(3)	40.5	.07	.49**	.12*	.38**			
Interreligious Exclusivism	3.76	0.93	.81(3)	63.7	.55**	-.07	-.33**	-.37**	-.15**		
Neuroticism	3.39	1.10	.75(6)	45.3	-.04	.12*	.09	.05	.05	.07	
Extraversion	3.58	1.27	.77(6)	62.0	-.02	.02	.06	.00	.05	-.03	-.18**

* As a rule of thumb, % represents the mean percentages of the responses which are >. 3.49 on a five-point Likert scale.

How Open is Muslim Youth to People of Other Faiths?

Table 13.2 Items of Interreligious Exclusivism, Interreligious Dialogue and Interreligious Pluralism, along with response percentages

The Scales of Interreligious Attitudes	Agree* %	Uncertain %	Disagree* %
Interreligious Exclusivism			
My religion or world view is the only access to authentic life	74.1	16.7	9.2
My religion or world view offers the only path for authentic life	64.6	18.9	11.9
Only in my religion or world view can people receive authentic life.	58.1	20.2	21.7
Interreligious Dialogue			
Authentic life can only be received through conversation between religions or world views	43.2	37.7	19.1
Authentic life can only be found when religions or world views communicate with one another.	44.2	32.8	23.0
The way to authentic life is only to be found when religions or world views have dialogue with one another.	43.4	34.2	24.4
Interreligious Pluralism			
Religions or world views are all equal, they are all directed to authentic life	13.1	26.0	61.0
All religions or world views are equally valuable, they represent different ways to authentic life.	21.0	23.9	55.0
There is no difference between religions or world views, they all stem from a longing for authentic life.	17.1	25.1	57.8

* *Agree strongly* responses have been combined with *agree* responses and *disagree* responses have been combined with *disagree strongly* responses.

In order to check whether the correlations between religious saliency and interreligious attitudes are spurious or not, the data were also subjected to multiple regression analysis, controlling for the effects of age, gender, extraversion, neuroticism, religious openness, and religious stress; with Interreligious Exclusivism and Interreligious Dialogue as dependent variables. This was done in two steps in each case. In the first step the effects of age, gender, and two personality factors were taken into account; and in the second step religious openness and religious stress were added into the model.

The results of this multiple regression analysis (Table 13.3) showed that men, people with less personal stability, and those with more religious saliency tend to be more exclusivist than do women, people with more personal stability, and people with less religiosity. By contrast, younger, more religious and more open adolescents tend to be more welcoming of interreligious dialogue than do older, less religious, and less open adolescents. An important point is that the lack of correlation between religious saliency and interreligious dialogue evaporates when introducing religious stress and/or religious openness into the model. This could mean that, in order to be open to religious dialogue, religious people should pass through a period of religious stress or have the experience of interreligious pluralism. It has already been seen in the correlation matrix that Interreligious Dialogue has positive correlations with both Religious Openness and Religious Stress, and no correlation with Religious Saliency.

Table 13.3 Multiple regression significance test with Interreligious Exclusivism and Interreligious Dialogue as the dependent variables

Interreligious Exclusivism

Predictors	Step 1 Beta	t	$p <$	Step 2 Beta	t	$p <$
Age	.051	1.146	NS	.073	1.580	NS
Gender	-.115	-2.584	.005	-.098	-2.130	.005
Extraversion	.010	.220	NS	.026	.552	NS
Neuroticism	.094	2.089	.005	.112	2.394	.005
Religious Saliency	.538	12.257	.001	.508	1.085	.001
Religious Openness				-.054	-1.157	NS
Religious Stress				-.095	-1.853	NS
Adjusted R^2		.310			.320	

Interreligious Dialogue

Predictors	Step 1 Beta	t	$p <$	Step 2 Beta	t	$p <$
Age	-.141	-2.618	.005	-.118	-2.441	.005
Gender	.028	.529	NS	.006	.132	NS
Extraversion	.015	.272	NS	-.005	-.112	NS
Neuroticism	.066	1.211	NS	.006	.116	NS
Religious Saliency	.102	1.916	NS	.131	2.497	.005
Religious Openness				.485	9.906	.001
Religious Stress				.080	1.497	.135
Adjusted R^2		.020			.270	

Table 13.4 Religiosity scales

Religious Saliency
My religion or worldview has great influence on my daily life.
If I have to take important decisions, my religion or worldview plays a major part in it.
My life would be quite different, had I not my religion or worldview.
I trust God never to abandon me.
God knows and understands me.
Muhammad received special revelations which led him to announce God's message.
Muhammad was called to preach God's teachings about faith and ethical demands.
Muhammad was sent by God as his prophet in order to proclaim his message.

Religious Openness
It is important to understand others through a sympathetic understanding of their culture and religion.
When I make a decision, I am open to contradicting proposals from diverse sources and philosophical standpoints.
I like to engage in conversation with people of other faiths and cultures that contradict my own.
We can learn from each other what ultimate truth each religion contains.
We need to look beyond the denominational and religious differences to find the ultimate reality.

Religious Stress
Education has led me to question some teachings of my religion.
I feel that I should not question my religion, but I sometimes do, anyway.
I am in danger of losing my faith.
I wish I could be sure my religious beliefs are correct.
Sometimes I feel guilty because of my lack of faith.
I cannot decide what to believe on religious matters.

Discussion and conclusion

It seems that adolescents showing religious saliency tend to be particularist, rejecting interreligious pluralism, and resisting cognitive complexity. However, they tend to be open (or certainly not closed) to interreligious dialogue. The positive link between religiosity and interreligious dialogue is consistent with a previous study (see Ok, 2006) which provided low but positive correlations with interreligious dialogue/openness. The reason behind the fact that religious students do not score highly on interreligious pluralism could be that interreligious pluralism is a rather neutral, if not a secular, position which neither denies nor confirms any single faith. This may not be attractive to believers who hold certain values to be true. To them, it can be argued, if something is true then its alternatives cannot be true, in a dualistic way of thinking.

In contrast to exclusivism, openness to other faiths requires a certain level of maturity or development (Streib and Klein, 2010). Providing that adolescents are largely at the conventional stage in terms of their faith development, i.e., that they are overwhelmingly imitating the faith of their parents (Fowler, 1981), the results of the survey should be taken tentatively. Religious stress may be taken as a temporary, tension-loaded, and transitory cognitive process in the move from conventional faith towards more openness.

In the present study the levels of both interreligious dialogue and interreligious exclusivism were found to be close to one another and relatively high (3.23 and 3.76 respectively). This result is similar to that of a Muslim German sample in which the mean score was found to be higher both in exclusiveness/inclusiveness (3.58) and in pluralism/dialogue (3.22) when compared with a Christian sample which showed relatively low mean scores in both dimensions (2.23 and 2.72, respectively) (Ziebertz, 2010).

The finding in previous studies that men are more exclusivist than women was confirmed in the present study. In addition, higher openness to interreligious dialogue among early adolescents can be explained by the characteristics of two periods of adolescence, early and late adolescence. In contrast to salient conventionalism among early adolescents, a struggle towards identity achievement (and thus a rebellion against conventions and a transition from stage 3 to stage 4) starts at a later period. According to the theory of faith development, 'simple and uncritical pluralism' can be found among conventional adolescents (stage 3) and is different in nature from the pluralism of stage 5 (Fowler, 1981).

It should be pointed out that Interreligious Exclusivism has been operationalized in this study in such a way that respondents claim the uniqueness of their faith compared to those of others, but they do not necessarily exclude others, at least directly (see the items in Table 13.2). In other words, its relation to exclusivism is indirect. If the items were constructed in an apparently exclusivist way, similar to the religious proximity scales, the results could be different. In fact, the notion of exclusivism is a rather broad conception: i.e., it includes one's absolute belief in the exclusive authenticity of one's own faith compared with the faith of others. It may also involve attempts by people to distance themselves from those of other faiths in terms of land or neighbourhood. It may even represent a belief that other faiths are evil. It is therefore important to take into account the measures utilized when evaluating the results of the surveys.

Briefly, then, Turkish Muslim adolescents tend to be highly committed to their faith and, perhaps as a consequence, are more particularist or exclusivist. However, at the same time, they seem to be open to interreligious dialogue but not to interreligious pluralism, which could be taken as another indication of their interreligious exclusivism. With regard to the implications of these results for religious education, it could be argued that religious education in Turkish secondary schools needs to improve its curriculum in order to promote positive attitudes towards people with other faiths. This suggestion is consistent with the lay political structure of Turkey, in which pluralism in faith is encouraged as state policy. It is known that the social structure in Turkey is rather homogeneous in terms of faith, with nearly 98 per cent regarding themselves as Muslims. The fact that Turkish society provides a relatively limited interreligious experience may contribute to interreligious particularism.

References

Argyle, M. (2000). *Psychology and religion*. London: Routledge.
Astley, J., and Francis, L. J. (2002). Christian education and openness: An empirical investigation among undergraduates. *Religious Education*, 97, 4–22.

Batson, C. D., Schoenrade, P., and Ventis, W. L. (1993). *Religion and the individual: A social-psychological perspective.* New York: Oxford University Press.

Baumeister, R. F., and Vohs, K. D. (eds) (2007). *Encyclopedia of Social Psychology.* London: Sage.

Becker, L. B. (1977). Predictors of change in religious beliefs and behaviors during college. *Sociological Analysis, 38,* 65–74.

Eysenck, H. J., and Eysenck, S. B. G. (1991). *Manual of the Eysenck Personality Scales.* London: Hodder & Stoughton.

Fowler, J. W. (1981). *Stages of faith: The psychology of human development and the quest for meaning.* San Francisco: Harper & Row.

Funk, R. A. (1967). A survey of attitudes toward religion and philosophy of life. In M. E. Shaw and J. M. Wright (eds). *Scales for the measurement of attitudes* (pp. 345–351). New York: McGraw-Hill.

Gennerich, C., and Huber, S. (2006). Value priorities and content of religiosity: New research perspectives. *Archive for the Psychology of Religion / Archiv für Religionspychologie, 28,* 253–267.

Hick, J. (1989). *An interpretation of religion.* London: Macmillan.

Hunsberger, B. (1995). Religion and prejudice: The role of religious fundamentalism, quest, and right-wing authoritarianism. *Journal of Social Issues, 51,* 113–129.

Jacobson, C. K. (1998). Religiosity and prejudice: An update and denominational analysis. *Review of Religious Research, 39,* 204–212.

Jelen, T. G. (2010). Particularism. In *Encyclopedia of Religion and Society,* <http://hirr.hartsem.edu/ency/Particularism.htm> (accessed 21 September 2010).

Nelson, N. N. (2007). Authoritarian personality. In Baumeister and Vohs (pp. 81–83).

Ok, Ü. (2006). Faith development and perception of diversity among Muslims: Construction and initial test of a measure for religious diversity in Islam. *Din Bilimleri, 6,* 221–247.

Ozdemir, Z. (2004). *Ergenlerde dini konulara ve dini cogulculuga karsi tutum: Sivas ili örnegi.* Unpublished Graduate Essay. Cumhuriyet Universitesi, Sivas, Turkey.

Saroglou, V. (2002). Beyond dogmatism: The need for closure as related to religion. *Mental Health, Religion and Culture, 5* (2), 183–194.

Spears, R. (2007). Ingroup-outgroup bias. In Baumeister and Vohs (pp. 483–485).

Stephan, W. G., and Stephan, C. W. (2007). Intergroup anxiety. In Baumeister and Vohs (pp. 492–493).

Streib, H., and Klein, C. (2010). From xenophobia to xenosophia: New empirical evidence. Paper presented at the International Seminar on Religious Education and Values, Ottowa.

Streib, H., Hood, R., and Klein, C. (2010). The religious schema scale: Construction and initial validation of a quantitative measure for religious styles. *International Journal for the Psychology of Religion, 20* (3), 151–172.

Williams, K. D., and Carter-Sowell, A. R. (2007). Ostracism. In Baumeister and Vohs (pp. 641–643).

Williams, K. D., Wesselman, E. D., and Chen, Z. (2007). Social exclusion. In Baumeister and Vohs (pp. 896–897).

Yapici, A. (2004). *Din kimlik ve ön yargi (biz ve onlar)*. Adana: Karahan.

Yapici, A., and Kayiklik, H. (2005). Ruh sağlığı bağlamında dindarlığın özsaygı ve kaygı ile ilişkisi: Çukurova üniversite örneği. *Değerler Eğitimi Dergisi, 3*, 177–206.

Yilmaz, H. (2006). *Türkiye'de muhafazakarlık, aile, din, Batı: Ilk sonuçlar üzerine genel değerlendirme*, <http://hakanyilmaz.info/yahoo_site_admin/assets/docs/HakanYilmaz-2006Mart-TurkiyedeMuhafazakarlik-Sunus-Turkce.28465359.pdf> (accessed 15 September 2010).

Ziebertz, H.-G. (2010). Religion and the right to freedom in the perspective of Christian and Muslim youth in Germany. Paper presented at the International Seminar on Religious Education and Values, Ottawa.

PART IV

Theological Critique

JEFF ASTLEY

14 A Theological Reflection on the Nature of Religious Truth

The problem?

Both the theology of religions and the practice of religious education (RE) raise questions about the use of the word 'truth' within religious traditions, and how this might affect the different relationships that obtain between the processes of education, on the one hand, and the self-understanding and practices of the religions, on the other. My approach to these issues in this chapter is broadly theological, in the sense that it analyses notions of truth and our perception of religion from the standpoint of an ultimate salvific concern that is the touchstone of meaning in the religious life.

My main anxiety is that the experience of 'belonging to', 'practising', and 'believing' a religion should be adequately captured in any study of the religions, as they must be in the induction of people into a particular religion. I believe that there is a real danger that the theology of religions may promote an inadequate and therefore misleading view of the nature of religion that shifts the focus of religious education away from certain significant dimensions of what it is to be religious.

Most religions contain or imply a metaphysical theology about the nature and activity of ultimate reality, including transcendent beings, as well as more mundane empirical truths (e.g. truths about historical figures and events). The theology of religions frequently focuses on these truth-claims. In this context, the *religious exclusivist* is one who claims that only one belief-system is true, the *inclusivist* that his or her religion includes the truths of other belief-systems, and the *pluralist* that religious claims are all on a par with respect to truth (Basinger, 2002; D'Costa, 1986, 1990; Griffiths, 2001; Hick, 1985, 1989, 1997; Knitter, 1985).

Some scholars distinguish questions of religious truth from the question of *salvation*, briefly 'who gets saved and how' (Griffiths, 2001, 53; cf. D'Costa, 1986, 29). Thus Christian inclusivism 'separates knowing the truth from receiving salvation', by arguing that 'some (or all) of those who do not in this life come to know the truth may nevertheless, by divine grace, either be counted now as "anonymous Christians" or may receive Christian salvation in or beyond death' (Hick, 1997, 610–611; cf. 1985, 46). This distinction works best if religious truth is limited to metaphysical and empirical truths, but it does not hold in the same way when we include other important areas of religious truth such as truths relating to spirituality, morality, and religious practice – and particularly to what we may call the subjective appropriation, or 'human pole', of salvation in this life. With regard to truths regarding religious conversion, enlightenment, ways of meditation and prayer, and sanctification and acceptance of grace, claims to truth clearly concern experiences that purport to be of the divine or the ultimate *in-relation-to-us* and *now* – rather than functioning as descriptions of the divine or the ultimate in itself, or accounts of its activity beyond our present experience. When religious people claim that their salvation comes about in such-and-such a way through these practices and experiences, they may be partly answering the question, 'Who then can be saved?' In doing so, however, they may not necessarily be making a judgement about who *cannot* be saved, for *that* judgement will depend on a higher-level metaphysical claim about the existence of other pathways to salvation. Yet the theology of religions often shifts the perspective of the religious practitioner away from what she would claim to know best, her own subjective appropriation of salvation, to engage her in theologizing about what she does not in the same way directly know – the general economy of God's ways with the whole of religious humanity.

I take it, however, that religions are *essentially* salvific (Burke, 1979, 40–41; Hick 1983, 86–87, 1989, ch. 17), interpreting 'salvation' very broadly so as to include the hunger for and realization of enlightenment, liberation, or some other spiritual ideal state. Others also use this word 'as a shorthand term for the end (goal, purpose) that all of us should want', concerned with what 'life is most fundamentally and comprehensively for' (Griffiths, 2001, 138, 140). Though we may refuse nowadays to speak of the essence of religion, isn't salvation a major aspect of what makes religions *religious*?

Even under this lesser claim, religion has priority over theology. It is possible to understand 'moral', 'spiritual', and 'salvific' truths as if they were identical to non-religious metaphysical or even empirical truths; but that would be to ignore their personal, affective, self-involving, and practical dimensions. But these 'contaminants' of pure cognitive religion are key ingredients in the mix. I would further argue that the empirical and metaphysical truths of religion are themselves dependent on these messier elements (in terms of inferential reasoning or psychological genesis), and that the former are badly misconstrued when taken in isolation from the latter. We should take seriously John Cottingham's claim that we 'entirely fail to capture what is involved in someone's adoption or rejection of a religious worldview if we suppose we can extract a pure cognitive juice from the mush of emotional or figurative coloration, and then establish whether or not the subject is prepared to swallow it' (Cottingham, 2005, 80–85). Religion is best understood through its affective, self-involving, passionate, and committed dimensions. It is visceral, a 'thinking with the blood' (Cupitt, 2006, ch. 13).

In particular, I believe that it is a mistake to distil out from the experiences of religious salvation, and its expression in narratives and practices, a rarefied fraction that we regard as its 'truth about salvation'. Invariably, this picture of the salvific activity of divinity (or of ultimate reality) will be shorn of the felt experience of salvation that is its origin, and to a large extent its point. Within religions most truths about salvation are only regarded as valid insofar as they relate – by expression or evocation – to the current, salvific experience of the religious believer. To find a religion to be salvific is to experience some sense of healing, illumination, or liberation *now*. It is to be saved *subjectively*. This is the switch that needs to be thrown to convert the religious equivalent of electrical potential into something that *flows*, that effectively *powers* people. Response, in religion, remains the crux – even in the most realistic of theologies. On this account, salvation must be about this world, whatever else it is about. Religious faith and hope, like religious practice, are *themselves* salvific. They are not just claims about the activities of transcendent beings or our future lives.

The theology of religions has traditionally seen the exclusivist and pluralist paradigms as two extremes of a spectrum, with some form of inclusivism located between them. Some have remarked that this analysis seems to treat the different religions as examination candidates who all sit down to answer the same question in their different ways. But if our focus is on salvation, it may well be that different individuals and traditions understand this state in such different ways that they are (in 'truth' terms) often answering different questions (D'Costa, 1986, 109). For good or ill, this leads many to think in terms of some form of salvific or soteriological relativism: that different people are saved in different ways from different things in different contexts (cf. Hick, 1989, 375).

Note, however, that I am not here endorsing an *ontological* pluralism, let alone 'the liberal theological principle that all religions are equal'. I agree with Philip Barnes that such a viewpoint can easily swamp a 'real respect for religious difference' (Barnes, 2009, 43–46). But I do want to insist that in order to understand objective theological cognitions properly we must bring to the fore their constitutive subjective dimension.

A focus on cognition alone lends itself to the distancing, objective discourse of authority and norms in religion. A concern for attitudes, emotions, behaviour, and experiences, however, locates the norms of faith within the religious response, rather than relegating them to the cognitive content of belief. Religion is 'tried and tested' by those who embrace it; religious norms point to things that have been found to 'work' in the hearts, souls, and lives of believers, as well as (and more than, and more significantly than) in their minds. For this view, religious truth is not the sort of truth that can be formulated or conceived independently of this human response. One might even say that religion only really *exists* in the context of this response.

> Religious truth is tied up with being truly religious, truly loving God, loving God in spirit and in truth (John 4:24) ... This is not like having the right scientific theory that covers all the facts and makes all the alternative explanations look bad. (Caputo, 2001, 111)

Significantly, Caputo adds that saying 'God is love' means that we are expected to *do* something – to 'make that truth *happen*'. On this account, *doing* the truth is 'what is true and truthful and honest about religious truth'; it is a deed, 'something that demands our response' (115–116). Dewi Phillips asks, 'What would it mean to say that one believed in God without this involving any affective state in one's life? Even if sense could be made of these "beliefs" divorced from active responses, *what would be particularly religious about them?*' (Phillips, 1993, 112, my italics; cf. 118–119; see also Jones, 2002, 73–77).

Truth telling

What do we mean when we claim that a proposition is true: that it 'corresponds' with the 'facts' or the 'actual state of affairs'; that it forms part of a consistent set of harmonious beliefs; that it is a reliable basis for action; or (on 'minimalist' or 'deflationist' views) simply that we have said what we have said, and that we endorse and stand by it? An holistic account appeals to me here. We should probably think of the human phenomenon of truth claiming as multidimensional, with these different 'theories of truth' (correspondence, coherence, pragmatic, performative, etc.) offering ways of foregrounding certain features. This might allow us to acknowledge particular functions of truth-claims without denying others (cf. Bhaskar, 2003, 705).

Problems arise when any one of these dimensions is promoted to fulfil the roles of all the others. In particular, some religious educationalists make much of the dangers of construing truth as wholly pragmatic (or instrumentalist). Pragmatic theories of truth recognize the close connection between belief in the truth of something and some kind of 'success' for the actions of the believer. True beliefs *work*, in some way or another. But is that what their truth entirely consist in? Recognizing the function of religion in people's lives is not the same as *reducing* religion to that function (Appelros, 2002, 171–172).

Righting Wright

Andrew Wright's *Critical religious education, multiculturalism and the pursuit of truth* offers a good defence of the core significance of the notion of ultimate truth within religious belief. His distinction between *truth* and *truthfulness* in RE is important, and his advocacy of a critical theological realism in religion compelling. But I want to qualify the rather too cool, abstract, and disinterested notion of religious truth with which he still tempts us, despite his claims that 'truth and truthfulness are ... two sides of the same coin', and that even the study of religion 'should not be a passionless affair' (2007, 225–226).

Wright holds that part of the task of the RE teacher is to enable pupils to 'orientate their lives appropriately' in response to their understanding of disputed claims about ultimate reality. 'Pupils need to feel the force of such claims', Wright argues, 'and learn to respond to them in an appropriate manner' (200–202). He means by this that they should cultivate sufficient religious literacy to 'modify their behaviour in an appropriate and responsible manner' in response to their own core beliefs (cf. 205). But this seems rather too rational and cognitive an account of what is involved in a religious response. Significant religious claims bear potential *spiritual* force. Unless the truth-claiming belief-systems of religion had captured and conveyed this transcognitive element, they would never have had any lasting effect.

For what it's worth, I too adopt a broad critical realism about God, and some sort of correspondence theory of truth. But I sense that there is much to be said about what is distinctive about religion that is not captured in these generic philosophical categories. It is something about which the radical non-realists and non-cognitivists, who oppose such orthodoxy, have had significant things to say.

Unlike them, I don't affirm a thoroughgoing religious expressivism or non-realism in religion. I do not claim that language about God does not refer to any transcendent reality but merely serves to express our attitudes and commitments. But I do insist that *even within a realistic analysis of religion* – one that recognizes some species of 'correspondence' between truths about the divine and ultimate reality – we should not downgrade religion's human component. This makes the story more complex in a number of ways.

The human component

(1) Truths about religion may be assented to or endorsed although the believer remains indifferent to religion. Wright distinguishes (2007, 2–3): (a) engagement with questions of ultimate truth within 'metaphysical space', from (b) 'the task of living truthful lives' within 'social and moral space'. This distinction is between (a) *pursuing (and describing) truth*, and (b) *being truthful* or *living truthfully* by responding to and living harmoniously with ultimate reality (ch. 1). 'Truthfulness' is our subjective response to truth. Wright regrets that much contemporary RE breaks the connection between the two by ignoring (a), the question of truth.

But there is surely another danger: that of underplaying the human response in order to make more room for 'engagement' with metaphysical questions. As Wright acknowledges, more traditional (confessional) forms of religious education allow 'an intimate relationship between truth and truthfulness' (57); but in religion we can't separate the inside from the outside of the teapot from whichever direction we start.

The point is well captured by the distinction in English between believing *that* x is the case, and believing *in* x. Briefly, 'belief-in' is 'belief-that' with attitude (and relevant behaviour). Thus believing in God involves a positive evaluation of God (one is 'for' God); a committed, trusting attitude; and a disposition to behave in a way that is appropriate to the belief that God exists. 'Coming to believe in God is coming to believe in a religious manner' (Holmer, 1967, 164). (Hence 'believing in baptism' is not simply a matter of having seen the action performed.)

Further, religious claims are never salvific truths, and therefore never fully *religious* claims, unless religious people are moved to hold them in a way that expresses their hope for healing, normally both in the present on earth and in some eschatological future. It is possible to believe that God will resurrect me to a life of greater intimacy with Godself and yet not to care about it, not to care for it, not to 'be saved' by this. I may also remain unmoved by, ungrateful for, even resentful of other truths that I acknowledge, such as God's gift of creation and of my life. (People *are* indifferent to gifts, even the gift of life from their parents. This is a fairly normal state of affairs among adolescents.) My argument undermines, I think, the idea that these are 'religious truths' in anything other than an etiolated, because a potential, sense.

In religion what really matters is not whether God's metaphysical nature and God's relation to the created world is of this, that, or the other kind, or not. Without a religious response there is little taste of a truly religious or spiritual truth in such claims. *What really matters to the believer is that these questions matter to the believer.* As Paul Holmer insists, the language *of* – not *about* – faith asks that we too 'have the pathos and the passion and that we let the categories of religion gain their dominance in our daily life' (Holmer, 1978, 71).

We are often informed that the religions arose solely to explain natural phenomena in a pre-scientific age; and that now (as these explanations have been proved to be otiose) religion should be abandoned. But that isn't what religion is about. Although they accept the scientific explanations, many still find that they cannot give religion up. Religion, we recall, is what *binds* us.

So when Wright argues, correctly, that a key role of religious language is to 'describe the ultimate order-of-things' (Wright, 2007, 92), he presumably should not be thought of as denying two significant qualifying factors. The first is that the ultimate order-of-things includes whatever is penultimate to it: that is, the world as well as God. And human religiosity is a part of this mundane reality. Hence, even in its descriptive mode, theistic language must also speak of religious humanity – of religious experience, religious reflection, and religious response, including spiritual yearning and struggling. Indeed, the descriptive religious language of ordinary believers is not much used to describe God *an sich*, but God-in-relation-to-us (cf. Astley, 2002, ch. 3). The second factor is that religious language does not just describe ...

(2) In fact a very great deal of religious language functions non-cognitively, in a manner that asserts no facts. Not only that, but it often performs these other functions *at the same time* as it renders the nature of God. So it could be a mistake, I believe, for us to attempt to study *religious* language by stripping off these evocative, expressive, action-directing, commitment-making, and other performative dimensions (Astley, 2004a, ch. 8). It is these components that help make religious language *religious*. That is the true bequest of the writings of D. Z. Phillips and Don Cupitt, and explains why many still regard them as truly religious – or, at least, as spiritual – authors (Astley, 2004b, 19). The 'positive thesis' of the non-cognitivist is that what makes something a religious statement, rather than merely a factual report, is that 'it expresses an attitude' (Moore and Scott, 2007, 3).

Although many religious beliefs are justifiable by their reference to religious realities whose existence is independent of religious believers, nevertheless there surely *is* much in religion that is humanly constructed. 'Religious experience ... while obviously involving imaginative projections, is at the same time a cognitive response to a transcendent reality' (Hick, 1997, 610). This is not surprising. After all, the hermeneutical perspective identifies the truth read out of religious texts as a new truth that is forged in the interpretative act of reading. The believer is always a co-creator of religious truth; and in that role her inventiveness may sometimes construct significant fictions of mythology or legend.

And religions are, in part, *ideals*. Neither St Christopher nor the Good Samaritan are simply instantiated. But that is part of their point: we must strive to create them in ourselves. Hence William Temple famously claimed that, although he believed in one, holy, catholic, and apostolic Church, he regretted that it nowhere existed.

Many other religious beliefs demand an analysis in terms of religious hope, which is not to be understood as on a logical par with secular hopes. Much in religious belief is properly the object of profound hope (cf. Pojman, 1986, 228), and not of clear, consistent, and comprehensive factual claims that fit well with the available evidence. People hope for an afterlife, an end to suffering, or some sort of conversion of the world. These are not to be understood in the way we understand secular hopes, as probabilistic expectations about the future. Religious hope is more of a fervent spiritual yearning, an 'earnest desiring'. It lies closer to – while yet transcending – my hope that I will be able to bear the pain of an illness, or that my long-left lover still remembers me. It is an expression of my wants, my needs, my deepest strengths and weaknesses – in a word, my very self-identity.

(3) In the case of cognitive religious claims, it must also be conceded that, according to the religions themselves, ultimate reality transcends our language. 'Articulating a mystery' through 'theological stammering' (to adopt Ian Ramsey's phraseology) is a process that sits uneasily with claims about religious truth couched in terms of 'the accuracy of [religious adherents'] descriptions of reality' (Wright, 2007, 138). Ramsey actually disavowed the use of the word 'descriptive' of our God-talk: not because he did not think that religious language referred, but because the term smacked too much of construing the 'odd logic' of religious language literally, as 'plain descriptions of fact' – a mistake that would eventually lead to atheism (Ramsey, 1961, 1, 1963, 65).

(4) The role of the will in religious 'choice' is poorly represented in many accounts of religious believing. A theology of religions that majors in empirical and metaphysical truths will also tend to misconstrue religious choice, as religious educators often do, as the outcome of a dispassionate study of factual truth-claims.

Let us first nail the loose talk about 'freedom of belief'. We cannot directly will to believe anything. The idea is psychologically bizarre and logically incoherent (see Astley, 1994, ch. 8; Griffiths, 2001, 27–28; Kinghorn, 2005; Plantinga, 1987; Pojman, 1986; Strawson, 1986; Swinburne, 2005; Ward, 1994, 323–324). However, we do have a limited, indirect freedom to entertain possibilities and to ignore or to seek out arguments and evidence (and to reflect critically upon them or not). Yet, in the end, we cannot but believe whatever these actions and the resulting processes deliver. *We are stuck with our beliefs.*

Not only that, but at base religious believing 'in the wild' is improperly characterized as the result of 'gathering evidence, weighing-up counter-evidence, making informed judgements' (Wright, 2007, 110). That model is only appropriate for a limited number of theological disputes within some religious traditions. No amount of piling up evidence and arguments concerning an empty tomb, nor any number of disciples shocked out of their despair, can deliver the spiritual response captured in the great Easter cry, *Resurrexit vere*. The adolescent's routine riposte expresses the issue well: 'So?' So the tomb was empty, the disciples transformed, the nascent Christian Church against all probability emboldened to resist persecution. But there are always going to be alternative, sometimes even more plausible, explanations for such facts. More important than that, it is always going to be possible for someone to claim that Christ was raised from the dead, and for it not to make any difference to that person's life. If the resurrection were solely about Jesus, it would leave me cold. To be religious, there has to be something here that is also about *me*. In order to be a Christian, I have to *embrace* it. And to do that, I have partly to want it. God can act decisively on every third day of the week until the end of time, but unless human beings respond spiritually to this 'objective truth' about God's objective activity, *there would be no Christian religion*. Neither adopting a religion nor seeing the point of a religion is solely a matter of adjudicating over evidence and argument (Basinger, 2002, 35–36).

(5) Finally, we should also note that very different theologies can undergird the same spiritual response. This suggests another reason why we should be cautious about fastening on metaphysical claims in isolation from human reactions. Within my own religious tradition there is much disagreement over, for example, the (meta)mechanics of sacramental theology and the (meta)physics of divinity. However, these distinctions rarely map tidily onto the actual spiritual attitudes and behaviours of Christians at their worship, or in their lives.

The truthful embrace

To affirm a *truth 'in' religion*, and not just 'about' it, I must step beyond religious texts and history and the second-hand description of religious concepts. In theistic faiths, this is the step towards prayer and worship. We might call this fundamental element of human religiosity the 'religious embrace'. I have argued that religious beliefs, attitudes, values, and practices may only be judged spiritual or salvific insofar as people relate to them in a certain way. Think of this in terms of enfolding another in one's arms.

Wittgenstein described 'a passionate commitment to a system of reference', as the learner runs to religious belief and grasps it for herself. The Christian 'seizes' on the message of the Gospels 'believingly (i.e. lovingly)', and with a certainty that is characteristic of this 'particular acceptance-as-true'. Wittgenstein calls this sort of certainty 'faith': 'faith is faith in what is needed by my *heart*, my *soul*, not my speculative intelligence' (faith, after all, 'is a passion'). What combats doubt here is therefore *redemption* (Wittgenstein, 1980, 32–33, 56, 64).

Although I illustrate my thesis with reference to Christianity, I strongly suspect that every tradition must contain, as a part of its normative claims about itself, a similar focus. If this is true, there is at least one thing that may be said to be common between religions, and that is the religious embrace; even though it may differ radically between religions with respect to the objects embraced and, perhaps, in some aspects of its form.

My argument is that no metaphysical or empirical truth, not even one that makes claims about salvation or the spiritual or moral realms, *counts as religious* unless it is embraced in a personal, affect-laden, and action-directing way. This is, of course, a normative claim. But it is one that is widely endorsed when religionists wish to distinguish nominal from 'real' or 'true' believers. I suggest that it is also implicitly adopted where teachers of religion construct syllabuses that select from the great range of phenomena associated with a religion, identifying those beliefs, practices, experiences, values, etc. that seem to them to lie *'at the heart'* of the faith concerned. This phrase may be understood in two senses. These elements

A Theological Reflection on the Nature of Religious Truth

occupy some sort of (actual or perceived) logical priority or comprehensive status within the religious system. But their salience may also be measured by their affective power, as the primary objects of the religious embrace (see Borg, 2003).

Selection is inevitable in the study of religion, as it is with any subject-matter. Certain elements are chosen for reflection and teaching, whereas other features from the same religious tradition are passed over. Theologies of religion do the same thing. In both activities, a major element of the selective focus is an implicit claim about what is significant or valuable in a religion (Astley, 1988). If salvation is what the religions are about, this must include an assumption about what human beings regard as salvific.

There are other criteria for syllabus selection, of course, including relying on representative surveys of the views held by the wide range of those who assess themselves as belonging to a particular religion. It is clearly important, for sound educational reasons, that we should know how the generality of self-confessed Muslims in Afghanistan – or Christians in Britain – understand and relate to their respective faiths. This sort of descriptive 'religious knowledge' is often very important for non-educational reasons, too. Taken seriously, it could affect our decisions about the funding of faith schools, or even about going to war.

But such descriptive information provides a woefully inadequate account of these religions *from a spiritual perspective*. Spiritual judgements tend to be normative claims about the 'real' or 'true' nature of religion. '*This* is what people (adults?) actually do and believe; but *this* is how they ought to be, for this is what is spiritual, moral, salvific' – that is, truly religious. Such positions may be represented only by a minority in a survey of self-identified religionists. But as Richard Pring has declared (admittedly in a different context), 'acquaintance only with the sociology of religion is not to see things from the religious point of view' (Pring, 2005, 57).

I want now to fill out this concept of the 'embrace', by relating it to other analyses of religion.

(1) The embrace is a major part of what makes a religion 'religious'. This has been characterized by Ninian Smart as a relationship to '"ultimate" value questions relating to the meaning of human life' (Smart, 1975, 20).

Metaphysical and religious worldviews provide meaning by keeping in place and enhancing – 'talking up' and raising up – certain values.

Many definitions of religion focus on this element of all-encompassing and deeply-felt *valuation*. Frederick Ferré defines religion as 'an institutionalized way of valuing most comprehensively and intensively' (1967, 73). Gavin Flood adds that these 'value-laden narratives and behaviours ... bind people in their objectivities to each other, and to non-empirical claims and beings' (Flood, 1999, 47). Jim Stone acknowledges the salvific dimension of valuing by defining religion as 'a system of practices meant to place us in a relation-of-value to a supermundane reality so grand that it can figure centrally in the satisfaction of substantial human needs' (Stone, 2001, 188).

(2) Values are types of attitudes, and attitudes are marked by a significant *feeling* component. The relationship between the 'mind' and the 'heart' in religion has often been debated; but too often those who emphasize the role of the heart are castigated for wallowing in subjectivity.

Yet, although Friedrich Schleiermacher employs the language of 'feeling' and 'affections', he grounds this in something more epistemologically respectable: 'intuition' and a 'sense and taste for the infinite'. His disciple, Rudolf Otto, more clearly articulates a veridical experience; and both allow religious experience to be schematized in concepts, and thus 'set forth in speech'.

Søren Kierkegaard, of course, strongly reacted against any philosophy of ideas expressed in detached and observational modes of thought. Christianity, especially, is not 'objective knowledge' to be manipulated in the disinterested fashion of the mathematician or scientist. It requires commitment. Kierkegaard perhaps goes too far when he adds that 'subjectivity is the truth' and writes of 'faith's crucifixion of the understanding' (Kierkegaard, 1846/1941, 206, 501). But some scholars claim that Kierkegaard's notion of 'being subjectively in the truth', by believing genuinely and deeply, should be understood as prescribing a road to veridical insight that is not available to impersonal procedures of enquiry (155; cf. Gardiner, 1988, 99).

Jonathan Edwards, William James, and John Henry Newman all steer a middle way between assessing religious truth solely by objective reason and claiming that God can only be known 'subjectively' by the heart. On this mediating view, the evidence for God can only be accurately assessed 'by men and women who possess the proper moral and spiritual qualifications': that is, whose 'cognitive faculties are rightly disposed' (Wainwright, 1995, 3).[1]

For James, human satisfactions are the pragmatic tests of faith. To be 'true to us', to 'ring true', our picture of the world must respect our passional natures as well as our theoretic side (Wainwright, 97). However, James also believed that the structure of our minds are 'in accordance with the nature of reality' (James, 1896/1956, 116). The desires and needs that count most are those that are universal and deep – e.g., the desire for significant action, or for meaning. Their 'satisfactions' (emotional solace, coherence with other beliefs, sense of meaning and moral significance, etc.) constitute 'truth for us', truth's 'cash value'. This 'truth for us, however, indicates that we are successfully dealing with reality and therefore possess truth simpliciter' (Wainwright, 1995, 100, n. 28).[2] Charles Taylor notes how our modern understanding of religion stresses this personal dimension: 'to take my religion seriously is to take it personally, more devotionally, inwardly, more committedly' (Taylor, 2002, 11) – as a religion of the heart, rather than just the head. Taylor reckons that William James was prescient in his take on religion; today's world is 'a paradigmatically Jamesian one' (111), not a Durkheimian one.

At its best, however, this view does not imply that this experience is individualistic, in the sense that society does not come first as the nurturing context of every person's experience, and of whoever teaches each individual

[1] They believe that: 'A converted heart, or a sensitive conscience, or a demand for meaning and the possibility of significant action are needed to approach the force of the evidence for religious truths. Each believes that (when properly disciplined) our passionate nature tracks the truth. "Passional reason" is reliable' (Wainwright, 1995, 5).

[2] Current research in neuroscience and the cognitive sciences appears to support the idea that most people live most of the time by a more holistic form of reason. This employs the emotions and affect-laden metaphors and stories, and is therefore much richer than the disembodied and dispassionate abstraction that defines the reason of the Enlightenment. 'Emotions seem to exhibit a kind of "global rationality" that saves pure reason from itself' (Evans, 2001, 52).

the language she uses to express and describe it. Nor does it imply any radically relativistic subjectivism, in which the only thing that matters is my response, and which therefore cannot be in any sense criticized provided it is sufficiently 'authentic' and self-fulfilling.

(3) For radical and postmodern theologians, religious truth is made within a religious life. But other theologians also claim that religious inquiry aims at 'practical' rather than 'theoretical' truth (see also Christian, 1964, 264; Ward, 1994, 232). Implicit in biblical literature itself is the claim that religious truth is to be appropriated (McGrath, 1997, 78–80).

> That you cannot analyse religious belief into knowing something and doing something, as though these were two separate independent elements in the same thing, is evidenced in the Bible. The knowledge of God, in the last analysis, the religious believer can say, is, 'That is how I live my life'. (Haymes, 1988, 179)

According to Michael Hand, in order to have a religion it is not enough just to believe that gods exist. 'A person must hold the gods she believes in to have *some positive relevance to her life*' (Hand, 2006, 97–98). In Stefan Huber's analysis of religiosity, religious beliefs must be *central* in the sense that they have an intense influence on experience and behaviour, and a broad influence on different areas of life (Huber, 2007, 213–214; cf. Huber and Klein, 2009).

What I have described above as spiritual, moral, or practical religious truths only become true in the religious embrace. They are typically truths of the form 'this practice, discipline, or experience releases my guilt / purifies my vision / empowers my love.' This is not to say that there are no objective truth-claims implied here. There are. But all religious truths concerning God (or Brahman) also possess a subjective component that implicates the yogi or devotee, and are often conditional on his or her stance or practice. In religion, as elsewhere, 'meaning arises when subjective attraction meets objective attractiveness' (Wolf, 1997, 211).

Relevance for religious education

Confessional religious education

To those concerned with confessional education into a religious tradition, I make two comments. First, that their teaching task is not the same as that undertaken by the teacher of religious studies in secular schools or of theology in a secular university, in that part of their task is to help people to engage in the religious embrace (by teaching towards religious conversion and commitment) and to help those in such an embrace to mature further (religious nurture). And, second, that in my experience it is helpful for members of a particular religion to gain some sense of how another faith might also seem to be salvific, because discovering more about the commitments of others can help you to understand better your own embraces.

I recall a Christian ordinand responding to a discussion of Hindu *advaita* (non-dualist) religious philosophy with the question, 'But why should anyone believe this?' He was not asking about evidence and argument – about 'reasons' in terms of grounds. He was asking about motivation. Why should anyone *want to* believe this? The answer that satisfied him was one that helped to evoke in him a sense that this 'metaphysical position' could serve people as a spiritual resource: that this way of seeing things could be salvific. And that happened when the answer was so framed as to resonate with his own salvific needs, and the resources he employed to meet them.

Do religious believers *need* a theology of religions? For many, I think, this is too cognitive a concern. What they need is a *religious response* to other faiths, rather than some improved rational reflection on their own position in the ultimate order of truths about reality. That is why current emphases on 'humility' and 'hospitality' often seem to hit the mark; whereas debates over the (theo)logical limits of tolerance and of religious relativism leave people cold, because the debates are themselves cold.

Non-confessional religious education

In teaching *about* a religion its truths will be portrayed, analysed, and critiqued. I welcome this cool, self-distancing exploration of religious beliefs. But for a proper understanding of religion, and therefore of the place of religious beliefs in the religious life, the student also needs to understand what is religiously special about this material. While pure empirical or metaphysical truth-claims about religion may be objective truths, they cannot be fully *religious* truths (truths in, and not just truths about, the religion) unless and until they are embraced. Metaphysics remains mere metaphysics until it is appropriated by those who find its truths to be salvific. The student thus needs an empathetic understanding of what is regarded as salvific by an alien (Christian, Hindu, Muslim, Buddhist) person and tradition. One condition of this understanding would seem to be some sense of what it is like to embrace religion at all. Teaching this may be the most difficult of the tasks of RE, and one that further blurs the distinction between its confessional and non-confessional modes.

Other issues may be raised here. Those who learn about different religions are bound to ask about the similarities between them. There are many such similarities, of course – many common beliefs, and many that are more similar than they appear at first blush. But, of course, there is a great deal that is wildly different.

Yet what is really important are the similarities represented by the key features of the human religious response: in particular, the way in which believers find value, meaning, or 'salvific relevance' in their putative experience of, or truth-claims about, a religious reality. It is there that they find a discernment of home, and a fulfilment of their true selves. The decisive similarity between religions thus lies in something about *us* (if we are religious) – something in our religious perspective, experience, feeling, and response.

By contrast, the principal differences between the religions lie in certain features of their religious objects, as the belief-system represents them. This is something about what is *not us*: the nature, actions, and intentions of ultimate reality / the divine; and the character of earth and heaven. As religious educators, and (where the cap fits) as religious believers, we need to articulate and discuss these different truths, and to negotiate their diversity and the options raised by agreements and disputes among these 'theologies'. But we really cannot neglect the widely shared reactions that mark these differences as *religious* differences, constituted by dimensions of our common humanity.

The theology of religions is often situated within some form of dialogue between religions. But the really significant religious dialogue for the *learner* is not that between the religions. It is the dialogue between, on the one hand, that individual himself or herself, with his or her own worldview; and, on the other hand, the variety of beliefs, values, and spiritual and moral practices of the plural world around them, especially where it takes on a religious form. If religions are fundamentally soteriologically oriented cultures, this educational dialogue is in principle open to developing into a salvific dialogue. It is therefore bound to lay the student open to risk – if that is the right word (and it isn't) – *the risk of religious embrace*.

But, as I have argued elsewhere, good religious education should never seek to immunize its students against the possibility of such a religious response (Astley, 2007).

References

Appelros, E. (2002). *God in the act of reference: Debating religious realism and non-realism*. Aldershot: Ashgate.
Astley, J. (1988). Theology and curriculum selection: A theoretical problem in teaching Christianity in religious education. *British Journal of Religious Education*, *10* (2), 86–91.
Astley, J. (1994). *The philosophy of Christian religious education*. Birmingham, Alabama: Religious Education Press.
Astley, J. (2002). *Ordinary theology: Looking, listening and learning in theology*. Aldershot: Ashgate.
Astley, J. (2004a). *Exploring God-talk: Using language in religion*. London: Darton, Longman & Todd.

Astley, J. (2004b). Religious non-realism and spiritual truth. In G. Hyman (ed.), *New directions in philosophical theology: Essays in honour of Don Cupitt* (pp. 19–33). London: Ashgate.

Astley, J. (2007). Crossing the Divide? In M. Felderhof, P. Thompson, and D. Torevell (eds), *Inspiring faith in schools: Studies in religious education* (pp. 175–185). Aldershot: Ashgate.

Barnes, L. P. (2009). *Religious education: Taking religious difference seriously*. London: Philosophy of Education Society of Great Britain.

Basinger, D. (2002). *Religious diversity: A philosophical assessment*. Aldershot: Ashgate.

Bhaskar, R. (2003). Truth. In W. Outhwaite (ed.), *The Blackwell Dictionary of Modern Social Thought* (pp. 705–706). Oxford: Blackwell.

Borg, M. J. (2003). *The heart of Christianity: Rediscovering a life of faith*. New York: HarperSanFrancisco.

Burke, P. (1979). *The fragile universe: An essay in the philosophy of religions*. London: Macmillan.

Caputo, J. D. (2001). *On religion*. London: Routledge.

Christian, W. A. (1964). *Meaning and truth in religion*. Princeton, New Jersey: Princeton University Press.

Cottingham, J. (2005). *The spiritual dimension: Religion, philosophy, and human value*. Cambridge: Cambridge University Press.

Cupitt, D. (2006). *The old creed and the new*. London: SCM.

D'Costa, G. (1986). *Theology and religious pluralism: The challenge of other religions*. Oxford: Blackwell.

D'Costa, G. (ed.). (1990). *Christian uniqueness reconsidered: The myth of a pluralistic theology of religions*. Maryknoll, New York: Orbis.

Evans, D. (2001). *Emotion: The science of sentiment*. Oxford: Oxford University Press.

Ferré, F. (1967). *Basic modern philosophy of religion*. London: Allen & Unwin.

Flood, G. (1999). *Beyond phenomenology: Rethinking the study of religion*. London: Cassell.

Gardiner, P. (1988). *Kierkegaard*. Oxford: Oxford University Press.

Griffiths, P. J. (2001). *Problems of religious diversity*. Oxford: Blackwell.

Hand, M. (2006). *Is religious education possible? A philosophical investigation*. London: Continuum.

Haymes, B. (1988). *The concept of the knowledge of God*. Basingstoke: Macmillan.

Hick, J. (1983). *The second Christianity*. London: SCM.

Hick, J. (1985). *Problems of religious pluralism*. Basingstoke: Macmillan.

Hick, J. (1989). *An interpretation of religion: Human responses to the transcendent*. London: Macmillan.
Hick, J. (1997). Religious pluralism. In P. L. Quinn and C. Taliaferro (eds), *A companion to philosophy of religion* (pp. 607–614). Malden, Massachusetts and Oxford: Blackwell.
Holmer, P. L. (1967). Religion from an existential standpoint. In J. C. Feaver and W. Horosz (eds), *Religion in philosophical and cultural perspective* (pp. 147–173). Princeton, New Jersey: D. Van Nostrand.
Holmer, P. L. (1978). *A grammar of faith*. San Francisco: Harper & Row.
Huber, S. (2007). Are religious beliefs relevant in daily life? In H. Streib (ed.), *Religion inside and outside traditional institutions* (pp. 209–230). Leiden: Brill.
Huber, S. and Klein, C. (2009). Faith or morality? Theological sediments depending on the centrality, content, and social context of personal religious construct systems. In L. J. Francis, M. Robbins, and J. Astley (eds), *Empirical theology in texts and tables: Qualitative, quantitative and comparative perspectives* (pp. 249–267). Leiden: Brill.
James, W. (1956). *The will to believe and other essays in popular philosophy*. New York: Dover. First published 1896.
Jones, S. (2002). Graced practices: Excellences and freedom in the Christian life. In M. Volf and D. C. Bass (eds), *Practicing theology: Beliefs and practices in Christian life* (pp. 51–77). Grand Rapids, Michigan: Eerdmans.
Kierkegaard, S. (1941). *Concluding unscientific postscript*. ET Princeton, New Jersey: Princeton University Press. First published 1846.
Kinghorn, K. (2005). *The decision of faith: Can Christian beliefs be freely chosen?* London: T. & T. Clark International.
Knitter, P. F. (1985). *No other name: A critical survey of Christian attitudes toward the world religions*. Maryknoll, New York: Orbis.
McGrath, A. E. (1997). *The genesis of doctrine: A study in the foundations of doctrinal criticism*. Grand Rapids, Michigan: Eerdmans; Vancouver: Regent College.
Moore, A. and Scott, M. (2007). Introduction. In A. Moore and M. Scott (eds), *Realism and religion: Philosophical and theological perspectives* (pp. 1–9). Aldershot: Ashgate.
Phillips, D. Z. (1993). *Wittgenstein and religion*. Basingstoke: Macmillan.
Plantinga, A. (1987). Justification and theism. *Faith and Philosophy*, *4*, 403–426.
Pojman, L. P. (1986). *Religious belief and the will*, London: Routledge & Kegan Paul.
Pring, R. (2005). Faith schools: Can they be justified? In R. Gardner, J. Cairns, and D. Lawton (eds). *Faith schools: Consensus or conflict?* (pp. 51–60). London: RoutledgeFalmer.

Ramsey, I. T. (1961). *On communicating religion*. London: National Society.
Ramsey, I. T. (1963). *On being sure in religion*. London: Athlone.
Smart, N. (1975). What is religion? In N. Smart and D. Horder (eds), *New movements in religious education* (pp. 13–22). London: Temple Smith.
Stone, J. (2001). A theory of religion revised. *Religious Studies, 37,* 117–189.
Strawson, G. (1986). *Freedom and belief.* Oxford: Clarendon.
Swinburne, R. (2005). *Faith and reason.* Oxford: Clarendon.
Taylor, C. (2002). *Varieties of religion today: William James revisited.* Cambridge, Massachusetts: Harvard University Press.
Wainwright, W. J. (1995). *Reason and the heart: A prolegomenon to a critique of passional reason.* Ithaca, New York: Cornell University Press.
Ward, K. (1994). *Religion and revelation: A theology of revelation in the world's religions.* Oxford: Oxford University Press.
Wittgenstein, L. (1980). *Culture and value.* ET Oxford: Blackwell.
Wolf, S. (1997). Happiness and meaning: Two aspects of the good life. *Social Philosophy and Policy, 14,* 207–225.
Wright, A. (2007). *Critical religious education, multiculturalism and the pursuit of truth.* Cardiff: University of Wales Press.

Contributors

Dr Z. Şeyma Arslan, Istanbul University, Turkey.
Dr Elisabeth Arweck, University of Warwick, Coventry, UK.
Professor Jeff Astley, North of England Institute for Christian Education, Durham, UK.
Dr Fernando A. Cascante-Gómez, Association of Hispanic Theological Education, Aurora, Colorado, USA.
Dr Marian de Souza, Australian Catholic University, Ballarat, Australia.
Professor Recai Doğan, Ankara University, Turkey.
Dr Mario O. D'Souza CSB, University of St Michael's College in the University of Toronto, Canada.
Professor Gloria Durka, Fordham University, New York, USA.
Associate Professor Kath Engebretson, Australian Catholic University, Victoria, Australia.
Professor Leslie J. Francis, University of Warwick, Coventry, UK.
Professor Eleanor Nesbitt, University of Warwick, Coventry, UK.
Dr Üzeyir Ok, Cumhuriyet University, Sivas, Turkey.
Dr Mandy Robbins, Glyndŵr University, Wrexham, UK.
Professor Friedrich Schweitzer, University of Tübingen, Germany.
Professor Mualla Selçuk, University of Ankara, Turkey.
Professor Hans-Georg Ziebertz, University of Würzburg, Germany.

Index of Names

Abbott, W. M. 28
Abdel Haleem, M. A. S. 104
Adnan Davudi, S. 132
Ahmed Zavi, T. 132
Aksakal, A. A. 115, 117
al-Cevheri, E. N. I. 122, 132
Ali, W. 187, 188, 190, 202
al-Isfahani, al-R. 122, 132
al-Razi, F. al-D. 124, 132
Altaş, N. 96, 104
Appelros, E. 245, 259
Argyle, M. 225, 236
Aristotle 53, 57, 59
Arslan, Z. Ş. 4
Arweck, E. 4, 136, 137, 145, 149, 150, 151, 152, 153
Aşikoğlu, N. 117
Aslan, E. 33, 44
Astley, J. 7, 34, 44, 203, 222, 223, 226, 236, 249, 250, 253, 259, 260, 261
Ata, A. 136, 141, 142, 152
Atkinson, T. 202, 203
Avis, J. 208, 219
Axinn, W. G. 136, 150, 153
Axworthy, T. 47, 59

Balasuriya, T. 25, 27
Ballard, P. H. 32, 44
Barnes, L. P. 224, 260
Basinger, D. 242, 251, 260
Bass, D. 83, 89
Bass, D. C. 261
Bates, D. 46
Bates, M. 208, 221

Batson, C. D. 225, 237
Baumann, G. 136, 152
Baumeister, R. F. 237, 238
Becher, H. 136, 152
Becker, L. B. 223, 237
Benedict XVI, Pope *see* Ratzinger, J.
Benner, D. 42, 44
Berger, P. L. 35, 44
Bhaskar, R. 245, 260
Bigelow, E. D. 208, 219
Binsse, H. L. 60
Blacker, D. 56, 59
Blair, C. 54, 60
Bloom, A. 56, 60
Borg, M. J. 253, 260
Borradori, G. 49, 60
Boyd, R. 83, 84, 85, 89
Boys, M. 83, 89
Brown, C. 78, 79, 89
Brzezinski, Z. 108, 117
Bucher, A. 34, 44
Burke, P. 242, 260
Burton, L. 208, 219
Busk, P. 219

Cabral, G. 208, 220
Cairns, G. G. 207, 222
Cairns, J. 261
Callan, E. 55, 60
Caputo, J. D. 244, 245, 260
Cargas, S. 208, 220
Carter-Sowell, A. R. 225, 238
Casanova, J. 35, 45
Cascante-Gómez, F. A. 2

Cassidy, E. I. 22, 27
Chen, Z. 225, 238
Christian, W. A. 256, 260
Clark, E. T. 121, 132
Clarke, D. 158, 183
Claxton, G. 191, 202, 203
Copley, T. 33, 37, 45
Coşan, E. 117
Cottingham, J. 243, 260
Craig, C. L. 208, 209, 213, 220, 221
Cronbach, L. J. 166, 213, 220, 229
Cropsey, J. 60
Cupitt, D. 243, 249, 260
Cush, D. 32, 45

D'Antonio, W. V. 14, 28
D'Costa, G. 242, 244, 260
D'Souza, M. O. 2
Daly, E. 54, 60
Davidson, J. D. 28
de Souza, M. 5, 6, 28, 191, 202, 203, 220
Delis-Bulhoes, V. 209, 220
Doğan, R. 3
Dolan, J. P. 11, 28
Duffy, S. J. 15, 28
Duncan, B. 208, 209, 220
Dupuis, J. 20, 21, 28
Durka, G. 1, 28, 46, 155, 158, 180, 203

Eck, D. L. 12, 28
Elsenbast, V. 44, 45
Engebretson, K. 2–3, 23, 28, 78, 89, 203
Eraut, M. 191, 203
Erricker, C. 34, 45
Erricker, J. 34, 45
Evans, D. 255, 260
Eysenck, H. J. 228, 237
Eysenck, S. B. G. 228, 237

Fabella, V. 27
Feaver, J. C. 261

Feinberg, E. W. 35, 60
Felderhof, M. C. 45, 260
Ferré, F. 254, 260
Fitzgerald, R. 208, 219
Flake, C. L. 132
Flood, G. 254, 260
Fortin, E. 53, 60
Fowler, J. W. 88, 89, 148, 152, 235, 237
Francis, L. J. 6, 203, 205, 208–209, 210, 211, 213–216, 218, 219, 221, 222, 223, 226, 236, 261
Franz, Th. 222
Franzmann, M. 78, 79, 89
Funk, R. A. 228, 237
Furlong, M. 136, 141, 142, 152

Gairdner, W. 51, 60
Gardels, N. 117
Gardiner, P. 254, 260
Gardner, H. 121, 132
Gardner, R. 261
Gautier, M. L. 28
Gearon, L. 28
Gennerich, C. 223, 237
Gent, B. 136, 152
Gerhardt, R. 209, 221
Girault, E. 208, 219
Griffiths, P. J. 242, 243, 250, 260
Grimmitt, M. 37, 45

Habermas, J. 35, 45, 60
Haigh, G. 186, 187, 194, 199, 203
Haji Baktash, W. 114, 116, 117
Hall, G. 213, 220
Hand, M. 256, 260
Harbaugh, G. L. 208, 221
Harman, W. 201, 203
Hatiboğlu, M. S. 99, 205
Hayes, D. 24, 29
Haymes, B. 256, 260
Hefling, C. 28

Index of Names

Heft, J. 29
Herms, E. 32, 42, 45
Hick, J. 28, 29, 41, 45, 81, 82, 89, 223, 237, 242, 244, 249, 260, 261
Hinnells, J. R. 153
Hogarth, R. M. 191, 203
Hoge, D. R. 28
Holmer, P. L. 247, 248, 261
Holsworth, T. E. 208, 221
Hood, R. 228, 238
Horder, D. 262
Horosz, W. 261
Hosteler, K. 50, 52, 60
Huber, S. 223, 237, 256, 261
Hull, J. M. 32, 45, 46
Hunsberger, B. 225, 237
Hutsebaut, D. 90
Hyman, G. 260

Ibn al-Esir 122, 132
Ineson, K. 209, 221
Iversen, G. Y. 34, 45

Jackson, R. 56, 60, 136, 147, 152, 203
Jacobson, C. K. 225, 237
James, A. 136, 152
James, W. 254, 255, 261, 262
Jelen, T. G. 223, 237
Joas, H. 35, 45
John Paul II, Pope 17, 22, 28
Jones, S. 245, 261
Jones, S. H. 208, 209, 210, 220, 221
Jung, C. G. 121, 208, 211, 220, 221
Justin Martyr 15

Kay, W. K. 164, 184
Kayiklik, H. 226, 238
Keirsey, D. 208, 221
Kierkegaard, S. 254, 260, 261
King, U. 26, 28
Kinghorn, K. 250, 261

Klein, C. 224, 225, 228, 235, 237, 238, 256, 261
Knitter, P. F. 15, 17, 18, 25, 28, 29, 73, 158, 159, 183, 242, 261
Kornman, A. 60
Küng, H. 17, 40, 45, 80, 82, 89, 109, 117
Kuschel, K. J. 109, 117
Kutlu, S. 112, 118

Law, S. 193, 194, 203
Lawton, D. 261
Lazari-Pawlowska, I. 54, 60
Lee, S. 83, 89
Lemkow, A. 121, 132
Louden, S. H. 209, 220
Lovin, R. 48, 60
Lucas, B. 191, 203
Luckmann, T. 35, 45
Luffman, G. 209, 220
Lyotard, J.-F. 181, 183

Mackay, H. 186, 203
McLaughlin, T. 55, 60
Maritain, J. 49, 50, 53, 60
McCaulley, M. H. 208, 221
McCoy, C. 50, 60
McGrady, A. 203
McGrath, A. E. 256, 261
McKenna, U. 152
Mels, S. 90
Miller, R. 120, 121, 132
Miller, R. C. 33, 45
Mitchell, G. 34, 45
Moore, A. 249, 261
Moran, G. 25, 28, 83–86, 90
Myers, D. G. 191, 192, 203
Myers, G. 83–85, 89
Myers, I. B. 208, 221

Nelson, N. N. 225, 237

Nesbitt, E. 4, 136–137, 145, 147, 149, 150, 151, 152, 153
Netto, B. 32, 45
Nipkow, K. E. 32, 44, 45
Nonneman, W. 90

O'Brien, D. J. 12, 28
Ok, Ü. 6, 227, 235, 237
Onat, H. 108, 118
Osmer, R. R. 32, 45
Østberg, S. 136, 153
Outhwaite, W. 260
Özarslan, S. 95, 105
Ozdemir, Z. 227, 237
Öztürk, Y. N. 102, 105

Pannikar, R. 21, 22, 28, 29
Payne, V. J. 208, 220
Pearce, L. D. 136, 150, 153
Phan, P. C. 12, 14, 18, 19, 21, 23, 24, 29
Phillips, D. Z. 245, 249, 261
Plantinga, A. 250, 261
Pojman, L. P. 249, 250, 261
Pollard, G. 34, 45
Pollefeyt, D. 222
Pope, S. J. 28
Priestley, J. 54, 60
Pring, R. 253, 261
Prout, A. 136, 152
Puett, T. 77, 90

Quinn, P. L. 261

Rahner, K. 15–17, 29, 157, 183
Ramsey, I. T. 250, 262
Ratzinger, J. 86, 90
Rausch, T. R. 14, 23, 29
Ragan, T. J. 130, 132
Reid, J. P. 54, 60
Ricoeur, P. 136, 153
Ricucci, R. 136, 146–148, 153

Riegel, U. 162, 164, 184
Robbins, M. 6, 203, 208–209, 219, 220, 221, 222, 261
Rodriguéz Garcia, D. 136, 153
Romain, J. 136, 141, 142, 143, 144, 153
Ross, C. F. J. 209, 211, 221, 222
Rothgangel, M. 33, 46
Ruether, R. R. 25, 29
Rummery, G. 88, 90
Ruokanen, M. 158, 183

Sadler-Smith, E. 191
Saroglou, V. 225, 237
Sauer, H. 222
Scheilke, C. T. 44, 45
Schoenrade, P. 225, 237
Schweitzer, F. 1–2, 32, 33, 34, 42, 44, 45, 46, 55, 60
Schwöbel, C. 33, 40, 42, 46
Scott, M. 220, 249, 261
Seager, R. H. 207, 222
Selçuk, M. 3, 95, 97, 105
Sen, A. 48, 61
Şener, A. 112, 113, 118
Shaw, M. E. 237
Sinclair, T. A. 59
Skeie, G. 55, 61
Slater, P. 208, 220
Smart, N. 33, 253, 262
Smith, P. L. 130, 132
Smith, S. 57, 61
Spears, R. 224, 237
Speelman, G. 136, 139–141, 145, 153
Stephan, C. W. 224, 237
Stephan, W. G. 224, 237
Stone, J. 254, 262
Strauss, L. 60
Strawson, G. 250, 262
Streib, H. 90, 224, 225, 228, 235, 237, 238, 261

Index of Names

Swidler, L. 83, 86, 90, 159, 184
Swinburne, R. 250, 262

Taliaferro, C. 261
Tan, B. 102, 105
Tanahi, M. M. 132
Taylor, C. 47, 57, 61, 255, 262
Taylor, H. 90
Teasdale, W. 207, 222
Thaidigsmann, E. 33, 46
Thompson, P. 260
Tidswell, T. 78, 79, 89
Tilley, D. 208, 220
Timmermann, C. 90
Tokuno, K. 205, 222
Torevell, D. 260
Torres, S. 27
Tosun, C. 117
Tracy, D. 26, 27, 29
Trudeau, P. 47, 59
Tsiolkas, C. 186, 187, 199, 203

van der Ven, J. A. 5, 165, 169, 184, 206, 222, 227
van Herck, W. 90
Ventis, W. L. 225, 237
Vermeer, P. 165, 169, 184, 206, 222
Village, A. 209, 221

Vohs, K. D. 237, 238
Volf, M. 261
von Tippelskirch, D. 40, 46
Vryhof, S. 54, 61

Wainwright, W. J. 255, 262
Ward, K. 250, 256, 262
Watson, J. 57, 61
Wellman, J. K. 205, 222
Wesselman, E. D. 225, 238
Whinney, M. 208, 220
Williams, A. 209, 221
Williams, K. D. 225, 238
Williams, R. 209, 221
Wilson, T. 192, 203
Winter, B. W. 158, 183
Wittgenstein, L. 252, 261, 262
Wolf, S. 256, 262
Wright, Alexis 186–187, 194, 199, 203
Wright, Andrew 80, 90, 188, 203, 246–248, 250, 251, 262
Wright, J. M. 237

Yaman, H. 101, 105
Yapici, A. 226, 238
Yasawî, A. 114, 116, 117, 118
Yilmaz, H. 227, 238

Index of Subjects

9/11 attack 13, 186, 226

Absolute, the 121 *see also* Real, the
absolutism 17, 20–22, 25, 49, 57, 79, 98, 109, 159, 160–161, 222, 225, 236
Ad gentes ('The Decree on the Church's Missionary Activity') 16, 158
affect 7, 77, 78, 83, 103, 128, 130, 139, 168, 191, 193–195, 202, 224–225, 243–244, 254–256, 258
Africans / Afro-Caribbean people 12, 23, 24, 65, 66, 67, 70, 71
agnosticism 79–80, 144, 150, 175
'Along the many paths to God' series 63, 65–67
analogy 27
'anonymous Christians' 18, 242
Anglicanism 5, 13–14, 175, 177–179, 198–199, 206
anxiety, intergroup 224–225 cf. 194
Asia 12, 23, 24, 71, 149
asylum seekers 185, 193
atheism 79–80, 144, 150, 250
Australia 6, 141, 185–202
autonomy, personal ix, 2, 58, 163
auxiliary function 6, 211–212, 216–218

Baha'ism 67, 212
belief, suspended 88
belief in ix, 14, 83, 95–96, 161, 228, 245, 247 *see also* faith
beliefs, religious *see* faith, religious; truth / truth-claims, religious
decentring of 74

belonging 51, 189
religious 21, 26, 143, 175, 180, 182, 224–225, 241, 252–256
binding, religious 248, 254
biodiversity 70
Britain *see* United Kingdom
Buddhism 12, 16, 21, 23–24, 67, 108, 110, 212

Calvinism 14
Canada 47–48, 52, 212, 226
Catholic Commission for Religious Relations with the Jews (CRR) 22
Catholicism, Roman 1, 5, 11–27, 41, 47, 65–66, 72, 83, 138, 155–183, 189, 195–196, 206
Catholic Bishops' Conference of India, the 17
catholicity 13–15, 161, 249
certainty 7, 26, 41, 96, 228, 252 *see also* faith, certainty of
charismatic experience 209
children's theology 34
choice 3, 93–95, 104, 129, 136, 141, 144, 250–251
Christian schools *see* religiously-affiliated schools
Christianity 5, 13, 14–22, 24–25, 32–34, 38, 44, 63–76, 77–89, 96, 108, 110, 136–141, 144–145, 149–151, 155, 157–169, 170–171, 175–179, 181–182, 189, 195, 198, 202, 206, 212, 225–227, 235, 241–262

Christian imperialism 32, 44, cf. 40
  see also Catholicism, Roman;
    Protestantism
Christians see Christianity
christic principle, the 21–22
Christocentrism 158–159
Church of England see Anglicanism
Church, the 14–17, 20, 25, 69, 157,
    160–162, 183, 249, 251
church schools see religiously-affiliated
    schools
citizenship education 57–58
coexistence 4, 36, 43, 110, 141
cognition see thinking; reason
cohesion, social 13, 77, 87, 174, 189, 196
common good 2, 47–59, 181
  fundamentalist understanding of 51
  privatized 50–51
communication 25, 42–43, 50, 52, 88,
    109, 163, 166–167, 174, 186, 211,
    231
Confucianism 12, 24
Congregation for the Doctrine of the
    Faith (CDF) 17, 21, 28
congregations 73–75, 209
conscience 3, 104, 107, 255 n.1
conversation see dialogue
conversion 17, 78–79, 85, 141, 242, 250,
    257, 259
Council of Trent 16
creation 75, 76, 95–96, 101, 107, 110, 115,
    121–131, 248
  human creativity 102–103, 121, 141,
    146, 187, 191–192, 201, 249, cf.
    224
  see also fitrah
critical realism 246–247 see also Real,
    the
critical reflection 24, 26, 40, 78, 80, 87,
    94, 99, 155–156, 168, 235, 246,
    250, 256

Croatia 5, 164, 170–175
culture 5, 6, 11, 12, 18, 32, 36, 40, 42, 46,
    48, 51–52, 55, 58, 70, 76, 79, 80, 81,
    87–88, 89, 93, 96, 97, 99, 102, 107,
    108, 110, 113–115, 121, 127, 130, 136,
    138–139, 143, 146–148, 150, 168,
    174, 185, 188–189, 192, 195, 197,
    201–202, 207, 234, 259
cultural fundamentalism 52

democracy 2, 36, 40, 41, 48–56, 98, 100
democratic square see public (square)
dialogue 1, 3, 7, 15–19, 22, 23–27, 33–34,
    36, 38–39, 40–44, 49, 57, 58,
    64–66, 68–70, 72–76, 77, 78,
    82–86, 88–89, 95, 139, 145, 150,
    156–160, 163, 166, 174, 182, 201,
    206, 208, 223, 226–227, 231,
    234, 259 see also Interreligious
    Dialogue Scale
'Dialogue and Proclamation' 16–17
difference ix, 5, 15, 23–24, 26, 36, 39–40,
    43, 48, 50, 54–58, 71, 73–74, 77,
    81, 85, 87, 108–110, 115–116, 140,
    142, 144, 182–183, 185, 188–189,
    190, 193–195, 196, 199, 202, 244,
    251, 258–259 see also diversity;
    individual differences; otherness;
    pluralism / plurality / plural(ist)
    society
differentiation 84–85
Dignitatis humanae ('Of the Dignity of
    the Human Person') 157
discrimination 36, 224–226
diversity 2, 15, 18, 19, 21, 23, 26, 47–61,
    74, 77, 81–82, 87–88, 109, 113, 116,
    121, 151, 160, 163, 167, 180–183,
    185, 201, 210, 226, 234, 244, 251,
    258–259
dogmatics 33–34, 44
dogmatism 33, 44, 98, 225–226

Index of Subjects

dominant function 6, 211–212, 216–218
Dominus Iesus / Jesus ('Lord Jesus') 17, 19, 28, 160–162, 183

'East is East' 138–139, 140, 147
embrace of strangers 188
embrace, religious 7, 55, 138, 144, 244, 251, 256, 257–259 *see also* conversion; truthful embrace
emotions *see* affect
empathy 6, 88, 102, 114, 190, 192, 196, 199–200, 226, 258
empirical theology 5, 6
ethnography 4–5, 135, 137
Europe 3, 12, 52, 66, 147, 155–183, 189, 197, 226
exclusivism *see* theology of religions, exclusivist
extraversion 6, 208–209, 211, 213, 214, 216–218, 228, 230, 232–233
extremism, religious 13, 88

faith, religious 2, 14, 33–34, 39, 77, 124, 243–244, 247–248, 252–256
  Catholic 14, 16, 161
  certainty of 41, 78–79, 88–89, 252
  choosing 136, 250–251 *see also* choice
  Christian 20, 73, 76, 167
  civic or secular 53
  Islamic 97, 99–100, 102, 125, 126
  lack / loss of 144, 150, 234
  mixed-faith families 5, 135–151
    responses to growing up in 146–150
    strategies of 139–145
  nature of 16, 40, 42, 75, 124, 125, 126, 243–244, 247–248, 252–253
  Protestant 14, 42
  and reason 41, 56, 94, 102, 158, 160, 243, 244, 246, 254–256, 257
  and religious education 41, 42, 55, 162–163 *see also* religious education

and theology 34, 38, 39–40, 41, 43, 156
  see also truth / truth-claims, religious
faith development 88, 148, 235
  and pluralist thinking 235
faith schools *see* religiously-affiliated schools
families 185, 201, 226 *see also* faith, religious, mixed-faith families
fate (*qadar*) in Islam 94–96
  Jabri view 95
  Mutazilite view 95
feeling types 6, 208, 210–211, 213–219
feelings *see* affect
fellowship 49
feminist theology / issues 24–25, 65–66, 70, 71–72, 207
Finland 5, 164, 170–175
fiqh 4, 112, 114, 116 *see also* Islam, Islamic law
fitrah (human nature, 'creation') 4, 117, 120, 122–131
flourishing, human *see* wellbeing, human
forms of life 34, 113
Francis Index of Theological Exclusivism (FITE) 6, 213, 214–217
Francis Psychological Type Scale 6, 208, 213
freedom 2, 3, 12, 34, 41, 52, 55, 57–58, 94–96, 116, 124, 127, 130, 197, 227, 250
fundamentalism 1, 15, 31, 36, 39, 42, 44, 51–52, 72, 78–79, 167, 177, 181

Gaudium et Spes ('Pastoral Constitution on the Church in the Modern World') 16
gender issues / differences 25, 65–66, 70–71, 140, 207, 225, 232–233, 235
Genesis 69, 76
Germany 5, 42, 164, 170–175

globalization 54, 63, 69 n.8, 107–109, 155, 158, 182
grace 15–19, 20, 70, 102, 161–162, 242

hadiths 100, 116
harmony ix, 13, 21, 23–24, 26, 58, 108, 121, 125, 142–144, 210, 247
hermeneutical processes 24–25, 66, 70, 156, 166, 249
hikmah (wisdom) 3, 100–102
Hinduism 12, 16, 21, 23–24, 26, 108, 110, 136–137, 144–145, 149, 162, 212, 257
holistic perspective
  on education 4, 119–131, 202
  on reason 255 n.2
  on religion 87
  on truth 245
hope 84, 109, 185
  religious 243–244, 248, 249–250
hospitality 24, 49, 69, 144, 257
human being / nature 3, 4, 16, 48–49, 56–59, 80, 119, 191, 192, 247–251
  in Christianity 21–22, 70, 73
  and the common good 50–59
  and equality 57–58, 103, 115–116, 180, 207 *see also* human rights
  as God's caliph 123–124
  in Islam 102, 114–117, 120 *see also fitrah*
  see also identity, human; individual differences; wellbeing, human
human rights 40, 48–49, 52, 55, 98, 103, 110–111, 113–114, 116, 147, 198, 207, 227
humility 116, 257

ideal types 5, 165, 168
ideals, religious 12, 57, 109, 130, 226, 242, 249
identity
  Australian 194
  British 147
  of Church 69
  citizen's 57
  differentiation 85
  (Roman) Catholic ix, 13–14, 24
  human 48, 51, 55, 78, 83–85, 235, 250
  multiple 48
  narrative 136
  religious 49, 50–53, 58–59, 85, 93, 135–136
  social 50, 53, 214
imagination 12, 26, 27, 81, 130, 191–192, 211, 249
immigration 11–13, 23–24, 47, 52, 143–144, 146, 186–187, 190, 200
inclusivism *see* theology of religions, inclusivist
incommensurability 21, 70
indifference, religious 79–80, 83, 146–148, 247–248
indigenous communities 12, 66, 70, 144, 186, 188, 190
individual differences 4, 6, 121, 123, 129–131, 165, 205, 208–211, 218
individualized religion 3, 93–104
  defined 94
indoctrination 37, 41–42, 94, 163
inerrancy of scripture 15 *see also* fundamentalism
insider / outsider perspectives ix, 33–34, 38, 41–43, 72
  in theology / religious studies 33, 38, 76
instrumentalism 245
  instrumental education 84–85, 87–89
intelligence 57, 59, 128, 252
  multiple intelligences 121, 131
interfaith 77, 139 *see also* interreligiosity; multifaith society; multi-religiosity; theology of religions, interreligious / interfaith model

Index of Subjects

interfaith dialogue *see* dialogue; theology of religions, interreligious / interfaith model
interfaith / interreligious education 2–3, 77–89, 162–163, 181–183 *see also* religious education
interreligiosity 7, 23–26, 40–41, 44, 58, 66, 68, 70, 74–75, 76, 77, 156, 158, 162–163, 223, 226–227, 229 *see also* theology of religions, interreligious / interfaith model
interreligious dialogue *see* dialogue; theology of religions, interreligious / interfaith model
Interreligious Dialogue Scale 228–236
Interreligious Exclusivism Scale 228–233, 235–236
Interreligious Pluralism Scale 228–232, 234–236
intrinsic religiosity 226
introversion 6, 208–209, 211, 213, 214, 216–218
intuition 6, 114, 191–193, 208, 211–213, 214–218, 254
intuitive types 6, 209, 210–211, 214–218
Ireland 5, 164, 170–175
Islam 3–4, 5, 6, 12, 13, 16, 23–24, 33, 75 n.12, 82, 85, Part II, 136–137, 138, 139, 141, 147, 149, 150, 151, 162, 169, 171, 173, 174–177, 179, 181, 186–189, 193, 196–200, 206, 212, 223–238
  Ahl al-Dhimma 112
  Ahl al-Kitab 112–113
  Islamophobia 225
  Islamic law / *Islam-sharia* (Islam-Islamic law) relationship 3, 4, 93, 97–100
  madrasas / Madrasa Islam 3–4, 111–114, 117, 138, 147

Mu'āhad, the 112
Musta'min, the 112
Rabb-abd (God-human being) relationship 93, 94
Sufi 114–117, 131
takkas / Takka Islam 3–4, 114–117
Islamic schools *see* religiously-affiliated schools
Israel 5, 22, 164, 169–175
Israeli Jewish Council for Interreligious Relations (IJCIR) 22
ISREV (International Seminar on Religious Education and Values) x, 219

Jesus (Christ) 14, 16–20, 25, 69, 71, 75, 82, 101, 155, 157, 159, 161, 198, 206, 251
  as sacrament 18
  as unique and universal 17–20, 25, 82, 159, 161, 167
  see also resurrection, of Jesus
Judaism 5, 13, 17, 22, 24, 33, 75 n.12, 82, 85, 108, 110, 162, 169, 171, 173, 174–177, 179, 181, 212, 226
judging types 6, 208, 210–211, 213, 214–218
justice 22, 43, 49, 59, 63–76, 86–87, 99, 100, 124, 207

Latin America 2, 12, 23, 24, 61–76
liberalism 48–52, 55–56, 177, 180
  liberal education 56–57
  liberal theology 157, 158, 244
liberation / liberation theology 2, 15, 25, 63–76, 205, 242–243
  pluralist 63–76
Logos theology 15, 16, 19, 20, 38, 69, 160
looking glass metaphor 11, 27, 194
love, God's 15, 73, 245

love and service, religious 22, 50, 65, 70–71, 73, 75, 76, 111–112, 114–115, 127, 144, 245, 256
Lutheranism 14, 174, 177

Madina, Constitution of / period 104, 110
Magisterium 160
Mass attendance 14, 175, 177
materialism 52, 54
meaning / meaningfulness 4, 26, 27, 78, 84, 94, 102, 107, 119, 124–125, 131, 148, 160, 167–168, 202, 225, 241, 253–254, 255, 256, 258
'Meeting God in Friend and Stranger' 25–26
metaphysics 53, 56, 111, 160, 241–243, 247–248, 250, 251, 252, 254, 257, 258
mission 12, 16–17, 26, 65–66, 69, 72, 159–160, 195
modernity / modernization 34, 35, 41, 48, 55, 56, 77, 93, 99, 104, 107, 120, 128, 144, 156–157, 167, 180–182, 255
   modern education 128, 130–131
monoculturalism 167, 190, 199
monoreligiosity 23, 37, 190 *see also* religious education, monoreligious; theology of religions, monoreligious model
morality
   bond 51
   communities 109
   development of 4
   education / training 114, 130
   influences 146–147
   plurality 54
   practice 20, 49, 102, 115, 259
   principles / rules 58, 97, 99, 108, 116
   relativism 79

   significance 255
   space 247
   teachings 14, 20
   truth 242–245, 256
   values / norms 107–108, 112, 117, 147, 253
   viewpoint 41, 48
   see also conscience; love and service, religious; responsibility
Muhammad, Prophet 97, 100–103, 110, 228, 234
multiculturalism ix, 32, 44, 47–49, 51–52, 56, 108, 110, 155, 182, 185, 197, 198 *see also* pluralism / plurality / plural(ist) society
multifaith education 77 *see also* interfaith / interreligious education; religious education
multifaith society ix, 13, 136 *see also* multireligiosity
multireligiosity 2, 23, 32, 44, 47, 68, 157, 190 *see also* pluralism / plurality / plural(ist) society; theology of religions, multireligious model
Muslims *see* Islam
mystery 26, 51, 70, 115, 161, 250
mystical experience 111–112, 209, 215

Netherlands, The 5, 164, 170–175, 227
neuroticism 228–230, 232–233
New Testament 14, 69, 71, 101–102, 159, 161
non-conscious learning *see* unconscious learning
non-realism, religious 246, 249 *cf. also* critical realism
Nostra Aetate ('The Declaration on the Relationship of the Church to Non-Christian Religions') 16, 22, 27, 28, 157

Index of Subjects 277

One, the 115
openness 6–7, 14, 15, 25, 26, 34, 36, 69, 73–74, 76, 79, 80, 82, 83, 88–89, 102, 115–116, 126–127, 156–163, 167, 174, 177, 208–210, 223–236, 259
   Religious Openness Scale 228, 229, 230, 232–235
ordinary theology 34–35, 44, 248–249
Orthodoxy 13–14
otherness / other, the 3, 5–6, 23, 36, 39, 41, 43, 83, 88, 93, 109–111, 113, 114, 116–117, 121, 141–143, 168, 187–190, 192, 193, 196, 199–202
Ottoman period 3, 107–117

papal authority 13, 32, 155, 157, 161–162, 206
parental effects / rights / wishes in religious formation / education 5, 55–56, 73 n.11, 113, 135–139, 143–151, 235 cf. 41, 227
Parliament of the World's Religions 6, 205, 206–208, 212, 214, 218–219
peace ix, 15, 22, 23–24, 26, 43, 63, 66, 69–70, 75, 76, 77, 87, 109–110, 142, 180, 205, 207, 226, 227
pedagogy
   as foundation for RE 162
   see religious education
perceiving types 6, 208–211, 213–216, 218
persecution 48, 71–72, 76, 251, 159
personality 6, 121, 127, 205–219, 228, 232–233
   authoritarian 225
philosophy of education as foundation of RE 2, 33
pluralism / plurality / plural(ist)
   society 2, 5, 11–12, 20–21, 23, 32, 35–36, 42, 44, 47–49, 51–59, 65, 67, 68, 70, 72, 76, 110, 113,

115, 141–142, 155–159, 160, 167, 168, 173–174, 180–183, 189, 190, 201–202, 223, 236, 259
   challenges of 19, 36
   exposure to 181, 232
   inclusive 21
   ontological 244
   principled ix, 1–2, 31–44 cf. 20
   Scale of Religious Pluralism 166, 228–231
   terminology 35–36, 110
   theology of 18–21, 244 *see also* theology of religions
   see also theology of religions, pluralist
pluralization 35–36
Poland 5, 164, 170–175
political and economic context 15, 25, 47–49, 50–59, 65, 76, 97, 104, 108, 110, 112–113, 181–182, 186, 193–194, 199, 205, 207, 237
poor 14, 63–76
Pope, the *see* papal authority
postmodernity 11, 54–55, 79–80, 181–182, 256
practical theology 38, 156, 182 cf. 256
   as foundation of RE 156
pragmatism 52, 245, 255
prejudice 87, 192, 196, 202, 224–226
proselytism 72, 88
Protestantism 1, 5, 13–14, 15, 17–18, 31–44, 65–66, 71–72, 158, 162, 170, 177–179
psychological type 208–212
public (square) ix, 2, 48, 156

qualitative studies 4–5, 135–153
quantitative studies 5, 6–7, 155–184, 205–238
Qur'an 3–4, 94, 97–104, 116–117, 120, 122–130, 138, 226
   Meccan verses 3, 93, 103–104

Rabb-abd (God-human being) relationship 93, 94
rational *see* reason
rationalization 35
RE *see* religious education
Real, the 81–82, 115, 121
reality, ultimate 81, 101, 121, 234, 241–243, 246–248, 250, 257, 258
reason 53, 56–57, 59, 99, 111, 158, 193, 246
    holistic 255 n.2
    passional reason 255 n.1
    and unconscious learning 190–196
    see also faith, and reason; faith, and theology
redemption *see* salvation
Redemptoris Missio ('Dialogue and Mission') 14, 16–17, 28
refugees 185
relativism *see* theology of religions, relativist
    salvific relativism 244
religio vera 157
religion
    and culture 18, 24, 42, 93, 117, 138–139, 259
    individualized 3, 93–104
    inside / outside perspectives on ix, 33–34, 38, 40–43, 160
    nature of 7, 13, 16, 24–25, 34, 35, 41, 48, 51, 55, 70, 71, 79, 81–82, 87, 94, 98, 102–104, 108, 110, 113, 116, 146, 156, 162, 175, 181, 205, 207, 225, 226, 241–259
Religion and Life-Perspectives of Youth in Europe Project 164
religious education ix, 1–7, 11, 23–27, 31–44, 53–59, 64, 71–76, 83–89, 93–104, 111, 128–129, 135, 136, 137, 145, 149, 151, 156, 161–163, 172–173, 178, 188, 201–202, 205, 236, 241, 245, 246, 247, 257–259

and the arts 14, 26
'confessional' / 'non-confessional' 7, 37, 41, 162, 180–181, 257–259
Christian 31–44, 77–89, 162–163, 182–183, 201–202
    in England and Wales / UK 31, 33, 37, 149, 172–173, 178
experiential dimension of 3, 7, 77–89, 145, 190–196, 200, 243–244, 258
instrumental 84–89
interfaith *see* interfaith / interreligious education
Islamic 93–104, 119–131, 138, 236, 257
learning about religion 39, 87, 137, 149, 258
learning from religion 39–40, 44
methods in 26, 56, 71, 111, 119, 120, 130–131 *see also* holistic perspective, on education
monoreligious 37, 165
multifaith 31, 162
risk in 259
selection in 253
teaching into religion 42
transformative 75, 77, 83–86, cf. 191
see also indoctrination
religious education development stages 84–85
religious language 249–250
    non-cognitive 246, 248–250
Religious Saliency Scale 228–230, 232–234
Religious Stress Scale 228–230, 232–235
religious studies 2, 31, 33, 37–39, 43, 80–82, 155, 162, 167–168, 241, 246, 253, 257
    as foundation of RE 2, 33, 162
religiously-affiliated schools 2–3, 77–89, 95, 128–129, 163, 195, 200, 236, 253, 257

Index of Subjects

respect 1, 5, 34, 36, 47, 54, 58, 66, 74, 77, 82, 111, 114–116, 124, 141–145, 168, 188, 207, 223, 244
   for life 207
   for passional human nature 255
   in religious education 87–88, 163
response, religious 7, 81, 242–245, 246–251, 252–256, 257, 258
   and religious education 257–259
responsibility
   individual 3, 55, 57, 94–95, 103, 104, 129, 188, 246 cf. 113, 124, 125 *see also* choice; freedom
   societal 53, 54, 57, 59, 109
resurrection
   of humans 103, 248, 251
   of Jesus 14, 251
risk 26, 76, 259

sacraments 14, 251
   body as 69
   Christ as 18
   Church as 20
salvation 15–21, 66, 70, 78, 82, 109, 157, 161, 166, 206, 223–225, 241–244, 248, 252–254, 257–259
   outside the Church / a particular religion 15, 109, 157, 162
   outside all religions 70
   salvific relativism 244
sameness 110, 113, 116, 188, 227, 244, 251, 258
secularization / secularity ix, 35, 51–53, 55–56, 58, 68, 70, 98, 107–108, 121, 128, 156, 169, 170, 175, 177, 179, 235, 249–250, 257
   post-secular 35
   secular faith 53
sensing types 6, 208–212, 213, 214–218
separation of Church and state 12
Sikhism 12, 136–137, 138, 143–144, 151, 212

similarity *see* sameness
socialization 24, 78, 135–136, 139, 147–148, 150, 162, 170
solidarity 1, 54, 75, 77, 188, 207
soul 102, 121, 126–129, 244, 252
spirit, human 124–128, 130
Spirit, the (Holy) 17, 19, 20, 65, 69, 70, 83, 101, 115, 124
spiritual truth 242–244, 246, 248, 250–256 *see also* truth / truth-claims, religious
spirituality 5, 14, 16, 20, 24, 34, 66–69, 71, 76, 108, 120, 130, 131, 185–202, 215, 249, 255, 257, 259
   interfaith / pluralist 65–66, 68, 69
state / secular / public schools 33, 41, 54–55, 145–146, 149, 162–163, 257, 258–259
stereotypes 151, 192, 224–225
Streib's Religious Schema Scale (RSS) 228
suspended belief 88
suspicion, hermeneutical 24–25, 33
Sweden 5, 31, 164, 170–174
symbolism 18, 77, 87, 148, 160

Taoism 12, 24
telos / end 48, 52, 80, 158, 242
terrorism 13, 22, 107–108, 186–187, 196–199, 206 *see also* 9/11 attack; extremism, religious; violence / non-violence
testimony 73–75, 108
'them and us' 187, 188, 194, 196 *see also* otherness
theocentrism 18, 158–159
theology 7, 12–13, 15–16, 33, 63–76, 155–165, 167, 183, 241–259
   academic 31, 34–35, 38–39, 43, 65, 74, 96, 100, 155–156, 159
   anthropology, theological 53

confessional 15, 37, 41, 43, 44, 67–68
  as foundation for RE 1–2, 33, 162
  interfaith 67–68
  planetary 64, 67–68
  postmodern 256
  post-religious / post-confessional 67
  and religious education 1–2, 31–44, 83, 95, 155–183, 257, 259
  see also Catholicism; Protestantism; theology of religions
theology of religions ix, 1, 2, 3, 5, 6–7, 14–27, 31–44, 63–76, 155–183, 205–219, 223–236, 241–245, 250, 251, 257
  acceptance model 19, 158, 160–161, 180
  Catholic 1, 5, 14–27, 71–72, 83, 155–183, 206
  conservative evangelical model 18 see also Protestant
  disinterested 246–248
  exclusivist 6, 16, 20, 70–71, 76, 78–79, 109, 157–159, 161–162, 166–167, 169, 175, 179, 206, 208, 210–211, 214–219, 223–236, 241, 244 see also Francis Index of Theological Exclusivism; monoreligious model
  fulfilment model 17, 18, 81, 158
  as fundamental theology 156
  inclusivist 3, 16, 21, 66, 69, 70–71, 82–83, 109, 157–158, 161, 166–167, 169, 175, 179, 206, 241–242, 244 see also monoreligious model
  incommensurability in 21, 70
  indifference 79–80, 83 cf. 146–148
  interreligious / interfaith model 5, 7, 65, 77–89, 165–170, 172–177, 179, 180–183, 206, 223, cf. 228–236 see also dialogue
  monoreligious model 5, 165–179, 182
  multireligious model 5, 64, 165–169, 172–3, 175–183, 206 see also mutuality model
  mutuality model 19, 158, 180 see also inclusivist; pluralist
  open Catholic model 18
  Ottoman 3, 107–117
  particularist 6, 109, 223, 226, 234, 236 see also exclusivist
  planetary 64, 67–68 see also pluralist
  Protestant 1, 5, 14, 15, 18, 31–44, 71–72, 158, 162, 170, 177–179
  pluralist 5, 7, 18, 20–21, 25, 31, 37, 40–41, 63–76, 81–82, 109–110, 158–159, 160–161, 163, 166, 178, 206, 222, 223–224, 229–231, 234–236, 241–242, 244 see also multireligious model
  and psychological type 205–219
  relativist 1, 21, 31, 36, 40, 44, 79–80, 83, 87, 110, 159–161, 167, 183, 225, 244, 256, 257
  replacement model 18, 158
  selection in 253
  super perspective in 40
  syncretistic model 206, cf. 87
  theocentric 18, 158–159
  see also absolutism
thinking 7, 21, 100, 126, 159, 162
  about 100
  critical 24, 94
  dualistic 235
  either/or, and/and 21, 159
  fundamentalist 167
  intuitive 191–192
  postmodern 181–182
  'them and us' 194
  visceral 243, 244
  Western 21
  see also reason

Index of Subjects

thinking types 6, 208, 210–211, 213, 214–218
tolerance 1, 23, 36, 37, 40, 43, 48–49, 65, 78, 82, 87, 110, 112, 114–115, 117, 157, 163, 168, 186, 198, 207, 224–226, 257
Torah 101–102 see also Genesis
tribalism 194
trust 54, 124, 125, 130, 234 see also faith
truth / truth-claims, religious ix, 2, 7, 18–19, 31, 33, 36, 41, 79–83, 88, 103, 109–110, 156–163, 166, 168–70, 174, 180–181, 206, 208, 215, 223, 225, 234, 241–259 see also theology of religions
  appropriation of 256
  and arguments 39, 158, 250–251, 257
  and evidence 73, 248, 249–250, 251, 254–256, 257
  central to life 256
  disinterested notion of 246, 255 n.2
  in / about religion 243, 248, 251, 252, 255–256
  moral 242–245, 256
  motivation for embracing 257
  objective 251, 256
  salvific / spiritual 242–244, 246, 248, 250–253, 256, 257, 259
  subjective 241–242, 244, 247, 254–256 cf. 210
  see also belief in; embrace, religious; response, religious
truth, theories of 158, 245, 246–247
truthful embrace 7, 252–256 see also embrace, religious
truthfulness 207, 246–247
Turkey 3–4, 5, 6, 99, 114, 117, 164, 169–175, 226–228, 236

unconscious learning 5–6, 183–202 cf. 57, 83–84, 87, 145, 181

uniformity 23, 182
United Kingdom 5, 25, 31, 37, 38, 135–153, 164, 170–174, 177–178, 212
United States 1, 11–29, 52, 56, 96, 155, 212, 226

value, ultimate 26, 40, 49, 253–254 see also meaning / meaningfulness
values, nature of 254
variety see diversity
Vatican, the 157, 159, 160
Vatican Council, First (Vatican I) 157
Vatican Council, Second (Vatican II) 11, 15–17, 66, 157–158, 160, 161, 162
violence / non-violence ix, 48, 107–108, 188–189, 197, 207

war against terror see terrorism
Warwick Religions and Education Research Unit (WRERU) 135–136
wellbeing, human 11, 49, 50–53, 75, 186, 189, 193, 196, 254–255
wholeness 4, 84, 119, 121, 126, 131, 161, 182–183 see also holistic perspective
Word see Logos theology
worldviews 32, 33, 36, 43, 77, 110, 119, 120, 121, 157, 181, 187, 189, 192, 193, 195, 210, 234, 254, 259
  religions as 77, 110, 181, 201, 243, 254, 259
worship 69, 75, 81, 97, 99, 103–104, 113, 124–125, 142, 146, 148, 251, 252
  school worship 145, 189

xenophobia 49
xenosophia 224

Zoroastrianism 12, 212

Religion, Education and Values

Debates about religion, education and values are more central to contemporary society than ever before. The challenges posed by the interaction between these different spheres will continue to increase as the effects of globalization and cultural pluralization impact on educational settings. Our radically changed and rapidly changing environment poses critical questions about how we should educate individuals to live in increasingly diverse societies.

Books in this series offer the most recent research, from a variety of disciplinary perspectives, on the interface between religion, education and values around the world. The series covers such themes as the history of religious education, the philosophies and psychologies of religious and values education, and the application of social science research methods to the study of young people's values and world-views.

Books within the series are subject to peer review and include single and co-authored monographs and edited collections. Proposals should be sent to any or all of the series editors:

Dr Stephen Parker (s.parker@worc.ac.uk)
The Rev'd Canon Professor Leslie J. Francis (Leslie.Francis@warwick.ac.uk)
Dr Rob Freathy (r.j.k.freathy@ex.ac.uk)
Dr Mandy Robbins (mandy.robbins@glyndwr.ac.uk)

Vol. 1   Jeff Astley, Leslie J. Francis, Mandy Robbins and Mualla Selçuk (eds):
Teaching Religion, Teaching Truth: Theoretical and Empirical Perspectives.
293 pages. 2012. ISBN 978-3-0343-0818-2